William Carew Hazlitt

**Old English Test-Books**

Vol. III. Reprints of the early and rare Test-Books supposed to have been used by

Shakespeare

William Carew Hazlitt

**Old English Test-Books**
*Vol. III. Reprints of the early and rare Test-Books supposed to have been used by Shakespeare*

ISBN/EAN: 9783744748421

Printed in Europe, USA, Canada, Australia, Japan

Cover: Foto ©Thomas Meinert / pixelio.de

More available books at **www.hansebooks.com**

# Old English Jest-Books.

## VOL. III.

# INTRODUCTION.

VERY little is needful by way of preface to the third volume of this collection of old English jest-books, inasmuch as whatever explanatory or other remarks seemed necessary have been prefixed to each article. It may be desirable, however, to point out that the following pages exhibit a farther instalment of seven curious pieces, the greater part of which are, in the originals, almost totally inaccessible. Of the tracts here brought together, four have never previously been reprinted, namely, *XII Mery Jests of the Wydow Edyth, Pasquils Jests, Certayne Conceyts and Jeasts,* and Taylor's *Wit and Mirth.* It is believed that this is also the first attempt to present to the modern reader, in their genuine form, the whimsical *Tales of the Mad-Men of Gotam;* and although the concluding section of the book, *Conceits, Clinches, Flashes and*

*b*

*Whimzies,* 1639, was republished by Mr. Halliwell in 1860, the impression was limited to six-and-twenty copies, thus placing the volume scarcely more within the reach of an ordinary purchaser than it was before.

In regard to *The Pleasant Conceits of Old Hobson,* 1607, which is included in the present volume, and which is composed of anecdotes, to the authorship of which the " Merry Londoner " had probably very slender claim, a passage may be quoted from Mr. Carrick's Memoir of the *Laird of Logan,* which is equally applicable to this and other attributions of the kind, originating in the desire of the writer to throw a halo of popularity round his facetious lucubrations:—"It appears to have been almost a general practice in collecting the jests or 'notable sayings' which have become current in a nation, to ascribe the merit of such sayings to some personage, real or fictitious, who is supposed to have distinguished himself for his ready wit, racy humour, and fertile imagination."

The copy of *A C. Mery Talys,* (reproduced in the first volume of this assemblage of facetiæ,) from which Mr. Singer printed his edition in 1815, is now in the possession of J. O. Halliwell, Esq., to whom Mr. Singer bequeathed it. No other is known to exist.

A perusal of the numerous collections of Tales brought together in this and the two former books is apt to lead to a feeling that in genuine home-grown humour, English literature is by no means wealthy. We shine indeed, but it is with borrowed light. Our jest-books are little beyond various readings to the Poggiana and other great stores of facetiæ; and if we should take away from the *C. Mery Talys* and its successors what is merely imported matter, it is to be feared that the residue would be compressible into a very slender compass. *Nihil Novi* should have been the motto of this publication; for to nothing in the entire circle of literature, science and art, is it more thoroughly applicable. There is scarcely a story which has not been told over and over again, with the change only of name, place, and circumstance. The germ and spirit are identical. Even the good things which the contemporaries of

Sydney Smith applauded in that excellent man, are in many cases discoverable in works which it is more probable than otherwise that Smith had read.

The *Wit and Mirth* of John Taylor, the Water Poet, although it can by no means claim complete exemption from the charge of plagiarism and larceny, is undoubtedly, as a collection, an unusually original and entertaining work, and there are many instances, in which it is the repository of curious anecdotes nowhere else preserved. In this respect, though of less remote antiquity than the *C. Mery Talys*, and of no direct Shakespearian interest, it is superior to the latter, and in point of raciness and comicality, the stories in the *Wit and Mirth* are hardly surpassed by any in the language. Those who came after the Water Poet certainly stole a great deal more from him than he had stolen from his predecessors; and one person, about the close of the 17th century, from an anxiety to testify his appreciation of the merits of Taylor's performance, reproduced the best articles, without a word of acknowledgment, as the " True and Diverting History of Tom of Chester." Selections from this tract are given by Mr. Halliwell in his *Palatine Anthology*, 1850, 4°.

Apart from their claim to originality, however, the old English jest-books ought to possess very considerable value in the eyes of the philologist and the student of early manners ; and the Editor hopes that he has performed a not unacceptable service in placing within the reach of the curious the most extensive assemblage of works in facetious lore ever published in this country.

# MERY TALES
## OF THE MAD MEN OF GOTHAM.

Merie Tales of the Mad Men of Gotam, gathered together by A. B. of Phisike Doctour. [Col.] Imprinted at London in Flet-Stret, beneath the Conduit, at the signe of S. John Evangelist, by Thomas Colwell. n. d. 12°, black letter.

*₄* See Halliwell's *Notices of Popular English Histories*, 1848.

The Merry Tales of the Mad Men of Gottam. Gathered together by A. B. of Phisicke, Doctor. [Woodcut of the hedging-in of the cuckoo.] Printed at London by B[ernard] A[lsop] and T[homas] F[awcet] for Michael Sparke, dwelling in Greene A[r]bor at the signe of the Blue-Bible, 1630, 12°. Black letter, 12 leaves, including title.

*₄* This edition, of which a copy is among Burton's books at Oxford, has been used for the present reprint. An earlier one, Lond. 1613, 12°, occurs in the *Harleian Catalogue*, but it seems to be no longer known.

The Merry Tales of the Mad Men of Gotam. By A. B. Doctor of Physick. Printed by J. R. for G. Coniers at the Golden Ring on Ludgate Hill, and J. Deacon at the Angel in Guilt-spur street without Newgate. n. d. 12°. bl. letter. With a similar woodcut on title of a Gothamite hedging in the cuckoo.

There is also a chapman's edition Printed and sold in London n. d. 12°, in the Bodleian, which possesses another impression without the title page, which may have appeared about the middle of the last century. Both these copies are in the Douce collection.

This facetious production, of which the earlier impressions appear to have perished, is generally and, probably, correctly ascribed to Andrew Borde who, according to Anthony Wood, published it in the reign of Henry VIII. That such was the case, is very likely, and when the excessive popularity of such a piece is considered, we can hardly wonder that all trace of the book in its original shape should have been lost. The Gothamite Tales were till lately, and may be still common as a chap-book in England, Scotland, and Ireland, and in 1840, Mr. Halliwell reprinted one of these editions. This reprint is itself scarce, and I have never met with it. But as a text it is, of course, of no value or importance.

Decker, in his *Guls Horn Book*, 1609, says :—"It is now high time for me to have a blow at thy head, which I will not cut off with sharp documents, but rather set it on faster ; bestowing upon it such excellent carving that, if *all the wise men of Gotham* should lay their heads together, their jobber-nowls should not be able to compare with thine."

Wither, in his *Abuses Stript and Whipt*, 1613, 8°, and many others among our early writers, allude to the hedging-in of the cuckoo, and Edward Dering, in his *Workes*, n. p. or d. 8°, numbers the Gothamite tales among the "witless devices" of the Elizabethan age.

Of Gotham, in Nottinghamshire, there is the following account in *England's Gazetteer*, 1751. "Gotham, in the S. W. angle of the County [is] noted for nothing so much as the ridiculous fable of the *wise men* here, who, 'tis said, went about to *hedge-in a cuckow*. What original it had does not appear, tho' at Court-Hill in this place there is a bush called Cuckow-Bush. The manor belonged anciently to the Beaumonts Earls of Leicester, who had a castle here. The family of Dives were Lords of this Town in the Reign of Henry II., and held it to the time of Edward III. It went thence by marriage to the family of St. Andrew, who were Lords of it till the Reign of King Charles I., when for want of issue-male it went by marriage to Gervase Piggot, Esq. of Thrumpton, from whom it has descended to his posterity.

# Here beginneth certaine merry Tales of the Mad-men of Gottam.

## The first Tale.

THERE was two men of Gottam, and the one of them was going to the Market to Nottingham to buy sheepe, and the other came from the Market : and both met together vpon Nottingham-bridge. Well met, said the one to the other. Whither be yee going? said he that came from Nottingham. Marry, said he that was going thither, I goe to the market to buy sheepe. Buy sheepe ! said the other, and which way wilt thou bring them home? Marry, said the other, I will bring them ouer this bridge. By robin hood, said he that came from Nottingham, but thou shalt not. By Maid marrian, said he that was going thither ward, but I will. Thou shalt not, said the one. I will, said the other. Let here, said yᵉ one. Shue there, said the other. Then they beate their staues against the ground, one against the other, as there had beene an hundred sheepe betwixt them. Hold in, said the one ; beware by leaping ouer the bridge of my sheepe. I care not, said the other.[1] They shall not come this way, said the one. But they shall, said the other. Then said the other : & if that thou make much to doe, I will put my finger in thy mouth. A **** thou wilt, said the other. And as they were at their contention, another man of Gottam came from the market with a sacke of meale vpon a horse, and seeing and hearing his neighbours at strife for sheepe, and none betwixt them, said : Ah, fooles, will you neuer learn wit ? Helpe me, said he that had the meale, and lay my sack vpon my shoulder. They did so ; and he went to the one side of the bridge, and vnloosed the mouth of the sacke, and did shake out all his meale into the riuer. Now, neigbours, said the man, how much meale is there in my sacke now ? Marry, there is none at all, said they. Now, by my faith, said he, euen as much wit is in your two heads, to striue for that thing you haue not.

Which was the wisest of all these three persons, judge you ?[2]

(1) By an inadvertence, *said the other* is repeated in the old ed.

(2) This story is also related in *A C. Mery Talys*, of which it is No. xxii ; and the reader may supply from the present source what is deficient in the earlier text.

## The second Tale.

THERE was a man of Gottam did ride to the market
with two bushells of wheate, and because his horse
should not beare heauy, he caried his corne vpon
his owne necke, & did ride vpon his horse, because his horse should not cary to heauy a burthen.
Judge you which was the wisest, his horse or himselfe.

## The third Tale.

.ON a tyme, the men of Gottam would haue pinned
in the Cuckoo, whereby shee should sing all the
yeere, and in the midst of yᵉ town they made a
hedge round in compasse, and they had got a
Cuckoo, and had put her into it, and said : Sing
here all the yeere, and thou shalt lacke neither
meate nor drinke. The Cuckoo, as soone as she
perceiued her selfe incompassed within the hedge,
flew away. A vengeance on her! said they; we
made not our hedge high enough.

## The fourth Tale.

THERE was a man of Gottam, the which went to
the market to Nottingham, to sell Cheese, and as

he was going downe the hill to Nottingham-bridge, one of his Cheeses did fall out of his wallet, and ran downe the hill. A whorsons ! said the fellow ; can you run to the Market alone? I will send the one after the other of you. Then he layd downe his wallet, and tooke the Cheeses, and did tumble them downe the hill one after another, and some ran into one bush, and some into another ; and at the last he said : I charge you all meet me in the Market-place. And when the fellow came to the Market-place to meet his Cheeses, he stayed there, till the Market was almost done. Then he went about and did enquire of his Neighbors and other men, if they did see his Cheeses come to the Market. Who should bring them? said one of the Market-men. Marry, themselves, said the fellow ; they knew the way well enough. He said : a vengeance on them all! I did feare to see my Cheeses run so fast, that they would run beyond the market ; I am now fully perswaded, that they bee now almost at Yorke ; whereupon he forthwith hired a horse to ride after to Yorke to seeke his Cheeses, where they were not. But to this day no man could tell him of his Cheeses.

## The fift Tale.

THERE was a man of Gottam, who bought at Nottingham a Treuet or a Brandyron, and as he was going home, his shoulders grew sore with the cariage thereof, & he set it downe; and, seeing that it had three feet, said : a whorson! hast thou three feet, and I but two? thou shalt beare me home, if thou wilt, and so set it downe on the ground, and sot himselfe downe thereupon, and said to the Treuet : beare me, as long as I haue borne thee : for, if thou doe not, thou shalt stond still for me. The man of Gottam did see, that his Treuet would not goe further. Stand still, said he, in the Mares name, and follow me, if thou wilt; I will tell thee the right way to my home. When he did come home to his house, his wife said : where is my Treuit? The man said : he hath three legs, and I haue but two, and I did teach him the way to my house; let him come home, if he will. Where left ye the Treuet, said the wife? At Gottam hill, said the man. His wife did runne and fetch home the Treuet her owne selfe, or else she had lost it through her husbands wit.

## The sixt Tale.

THERE dwelt a Smith at Gottam, who had a Waspes nest in the strow in the end of his Forge. There did come one of his neigbors to haue his horse shood, and the Waspes were so busie, that the fellow was stung with a Waspe. He, being angry, said : art thou worthy to keepe a forge or no, to haue men stung here with wasps? O, neighbour, said the Smith, be content; I will put them from this nest by and by. Immediately he tooke a Coulter, and heated it in his Forge glowing hot, and he thrust it into the straw in the end of his Forge, and so he set his Forge a fire, [and] burnt it vp. Then said the Smith : and I told thee I would fire them forth of their nest.

## The seuenth Tale.

WHEN that good-Friday was come, the men of Gottam did cast their heads together what to do with their white Herring, their red Herring, their Sprats and salt Fish. One consulted with the other, and agreed that such fish should be cast into their Pond or poole (the which was in the middle of the Towne), that it might increase against the

next yeere; & every man that had any Fish left,
did cast them into the Poole. The one said : I
haue thus many white Herrings; another said : I
haue thus many Sprats; another said : I haue thus
many red Herrings; and the other said : I haue
thus many salt Fishes. Let all goe together into
the Poole or Pond, and we shall fare like lords y°
next Lent. At the beginning of the next Lent
following, the men did draw the Pond to haue
their Fish, and there was nothing but a great Eele.

Ah ! said they all, a mischeife on this Eele ! for
he hath eate vp all our Fish. What shall we doe
with him, said the one to the other? Kill him,
said the one of them; chop him all to pieces,
said another. Nay, not so, said the other, Let
vs drowne him. Be it so, said all.

They went to another Poole or Pond by, and
did cast in the Eele into the water. Lye there,
said they, and shift for thyselfe : for no helpe thou
shalt haue of vs; and there they left the Eele to
be drowned.


## The eight Tale.

ON a time, the men of Gottam had forgotten to
pay their rent to their landlord. The one said to
the other : to morow is our pay day, and what

remedy shall we find to send our money to our
Lord? The one said: this day I haue taken a
quicke Hare, and he shall carry it: for he is light
of foot. Be it so, said all, he shal haue a Letter
and a purse to put in our money, and we shall
direct him the ready way; and when the Letters
were written, and the mony put in a Purse, they
did tye them about the Hares necke, saying:
first, thou must goe to Loughborow, and then to
Leicester, and at Newarke there is our Lord, and
commend vs to him, and there is his dutie.[1] The
Hare, as soone as he was out of their hands, he
did run a cleane contrary way. Some cried to
him, saying: thou must goe to Loughborow first;
some said: let the Hare alone, hee can tell a
neerer way, then the best of vs all doe, let him
goe. Another said: it is a subtle Hare, let her
alone, she will not keep the highway for feare of
dogs.

## The ninth Tale.

ON a time, there was one of Gottam was a mowing
in the meads, and found a great Grashopper:[2]
he cast downe his sithe, and did run home to his
neighbours and said, that there was a Diuell in

(1) *i. e.* his due.   (2) *i. e.* a *Cicada.*

the field that hopped in the Grasse. Then there was euery man ready with Clubs and Staues, with Halberts and other weapons, to goe and kill the Grashopper. When they did come to the place, where the Grashopper should be, said the one to the other : let euery man crosse himselfe from the Diuell, or we will not meddle with him. And so they returned againe, and said : we were well blest this day that we went no further. Ah ! cowards, said he that had the Sithe in the mead ; helpe me to fetch my Sithe. No, said they, it is good to sleepe in a whole skin ; better it is to loose thy Sithe, than to marre vs all.

## Ƭhe tenth Ƭale.

ON a certaine time, there were xii. men of Gottam, that did goe a fishing, and some did wade in the water, and some stood vpon dry land, and when that they went homeward, one said to the other : we haue ventured wonderfull hard this day in wading ; I pray God, that none of vs that did come from home be drowned. Marry, said the one to the other, let vs see that, for there did twelue of vs come out : and they told themselues, and euery man did tell eleuen, and the twelfth man did neuer tell himselfe. Alas, said the one to the other, there is one of vs drowned. They went backe to the Brooke, where that they had beene fishing, and sought vp and downe for him that was drowned, and did make great lamentation. A Courtier did come riding by, and he did aske what it was they did seeke, and why they were so sorry. O, said they, this day we went to fish in this Brooke, and there did come out twelue of vs, and one is drowned. Why, said the Courtier, tell how many be of you. And the one told eleuen, and he did not tell himselfe. Well, said the Courtier, what will you giue me, and I will find out twelve men ? Sir, said they, all the money that we haue. Giue me the money, said the Courtier : and hee began with the first, and did giue him a recombendibus ouer the shoulders that he groaned, and said : there is one. So he serued all, that they groaned on the matter. When he did come to the last, he payed him a good [blow], saying : here is the twelfth man. Gods blessing on your heart, said all the company, that you haue found out our neighbour.

## 𝕮𝖍𝖊 𝖊𝖑𝖊𝖚𝖊𝖓𝖙𝖍 𝕮𝖆𝖑𝖊.

THERE was a man of Gottam, that did ride vpon
the high way, and there he found a Cheese, and he
puld out his sword, & pored and pricked with the
poynt of his sword, to take vp the Cheese. There
did come another man by, and did alight, and tooke
vp the Cheese, and did ride his way with it. The
man of Gottam did ride backe to Nottingham to
buy a long sword to take vp the Cheese, and when
he had bought this sword, he returned backe, and
when he did come to the place, where the Cheese
did lye, he pulled out his sword, and pricked the
ground, saying : a murrion take it ! if I had had
this sword, I had had the Cheese myselfe, and now
another hath got it.

## 𝕮𝖍𝖊 𝖙𝖜𝖊𝖑𝖋𝖙𝖍 𝕮𝖆𝖑𝖊.

THERE was a man of Gottam, and he did not loue
his wife ; and hauing a faire haire, her husband
said diuers times, that he would cut it off, and
he durst not doe it, when she was waking, but
when she was a sleepe. So, on a night, he tooke
up a paire of sheeres, and layd them vnder his
beds head, the which his wife perceiued. And
then she did call to one of her maids, and said ;

goe to bed to my husband : for he is minded to cut off my haire to night ; let him cut off thy haire, and I will giue thee as good a kertle as euer thou didst weare. The maid did so, and fained herselfe asleepe, the which [when] the man perceiued, [he] cut off the maid's haire, and did wrap it about his sheeres, and laid it vnder his beds head, and fell asleepe. The wife made her maid to rise, and tooke the haire and the sheeres, and went into the hall, and there burnt y⁰ haire. The man had a horse, the which hee did loue aboue all things (as shee did well know). The good wife went into her husbands Stable, and cut off the horse taile, and did wrap the Sheeres in the Horse taile, and laid them vnder her husbands head. In the morning, shee did rise betimes, and did sit by the fire kembing of her head. At last, the man did come to the fire ; and, seeing of his wife kembing of her head, marvelled much thereat. The Maide, seeing her Master standing in a browne study, said : what a diuell ailes the horse in the stable : for he bleedeth sore ? The good man ranne into the stable, and found that his horse taile was cut off; he went to his beds head, and did find the sheeres wrapt in his horse taile, and did come to his wife, saying : I cry thee mercy, for I had thought that I had cut off thy haire to night, and I haue cut off my

horse taile. Yea, said shee, selfe do, selfe haue :
many a man thinketh to doe another man a shrewd
turne, and it turneth oftimes to his owne selfe.

## The thirteenth Tale.

THERE was a man in Gottam, that layd a wager
with his wife, that shee should not make him cuckold. No, said she, but I can. Spare not, quoth
he, doe what thou canst. On a time, shee hid all
the Spiggots and Fausets in the House, and shee
went into her Buttery, and set a Barrell abroach,
and cryed to her husband, and said : I pray you,
bring me hither a spiggot and a fauset, or else all
the Ale will run out. The good man sought vp and
downe, and could find none. Come hither, said
she then, and hold your finger in the tap-hole. She
pulled out her finger, and the good-man put in his.
Shee then called to her Taylor, which did dwell at
the next doore, with whom she made a blinde bargaine ; and within a while shee came to her husband,
and did bring a Spiggot and a Fauset with her,
saying : pull out thy finger out of the tap-hole,
gentle Cuckold : for you haue lost your bargaine.
I beshrew your heart for your labour, said the goodman. Make no such bargaines then, said she,
with me.

## The fourteenth Tale.

THERE was a man of Gottam, that had taken a Bustard,[1] and to the eating of it did bid foure or fiue Gentlemen's seruants. The wife had killed an old brood Goose, and she & two of her Gossips had eaten vp the Bustard, and the old Goose was layd to the fire for the Gentlemens seruants : and when that they were come, and that the old Goose was set before them : what is this, then? said one of the men. The good man said : a good fat Bustard. A Bustard! said they; it is an old Goose, and thou art a knaue to mocke vs; and in great anger they departed out of his house, and went home. The fellow was sorry, that the Gentlemens seruant[s] were angry, and did take a bagge, and did in the Bustards feathers, and thought to goe to them, and shew them the feathers of the Bustard, and so to please them. The wife prayed her husband, ere hee went, to fetch in a blocke to the fire ; and in the meane space she did pull out all the Bustards feathers, and did put in the Goose feathers. The man, taking his wallet or bagge, went to the Gentlemens seruants, and said : pray you, bee not angry with me, for you shall see here,

(1) All the old eds. have buzzard, wherever the word occurs.

that I had a Bustard, for here be the feathers ; and he opened his bag, and did shake out all the Goose feathers.  The Gentlemens seruants, seeing the Goose feathers, said : why, thou knaue, couldest thou not be contented to mocke vs at thine owne house, but art come to mocke vs here.  The one tooke a waster [1] in his hand, and did giue him a dozen stripes, saying : take this for a reward, and hereafter mocke not vs any more.

## The XV. Tale.

THERE was a young man of Gottam, the which should goe wooing to a faire maid.  His mother did warne him beforehand, saying : when thou dost looke vpon her, cast a sheepes eye, and say : how doe you, sweet pigs-nie ?  The fellow went to the Butchers, and bought seuen or eight sheepes eyes, and when this lusty wooer did sit at dinner, hee would looke vpon his faire wench, and would cast in her face a sheepes eye, saying : how doest thou, my pretty pigs-nie ?  How doe I (said the wench), swines face ?  why dost thou cast the sheepes eye vpon me ?  O sweet pigs nie, said he, haue at thee another !  I defie thee, swines face,

(1) A cudgel.  See *A C. Mery Talys*, No. 2, *note.*

saith the wench. The fellow, being abashed, said : what, sweet pigs nie, be content : for, if thou doe liue vntill the next yeere, thou wilt be foule Sowe. Walke, knaue, walke, said she : for, if thou liue till the next yeere, thou wilt be a starke knaue, a lubber, and a foole. Here a man may see that for a mans good will, he shall haue euill will and displeasure.

## The XVI. Tale.

A MANS wife of Gottam was brought a bed of a Man-child; the father did bid the Gossips, the which were children of eight or nine yeeres of age. The eldest childs name that should be Godfather was named Gilbert; the second child was named Humfrey; and the Godmothers name was Christabel. The friends of them did admonish them, saying, that diuers times they must say after the Priest. When all were come to the Church doore, the Priest said : be you agreed of the name ? Be you, said Gilbert, agreed of the name ? Be you, said Humfrey, agreed of the name ? Be you, sayd Christabel, agreed of the name ? The Priest said : wherefore be you come hither ? Gilbert said : wherefore be you come hither ? Humfrey said : wherefore bee you come hither ? Christabel

said : wherefore bee you come hither? The
Priest, being amazed, could not tell what to say,
but whistled, and said whew. Gilbert whistled &
said whew ; Humfrey whistled and said whew, and
so did Christabel. The Priest, being angry, said :
goe home, fooles, goe home. Goe home, fooles,
goe home, said Gilbert. Goe home, fooles, goe
home, said Humfrey. Goe home, fooles, goe home,
said Christabel. The Priest then prouided new
Godfathers and Godmothers. Here a man may
see, that children can doe nothing without good
instructions. And they bee not wise that will
regard childrens words.

## The XVII. Tale.

THERE was a man of Gottam, the which should
bee married ; and when the day of marriage was
appoynted, and the time came that they should be
married together, the Priest said : say after me.
The man said : say after me. The Priest said :
say not after me such words, but say after me, as
I will tell thee. The fellow said : say not after
me such words, but say after me, as I will tell
thee. The Priest said : thou doest play the foole
and the knaue, to mocke with this holy Sacrament
of Matrimonie. The fellow said : Doest thou play

the foole and the knaue, to mock with this holy Sacrament of Matrimonie ?  The Priest could not tell what to say, but sayd : what shall I doe with this foole ?  The fellow said : what shal I do with this foole ?  Farewell, said the Priest, I will not marry thee.  Farewell, said the fellow, I will not marry thee.  The priest departed ; howbeit, the fellow by other men was instructed how to doe ; [and] after that, he was married.  And I heard say, such a foolish pranke was played at Kingstone of late dayes.

## The XVIII Tale.

THERE was a Scottish man, the which did dwell at Gottam, & hee had taken a house, [a] little from London, and of it hee would make an Inne ; and to his Signe hee would haue a Bores-head. And hee went to London to haue a Bores-head made.  Hee did come to a Caruer or a Joyner, saying in his mother tongue : I say, speake, canst thou make me a Bare-head ?  Yea, said the Caruer. Then said the Scottish-man : make me a Bare-head anonst Youle, and thouse haue twenty pence for thy hire.  I will doe it, said the Caruer.  On S. Andrews day before Christmas, the which is named

Youle in Scotland (and in England in the North) the Scottish man did come to London for his Boreshead, to set it at the doore for a signe. I say, speak, said the Scottishman, hast thou made the bare-head? Yea, said the Caruer. Then thouse a geude fellow. The Caruer went, and did bring a mans head of wood, that was bare, and said: Sir, here is your bare-head. I say, said the Scottish-man, the mickle Diuell is this a bare-head. Yea, said the Caruer. I say, said the Scottishman, I will haue a bare-head, sicke an head as doth follow a Sew that hath Gryces. Sir, said the Caruer, I cannot tell what is a Sew, nor what is a Gryce. What, herson, kenst thou not a Sew, that will greet and grone, and her Gryces will run after her, and cry: aweeke, aweeke. Oh, said the Caruer, it is a Pig. Yea, said the[1] Scottishman, let mee haue his fathers head made in timber, and make me a bird, and set on her scalpe, and cause her to sing: whip whir, whip whir. The Caruer said: I cannot cause her to sing: whip whir. Why, herson, said the Scottishman, gar her as shee should sing: whip whir.

Here a man may see, that euery man doth delight in his owne senses, or doth reioyce in his fantasie.

---

(1) Old ed. reads *thy.*

# The XIX Tale.

IN old tyme, when these aforesaid iests (as men of the Countrey reported) and such fantasticall matters were[1] done at Gottam, which I cannot tell halfe, the wiues were gathered together in an Alehouse, and the one said to the other, that they were profitable to their husbands. Which way, good Gossips, said the Alewife ? The first said : I shall tell you all, good Gossips. I can neither bake, brew, nor can I doe no worke, wherefore I doe make euery day holyday, and I goe to the Alehouse, because at all times I cannot goe to the Church ; and in the Alehouse I pray to God to speed well my husband, and I doe thinke my prayer shall doe him much more good then my labour, if I should worke. Then said the second : I am profitable to my husband in sauing of Candles in winter : for I doe cause my husband and all my household folkes to goe to bed by day light, and to rise by day light. The third wife said : and I am profitable to my husband in spending of bread, for I will eate but little : for to the drinking of a gallon or two of good Ale, I care for no meate.[2] The fourth

(1) In old ed. this word is erroneously repeated.

(2) This reminds us of the capital song of *Back and Side go bare, go bare*, in "Gammer Gurtons Needle," 1575.

wife said : I am loth to spend meate and drinke
at home in mine owne house, wherefore I doe goe
to the wine Tauerne at Nottingham, and so take
wine and such things, as God shall send me there.
The fift wife said : a man shall haue euer more
company in another mans house then in his owne,
and most commonly in an Alehouse is the best
cheare in a Towne ; and for sparing of meat and
drinke, and other necessaries, I goe to the Alehouse. The sixt wife said : my husband hath
Wooll, and Flaxe, and Towe ; and to spare it, I
goe to other mens houses to doe other mens worke.
The seuenth wife said : I doe spare my husbands
wood and cole, and doe sit talking all the day by
other mens fires. The eight said : Beefe and
Mutton, and Porke is deare ; wherefore I doe spare
it, and do take Pigge, Goose, Hen, Chicken, Coney,
and Capon, the which bee of lower price. The
ninth said : and I doe spare my husbands Sope
and lye : for when hee should be washed once in
a weeke, I doe wash once in a quarter of a yeere.
Then said the Ale-wife : and I doe keepe my
husbands Ale, that I doe brew, from sowring : for,
whereas I was wont to drinke vp all, now I doe
leaue neuer a drop.

## 𝕿𝖍𝖊 𝖃𝖃 𝕿𝖆𝖑𝖊.

ON Ashwednesday, the Priest of Gottam would haue a collation to his Parishioners, and said : Friends, the time is come, that you must vse prayer and fasting & almesdeedes, and this weeke come you to shrift, and I will tell you more of my mind : for, as for prayers, I thinke there bee not two persons in the Parish can say halfe their Paternoster ; as for fasting, you fast still : for you haue not a good meales meate through the whole yeere ; as for almes-deedes, what should you doe to giue anything, that haue nothing to take to ? But when that you come to shrift, I will tell you more of my mind after Masse. The good man, that did keepe the Ale-house, did come to shrift, and aboue all things he confessed himselfe to be drunke diuers times in the yeere, specially in Lent. The Priest said : in Lent, thou shouldest most refraine from drunkennesse, and abstaine from drinke.

Not so, said the fellow: for it is an old Prouerbe, that fish must swim. Yea, said the Priest, it must swim in water. I cry you mercy, quoth the fellow, I thought it should haue swom in good Ale.

So, one after another, the men of Gottam did come to shrift : and when they were shriuen, the

Priest said: I cannot tell what penance to giue you. If I should enioyne you to prayer, there is none of you that can say your Pater noster, and you be now too old to learne ; and to enioyne you to fast, it were but foolishnesse : for you doe not eate a good meales meat in a yeere ; wherefore I doe enioyne thee to labour well all the weeke, that thou maist fare well to dinner on the Sundayes, and I will come to dinner, and see it to be so, and take part. Another man he did enioyne to fare well on Munday, and another, the Teusday ; and one after another, that one or other should fare well once a weeke, that hee might haue part of [his] meat. And as for Almes-deedes,

The Priest said : You be but beggers all,
except it be one or two ; therefore bestow your almes
on your selues.

\* \*
\*

**ffinis.**

# XII MERY JESTS
## OF THE WYDDOW EDYTH.

The Wydow Edyth : Twelue mery gestys of one called Edyth, the lyeing wydow whyche still lyueth. Emprynted at London at the sygne of the mere-mayde at Pollis gate next to chepesyde by J. Rastall. 23 March, MDXXV. Sm. folio, bl. letter.

*⁎* Of this edition not more than 3 copies are known. It extends to sign D. iii.

xii Mery Jests of the Wyddow Edyth. [Col.] Imprinted at London in Fletelane by Richarde Ihones, 1573, 4°, bl. letter. 32 unnumbered leaves, including title.

*⁎* Of this edition it is doubtful whether more than 2 copies be extant; the copy which has been used on the present occasion is among Selden's books in the Bodleian. The title is within a neat border. The running title is in Roman capitals, the title, table, and preface contain three leaves ; there are catchwords and signatures.

This singular tract is not strictly a *jest book*, but rather a relation of the tricks and deceptions practised by the heroine (among others) on one Walter Smith, who published them for the information of his contemporaries and posterity. The impression by Rastell is described at some length in Herbert's edition of Ames, and as all that is known of this female sharper is derived from the tract itself, it is unnecessary to do more than refer the reader thereto.

# XII. mery Jests of the wydowo Edyth.

THIS lying widow, false and craftie,
Late ī England hath deceiued many :
Both men and women of euery degree,
As wel of the Spiritual, as temporaltie :
Lordes, Knights, and Gentlemen also :
Yemen, Groomes, and that not long ago :
For, in the time of King Henry the eight,
She hath used many a suttle sleight.
What with lieng, weepyng and laughyng,
Dissemblyng, boastyng, and flatteryng,
As by this Booke hereafter doth appere.
Who so list the matter now for to here,
No fayned Stories, but matters in deed
Of xii. of her Jestes, here may ye reede.
Nowe newly printed this present yeare,
For such as delite mery Jests for to here.

1573.

## 𝕿𝖍𝖊 𝕮𝖔𝖓𝖙𝖊𝖓𝖙𝖊𝖘
## of these xíí. merꝑ 𝕵𝖊𝖘𝖙𝖊𝖘 folowꝑng.

THE first mery Jest declareth, how this faire and merye Mayden Edith was maryed to one Thomas Ellys, and how she ran away with another, by whom she had a bastard Doughter, and how she deceiued a Gentleman, bearynge him in hand, how her Doughter was Heire to faire Landes and great Richesse.

The second mery Jest : how this lying Edyth made a poore man to vnthatch his House, bearyng him in hand, that she wold couer it with Lead : and how she deceiued a Barbour, makyng him beleue she was a widow, and had great aboundance of Gooddes.

The thyrd mery Jest : how this wydow Edyth deceiued her Hoste at Hormynger, and her Hoste at Brandonfery, and borowed money of them both, and also one mayster Guy of whome she borowed iiii. Marke.

The fourth mery Jest, how this wydow Edith

deceiued a Doctor of diuinitie, at S. Thomas of
Akers in London, of v. Nobles he layd out for
her, and how she gaue hym the slyp.

The fifth merye Jest : how this wydow Edyth
deceiued a man and his wife that were ryding on
Pylgremage : of iiii Nobles that they laid out for
her : and how she deceiued a scriuener in London, whose name was M. Rowse.

The sixt merye Jest : how this wydowe Edyth
deceiued a Draper in Lōdon of a new Gowne and
a new Kyrtell ; and how she sent hym for a Nest
of Gobblets and other Plate to that scriuener
whome she had deceiued afore.

The vii mery Jest : how she deceiued a seruāt
of Sir Thomas Neuells, who in hope to haue her
in Mariage, with al her great richesse, kepte her
company, tyl al his money was spent ; and then she
tooke her flight, and forsooke him.

The eight mery Jest : how this wydow Edyth
deceyued a seruaunt of the Bysshop of Rochesters,
with her coggynge, and boastynge of her great
Richesse ; who like wise thought to haue had her
in Maryage.

The ix mery Jest : how she deceiued a Lord, sō-tyme Earle of Arūdell : and how he sent v. of his men seruantes and a handmaid to bere her company, and fetch her Daughter, who, as she boasted, was an Heire of great Landes.

The tenth merye Jest : how she deceiued three yong men of Chelsey, that were seruantes to Syr Thomas More, and were all three suters vnto her for Maryage : and what mischaunce happened vnto her.

The xi. mery Jest : how she deceiued three yong men of the Lord Legates seruants with her great liyng, crakyng and boastyng of her great Treasure and Jueiles.

The xii. merye Jèst : how this wydow Edyth deceyued the good man of the three Cuppes in Holburne, and one John Cotes : and how they both ryd with her to S. Albans to ouersee her houses & landes : and how thei were rewarded.

FINIS.

# The Preface.

In the Cittie of Exceter by Dell[1] a way
The tyme not passed hence many a day,
There dwelled a Yoman discrete and wise,
At the signe of the Flowerdelyse,
Which had to name John Haukyn,[2]
Discended he was of an honest line :
A Man but of a meane stature,
Full well compact in euery feature.
Broad he was from pine to pine,
And red in the face when he dranke wine.
Blacke was his Haire, and hooked his nose,
And now and then, had the cough and the pose.
A sycknesse rayned vpon him aye,
Which troubled him sore night and daye :
Beside the cough, a bloudy flyr,
And euer among a deadly yer,
Which brought him to his finall day.
But ere that tyme, I wyll you say
He dyd espouse within that countrie
In processe of yeares Wiues three :
Each after other, in mirth and game,
Women of great substaunce and fame.

(1) Ed. 1525 has *West*.    (2) Ed. 1573 has H*a*kyn.

3.    D

And namely the last weddes wyfe,
With whom he liued, withouten stryfe,
The space of full fyfteene yeere,
By than he was layd on a Beare.
A Daughter he had within band of maryage
By his last Wife, a worthy caryage,
Which named was Edyth at the Fontstone,
Of ii women and a man, of blood and bone,
And when that her Father was layd in graue,
From fyre and water her to saue.
Her Mother aye dyd her busy cure,
As Mothers done by course of nature :
And vertuously, as I haue hard say,
She brought vp her doughter night and day,
Charging her vpon her blessyng,
That she ne should medle with anything,
That sowned vnto good huswyfry ;
But aye study to forge and lye,
And counternaunce it right well therto,
In euery place where she dyd go.
This Childe, obeying her Mother deare,
Answered to her as you shall heare :
Mother, she sayde, I am your Daughter,
I wyll endeuour myselfe there after :
While that I liue, I shall resigne
All such as pertayne to verteous dicyplyne :
My study shalbe how I may conclude

In things the people to delude.
Thus is the Mother and Daughter agreed ;
Now go, sayd the Mother, God thee speed !
Thomas Ellys loueth thee well, perfay,
And woeth thee fast day by day :
His desyre is to haue thee to wyfe,
And to liue together all your lyfe.
Wed him hardely, spare not a dele,
And take another, when he hath not his hele :
Daughter, make mery, whiles thou may,
For this world wyll not last alway.
She promised her Mother to doo full well
Euery thing after her counsell.

**ﬀinis.**

## The fyrste merye Jest:

declareth how this faire & wel nurtured Damsel
Edyth was maryed to one Thomas Ellys: and how
she ran away with another, by whome she had a
bastard Doughter : and how she deceyued a Gentleman, who (for her worthinesse) preferred her to
Sir Thomas Deñys, before whom
she auouched her Doughter to
be Heire of fair landes.

———❧———

THOMAS ELLYS she maryed for a yeare or two,
And then left hym, and away dyd go
With a seruant of the Erle of Wyltshyre,
The which payd her well her hyre.
By hym in advoutry a childe she had,
Which dyed, when it was but a Lad :
Than her Lemman cast her vp,
Go where she wold : gup queane gup.
She toke her way from then ouer
To a Towne called Andouer.
And there she made a Gentylman
Beleue that she was from hym gone,
To seeke her a friend, which in her right

Would defend her with mayne and might :
For great wrong she said she had,
And by mighty hand was sore bestad ;
And by mighty hand wrongfully reft
Both house and lande, and nothyng to her left ;
And what so he were, that of good affection
Wolde her helpe, the whole disposition
Of her onely Doughter he should haue,
Which is a great Heyre, God her saue.
This Gentilman went [in] her right
To Syr Thomas Dennis, a worshipfull Knight,
Informyng hym, how that it stood
With this wydow of gentle blood,
And how that she had a Doughter and Heire,
Tender of Age, goodly and fayre :
Which should inherite successiuely
Both house and lande, and that good plentie ;
And who that would help her to her ryght,
Should haue her Doughter day and nyght,
In honestie to vse, and her selfe both ;
Whiche thyng she bound with a great Othe.
The Knight, hearyng this euery dell,
Bad the gentylman no longer to dwell,
But walke with her, and fet her Doughter,
And we shall commyn more hereafter.
Then they departed, and wandred right foorth,
Tyl they w^t good speed cam both to Wainswōrth ;

And there the gentylman full well did espie,
How the coggyng queane most falsly dyd lye.
Then would he no longer geue heede to her talke,
But bad her be packyng w$^t$ a vengeance, & walke,
And neuer to come in his sight any more :
Syr, no more I wyl not (quoth she), & god before.

## 𝕿𝖍𝖊 𝖘𝖊𝖈𝖔𝖓𝖉 𝖒𝖊𝖗𝖞 𝕵𝖊𝖘𝖙:

how this liynge Wydowe Edyth made a poore man
to vnthatch his House, and bore him in hand, she
would bestow the coueryng of it with Lead : And
how she deceiued a Barbour, makyng hym
beleue she was a Wydowe, and had
great abundance of Richesse.

———❧———

FROM Wainsworth, than, she tooke her way,
To Kew, where thē y$^e$ Lord Chamberlayn lay.
And not far from his place, a good long space
In a poore mans house lodged she was,
And was in good credence with him in deede.
She, seing the house couered with reede,
Sayd to her Hoste, vpon a day:
Mine Host (quod she), next to the hye way,

Take ye the thak of your house a downe ;
It is a foule sight buttying on the towne :
Haue it away fast, leaue the Rafters bare,
And for a new couering take ye no care ;
It shalbe hilled agayne, ere it be long,
But loke ye wel that the Rafters be strong :
For I tell you they shall beare a great weight.
Hoste (quod she), I sweare by this light,
I wyll haue that end couered with Lead ;
Came neuer such a coueryng ouer thy head.
Nor none of thy kin, I may say to thee.
It lyeth in my Storehouse, so mote I thee,
In fayre playne rolles new melt with glede.
My Plommer bestowed it, I pray God hym spede,
An honest man is he, and expert in that Art.
The selfe same day that he did depart
A way from my house, I cannot tell where,
Many a fayre Noble with him he did bere.
Her Hoste, when he had hard this tale,
With his hands his cap he gan avale,
And with his knees flexed, sayd vnto her there :
I cry you mercy, Mistris, what do you here
In this poore cotage which is not meete for you ?
Holde thy peace (quod she), for I wil not be kno,
What I am as yet, and for consideration ;
Go thou thy way, and worke after the facion,
As I haue sayd : & looke thou speke no worde ;

But is none of my Lords seruants at bord
With you (quod she), nor hawnte they not heare ?
It is lyke yᵗ they should, for you haue good beere.
Yes (quod her hoste), now and then among
My Lords Barbour is here, wᵗ many a good song ;
A liuely yong man, I tell you, & full of corage ;
Somtyme we haue here our whit wine wᵗ borag,
And wafers pypyng hot out of the glede.
We chat and laugh it out, so God me spede !
Mistresse, folke must nede be mery somtyme.
Hoste, ye say true, by holy Saint Sym,
Quod the wydow, but let us go to dinner,
It is xii of the cloke, and som what ouer.
    Into the house they go, and take refection,
And after that they fell in further communication.
This yong mā yᵉ barbour, as he was accustomed,
Came in sodenly, and biddeth them God spede :
Welcome my guest (quod yᵉ good man of yᵉ house),
How haue you done, since we eate the souse,
The last night, ye remember, to bedward ?
Tut, and it were a stone neuer so hard,
Quoth this barbour, it should digest with me :
For somtime, when it wyll not forge,
I drinke a little lamp Oyle, & cast up my gorge,
And then forthwith I am as hole as a trout.
But Hoste (quod he), what woman went out
At the Dore now ? doe you know her well ?

By gods body, Thomas barbour, I shal thee tel.
She is a widow of late come to towne ;
But at al aduentures I had leuer thā my gowne
Thou were sure to her : for she to me sayd,
She is worth a M. li. and euery man payd ;
Besyde land, I cannot tell how mych.
The barbour gan to claw there it did not ych.
Holde your peace (quod he), she cōmeth in againe :
Mistresse, sayd Thomas, wil it plese you to drink ?
And be ye mery, and vse not to think :
Me semeth, it becōmeth a wel fauoured wight,
And namely a woman, to be glad and light.
Yong man (quod she), I thank God of his loue,
I haue no great cause to make any moue :
I knowledge this, that God hath indewed me
An hundred folde better than I am worthye,
And I pray to hym, that I neuer do the thing,
Which is contrary vnto his hye pleasyng.
Gods blessīg haue you (sayd Thomas barbour),
Forsooth ye speake lyke a good Cristian creature ;
But let vs leaue al this, & make some good cheare.
Ostes, fyll vs an other pot with beere,
Quod yᵉ Barbour, and bid this gentilwomā welcōe
Mistrisse, sayd yᵉ good wife, this is all & some,
Ye be hartely welcome euen at one worde ;
And therewith she droue yᵉ Cat of the borde,
And made rome for a dish or two more.

This wydow had vnder her chin a sore,
That Surgeons cal Noli me tangere,
Which when the barbour did espye,
He sayd : Misterisse, may I be so bolde ?
Nay yet I will not touch it, for my hand is colde ;
I pray you what is this, God saue the mark ?
A thing (quod she), y$^t$ I wyll take no. great cark
For surgery therto : for I was borne so,
I thank God whether I ryde or go.
It doth not greue me otherwise than you see.
And it is no great blemysh, so mote I thee,
Quod the Barbour, but a lytell eye sore :
Now, Mistresse, do ye gladly, I can no more.
I trust we shall make better chere than this,
And then he began for to coll her and kysse.
So long they were dalliyng both day and night,
Tyll eche had others their trouth yplyght,
Whiche was the same day, as I hard say,
That the thatch of the house was pulled away ;
And asked they were in holy Churche,
Where Christ's workmen do wurche.
But when he, by long communication,
Knew her falshod and dissimulation,
And after he perceiued he was begyled,
In all the haste his wife he exyled,
Ratyng her with termes somthyng rude,
And here of hym I wyll conclude.

## 𝕮𝖍𝖊 𝖙𝖍𝖞𝖗𝖉 𝖒𝖊𝖗𝖞𝖊 𝕵𝖊𝖘𝖙 :

how this Wydow Edyth decyued her Hoste
at Hormynger, and her Hoste at Brandonfery,
and borowed money of them both : and
also, one Mayster Guy, of whom she
borowed iiij Marke.

———&———

THIS wydow then walked withouten fere,
Tyll that she came to Hormynger,
Within two myles of S. Edmunds bery,
And there she abode, full iocunde and mery,
For the space fully of vi weekes day ;
And borrowed money there as she lay.
Her old lyes she occupted styll,
The people gaue credence her untyll ;
At Thetford she sayd her stuffe lay,
Which false was proued vpon a day ;
Than one master Lee committed her to ward,
And little or nought she dyd it regard ;
On the vi. day after deliuered she was,
And at her owne lyberty to passe and repasse.
Then straight way she toke to Brandonfery,
In all her lyfe was she neuer so mery,
And there she borrowed of her Hoste

Thirteene shillings, with myckle boste
Of her great substance, which she sayd she had ;
To Bradefolde straight her Hoste she lad,
Where she sayde that she dwelled as than.
And when she came thyther, she fild him a can,
Full with good Ale, and sayd he was welcome.
For his thirteene shillings she bad him bum,
And laughed tyghe : no more could he haue.
An oth he sware, so God hym saue,
The Justice should know of her deceyt,
A wh***! (quod he) heyt, wh***, heyt !
The Justice name was master Lee,
He sent her to Saint Edmonds berye.
And there in the Jayle halfe a yeare
She continewed without good cheare.
But after she was deliuered out
Upon a day, withouten doubt,
By Lorde Abbot commanded it should so bee,
When he was remembred of his charitye.
From thence she departed, and to Coulme she come,
Wher with her lyes, all and some,
She sudiorned, and was at borde
In an house of my Lord of Oxenforde,
Wherein a seruant of his owne did dwell,
Which brewed bere, but none to sell.
The Brewer was called John Douchmon,
With whom vi. dayes she dyd won.

Then after to Stretford at the bow
She repayred right as I trow,
And vii. dayes there she abode,
Spreding her lyes all abrode.
In which tyme one Maister Gye,
Supposing nought that she did lye,
And trustyng of her to haue some good,
Foure Marks, by the swete roode,
He lent her out of his purs anon,
And asked ay, when she wold gon
To the place where her goods were layd,
Which was at Barking (as she sayd).
Master Guy and his sister both
To ride with her they were not loth,
Ne grudged nothing, till they perceiued,
That she had them falsly deceiued.
Than Master Guy, with egre moode,
In the place there as they stoode,
Raft her both Kyrtle and gowne,
And in her Peticote to the Towne
He sent her forth, Mahound her saue!
For his iiii. Marks no more could he haue.

**ﬃnis.**

## 𝕿𝖍𝖊 𝖋𝖔𝖚𝖗𝖙𝖍 𝖒𝖊𝖗𝖞 𝕵𝖊𝖘𝖙,

how this Wyddow Edyth deceiued a Doctor of
Diuynitie at S. Thomas of Akers in London of fiue
Nobles, that he lay out for her, and how shee
gaue him the slip.

———◦◦———

To Barkyng than she tooke her gate,
And lodged she was at the Abbay yate
For a day or two, till she could prouide
A Gowne : and then wolde no lenger byde
In that quarter ; she thought it not best ;
She deemd her profyt there did not rest,
Namely so neare the Nunnes nose.
In a mornyng she get her ouer the close,
Westwarde she yede, the soth to saye,
And came to London that same daye.
At London stone she was hosted,
And there she prated and she bosted
Of much fayre stuffe that she had,
The which stuffe she wolde be glad
For the loue of Christ to forsake,
And Mantle and Ring for to take.
She prayed her Hoste after a day or two,
To let his worke, and with her to go :

And bring her to some discrete man,
The which full well tell can,
What belongeth vnto that thing,
I meane the Mantle and the Ring.
Of him she sayd she would confessed be,
Desyring the hole Trinitie
To be her ayde in that foresayde mater.
Her Host brought her to S. Thomas of Aker,
And there she was prouided anone,
I tell you for trothe, of such a one,
As knew by learning what was to do
In such busynes, and what longeth therto.
A Doctor he was of hie deuinytie,
Called deuote and ful of charitie :
A good publysher of God's word
In Church and Towne, and sitting at the Bord :
This world dispising night and day :
All mundayne glory, he wold saye,
I wholy defye, and vtterly forsake :
The Deuyll (quod he) shall them al take,
That loueth these riches and pomp temporall,
More then God that sent them all.
They shall neuer see their maker in the face :
With Sathan prepared is their place,
In the dark dongeon, in the region alow,
Of ioy and blis neuer for to know :
More sinfull liuyng was neuer vsed,

Than is now a dayes : no vice refused :
And worst of all, with vs of the Church,
That should teach other, how they should wurck,
And to shew them the way to heauens blisse,
Where our Sauiours dwelling is.
O God, why doe we not so ?
Why doe we not let these Beneficies go ?
Why do we retayne more then suffises ?
Why do we not geue vnto them that cries ?
Why fyll we our Bellyes, and let other go wᵗoute ?
Why doe we not walke out all aboute ?
Why doe we not pray and watch all night ?
Why doe we not our duty, as it is right ?
Why doe we not let other mens wiues alone,
And sylly poore wenches, making their mone ?
Why obserue we not the precepts of God ?
What yf we be punished with our owne rod,
Whom shall we erecte the fault vnto,
But to our selfes that can neuer say no ?
And one thing ther is, yᵗ maketh my hart to blede,
As oft as I think thereon, so god me spede.
This coueitousnesse vsed with men of my facultye,
Oh, what meane they ? Christs holy benedicitie !
Can they not be content wᵗ iiii. nor wᵗ fyue ?
I trow they wold that no man should thriue,
But them selfes onely, an heauy case !
I know one man, wheresoeuer he was,

That hath vi. benefices, and yet not content,
And the least of them is xx. li. rent.
I meane by the yeare, and the cure serued,
And no good is don, but all reserued :
It is maruell to see the vnsaciable mind,
That can neuer be fulfylled, before nor behind :
I assure you, I could be wel pleased
With iiii. such promocions : & hold me wel eased
As for a certayne time, tyl an other fall,
Welcome, good wyfe, what say you to all
This world ? now (quod he) haue done let see.
Sir, sayd this widow, vnder benedicitie,
I haue for to speak, if it lyke you to heare.
Come your wayes (quod he), & be of good cheare ;
Dispayre not, what so euer the matter bee :
I shall go betwene the Feend and thee ;
And eke discharge thee agayne our heauen king,
If that you wyll doe after my teaching.
Wherfore begin ye in Christs holy name ;
Breake your mind hardly, auoyde all shame.
She kneeled thē a down on her knees deuoutly,
And tolde her confessour many a great lye :
And of the treasure that she had in store ;
And when that she could tell no more,
Master Doctor bad she should be mery ;
He sayd : Ego absoluo te :
Forte sic, forte non.

3.                         E

And when that they had al done,
Out of the Church they went both.
She promised him a Gowne of cloth,
Of Scarlet coulour, very fine in grayne,
And a hood thereto, to kepe him from the rayne.
She promised him, beside all that,
He should haue ye mary algate :
Of Goblets no more but a nest,[1]
And of other things she made him hest.[2]
So that[3] he wolde, while she were in towne,
Walke with her vp and downe,
And lay out mony alway as she neede,
And three times double ; so god her speede,
He should haue agayne within three dayes ;
Therin should be made no delayes.
Master Doctor was well content,
And in the Cittie before her he went,
So long tyll that he had out layd
Of his owne money, and for her payd,
Fiue Nobles, if the reknyng be right,
And then anone she stale a way by night.
Master Doctor thought great vnkindnes,
That he was so serued for his gentylnes ;
But she is gone : what remedy now?
His money shalbe payd hym, I wot neuer how.

(1) A set of goblets of different sizes, fitting into each other, commencing with the largest in use, and descending to the smallest by regular gradations, was termed *a nest of goblets.*  (2) Promise.  (3) Old ed. has *thas.*

## 𝕿𝖍𝖊 𝖋𝖞[𝖋]𝖙𝖍 𝖒𝖊𝖗𝖞 𝕵𝖊𝖘𝖙

how this wydow deceyued a man & his wife
that were goynge on pilgremage : who layd out
for her iiij. nobles : and how she deceiued
a scriuener in London, whose name
was Rowse.

———🙢🙠———

But more wyll I tel you in very deede
Of this wydow, whom I pray god speede.
Shortly after she walked by the Thems side,
Not far from a way where folke did ride.
A mong all other, a man and his wife
She saw riding withouten stryfe,
Both being of meetly good age :
It semed that they were on pilgremage
Toward Canterbery, or some other place,
Where as it pleased god of his grace.
But where ere they ryd, or to what end,
Right soone she made them both discend
Downe from their caple to the cold ground :
For she fared as she wold her selfe drownd.
This goodmans name was called John Frank,
His wyfe Annes, a Dame full crank :
Both they came ronning in great hast
Toward this wydow, full sore a gast :

Leest that she, ere they come neare,
Wolde spill her selfe, she made such cheare.
John Frank cryed : woman, remember thee,
What intendest thou ? aye benedicitie !
Thynk on God, and banysh the fowle feend ;
Beware of dispayre, thy selfe not shend.
She stayed at that, and sighed sore,
And sayd : blessed be you, I can no more :
For had ye not come the sooner, verely
I should haue been damned perpetually,
But I pray you now tel me what I shal doe.
Quod this frank : come away & with vs go,
And tell vs further of your estate.
Then (quod she) I haue great hate ;
God I take to iudge for mine owne right,
My goods are taken away by might :
Vndone I am, standyng on this ground,
I am scarcely left worth iii. hundreth pound,
As in mouable substance, beside a lytell lande,
Whiche mine husbande left vnto my hand :
For she sayd, that her husbande was a great man
Of lande, and sayd that he was dead than.
God assoyle his soule ! (quod she) he was kind to me,
And I trust I quyt his kyndenes (quod she) :
For all folke saiyng, God forgeue them !
This Frank desyred her to walke with hym
As farre as London and he would do his payne,

That she might be restored a gayne,
And the malefactors punished, what so euer they be;
Wydow, dread ye nothyng, quod he,
But come on this way, in the name of our lorde,
And I shall bryng you, where ye shall be at boord
With a frende of myne, in an honest howse :
The good mannes sir name is called Rowse.
There ye shall be honestly entreated ;
But where is the stuffe, wherof ye speaked ?
At Kyngston, at Kyngston, then quod she ;
I care not muche for it, so mot I thee,
Ne for all this world ; and therwith she gan wepe.
This Frankes hart than in his body lepe :
This game, thought he, goeth fayre and well,
He requyred her no more to tell
As at that tyme, but went foorthryght,
And came to their lodgyng before nyght
To Frankes frende, as I tolde you before.
A scryuener he was, and wrought full sore,
To hym they were welcome, and welcome agayn,
And specially, whē Frank had tould him certain,
What woman she was, and of what substance.
Then she tould the scryuener of the great dystance,
That she was at for her ryght,
And much wrong she had by meanes of a knight
Whiche shallbe nameles as yet (quod she),
Tyll I see my tyme auenged for to bee.

God wyll sende me once a frende, I truste,
Before whiche tyme I can take no rest,
Nother in body, nor in conscience.
Tarry ye here, sayd y° scryuener, go ye not hence,
And we shall haue frendes ynow for money.
I wyll not sticke for that truely, quod she,
Howbeit my money is almost spent, .
But I haue other thynges, whiche shalbe hent,
And money made therof me to defende.
I neuer had that jewell, so God me mende,
In all my lyfe, but could finde in myne hert,
In tyme of neede, therwith to depart.
At Kingston on Temmes I haue certayne Plate,
XL. poundes wurthe, for all this mortall hate,
And other thynges withall, els I beshrewe some.
She desyred her Hoste to her for to come :
I haue, quod she, to tell you in priuitie :
Step ye a lytell apart, let your busynes bee.
Into the shop they go out of the hall,
And then she began for to tell hym all,
And more, too, by a an hundreth lyes.
The scryuener thanked her xl. sythes :
For she had made to hym graunt
Of part of her Plate wherof she made vaunt ;
And the keepyng of al together he shuld haue.
An Othe she sware, so God her saue,
Of all her treasure she cared not a myte,

So that she might her enemyes acquyte.
But Hoste, quod she, my friende leefe and dere,
I pray you of your good counsell here :
This wretched worlde I am mynded to forsake,
And chastytie for to avowe and take ;
All my causes I am content to resine .
Into your handes, myne owne Hoste myne ;
Doo as ye lyst, be it good or yll,
Ye shall haue all to order at your wyll.
The scryuener sayd : gramercy, Maistresse,
Forsothe, quod he, ye intende well doubtlesse ;
If ye wyll do as ye say, I holde well withall.
Than he called John Franke out of the Hall,
And made hym preuie vnto euery thyng.
She said unto thē both, that she ought offeryng
To Sainct Sauiours, and she would very fayne
To pay her offeryng, and then returne agayne.
And after she said, that she would desire
Her Hoste to write her Testament for hyre,
And last wyll, whyle she were in good mynde,
So discretly, that as for vnkinde
Her frendes should not hold her another day,
Whun that her presence is hence away.
The scryuener & Frank both praysed her gretly
For her good purpose, and said to her truely :
To performe your pylgremage, it is well done,
And I myselfe shall wayt you vpon,

Quod John Franke, and eke I wyll prouyde
A Mayden seruant, to walke by your side.
To ward Saynt Sauiours in haste she yede,
As ye haue heard beyng accompanied.
Rowsys wyues best Kyrttyll and Gowne
She weared on her backe throw the towne,
Which was lent her of good affection,
Because that her owne was welnye done.
Frank was her amner,[1] and layd out to the poore
By the way as they went, and at the Church dore,
Of his owne proper money, which did amount
To the some of ii. Marks by true account.
And while they were forth, this Rowse y^e scriuener
Sent to Kingston, for to enquyre
Of her treasure there being in mew;
But in all the towne she was not worth a q,
How be it she was there; full well I know,
The people laughed all on a row.
Home goeth the messenger, and told in hast
Unto the scriuener all this quoynt cast.
By coks soule (quod he), it is not so, I hope.
Els (quod the seruant), hang me with a rope.
For I have enquyred substancyally
In euery place, I tell you, by and by.
By our Lady masse, then, all is not right;
But whist! no more, she wyll be here to night:

(1) Almoner.

My cosen Frank wyl not let her depart away.
Thou shalt heare other tidings to morrow or day.
At fiue of the clocke in the after noone,
These Pilgrims came home full soone,
And anon was layd to this widows charge,
With hye words out at large,
Her false deceipt from poynt to poynt.
Than strode she in great disioynt,
And no reason could she aledge nor say,
For her excuse but gan for to pray.
Nay then, sayd y<sup>e</sup> scriuener, god geue me sorow,
How be it thou shalt tary heare tyl to morow,
And then forth shalt thou sterk belly naked,
With dogs, arrand quen, thou shalt be bayted.
The scriuener was halle ashamed of this,
And at iii of the cloke, when he rose for to p***,
He put forth his gest on the backside,
Without company or any guide.
Her Gowne and her Kyrtle he tooke away,
And Frank went to Fullam on the next day,
Deferryng his pylgremage to Caunterbery,
Full sad he was and nothyng mery.
His mony was gone and spent indede,
The blessed Marter quit him his mede!

## Finis.

## The sprth mery Jest,

how this wydow Edyth deceiued a Draper
in London of a new Gowne and a new Kyrtell, and
how she sent him for a nest of Goblets to the
Scriuener, that she had deceiued afore.

———◦◦———

HERE wyll I tary no lenger while,
But to the wydow agayne my stile
I shal direct : and tell some deale more
Of her pastime, and God before.
In the Cittie she walked in her Peticote :
Yet, at the last, acquayntaunce she gote,
Out of her old walke, on the other side.
A Draper there was that loued no pride,
To whom she preferred her accustomed craft,
Lye after lye, and sayd she was beraft
A greate part of her goods full wrongfully.
Alas, (quod the Draper ful piteously)
It is ruth to see you go so slender.
I shall mend it (quod she), when I come yender
To winsore (I trust), where my staff is ;
Gods curse haue they, that make me doe this.
Master mine (quod she), I pray you be not wroth,
Might I be so bolde as of your hole cloth
To desire you for to deliuer vnto me

As much as wyll suffyse (quod she)
To make a large Gowne and a Kyrtell,
And I shall pay you therfore full well,
When I come to winsore, & after your owne price,
So that ye set not on me all the dice,
But let me haue a penyworth for a peny.
Mistresse, sayd the Draper, if there be any
Ware in the shop that wyll doe you good,
You shal haue it, I swere by the roode,
So that ye put me in good suretie
For my money : for I know you not, truely.
Syr, sayd the wydow, if it be your pleasure
To commaund your seruant to ride to Wynsore,
In my company, within these vi. dayes,
You shal haue your money without any delayes,
And a pleasure [1] withall for your good wyll.
Forsooth, sayd y° Draper, you speake good skyll ;
And shortly, without any interogation,
He deliuered vnto her at the mocion
Of broade cloth iiii. yardes ful wely mote,
And eke as much as wolde make her a cote,
A Kyrtell, I wolde say, of good wolstet, [2]
And commanded his seruant for to beare it
To the Taylour to be made in hast.
And on the 4. day after, whē she had toke repast,
The Draper sent a Jurneyman of his

(1) A gratuity.          (2) Worsted.

With her to Winsore, the way they did not mis.

A gardeuyaunce [1] the seruant with him bare,

Therin to bring thence all the short ware,

That she had promised the Draper before,

He should haue in keeping, I can no more.

To winsore they came ii houres before night,

And at a dore off her horse down she light;

And in she goth, no more but for a countenaunce,

And came out agayne, saying w^t a vengeaunce,

They must go by water and the way so fayre,

But I think they lacked horse to repayre.

The seruant, abroade walkyng the horses,

Hard her wel, when she sayd al this :

No force (quod he), I shall haue the lesse to cary.

So you shall, sayd she, nor ye nede not to tary.

But set vp your horse therfore anon

In some Inne, and in the meane season

I shal hastely go wright a skrow,

To certyfie your master shortly, as I trow.

The seruant to an Inne the horses had,

While she caused the letter to be made,

And then gaue it him, and bad him go to bed

To Colbroke, wher his horse better might be fed ;

And syr, she sayd, I thanke you for your payne ;

Your master wylbe plesed, this letter whē he hath
    saine.

1) A trunk.

A cup wᵗ ale at yᵉ dore she made him drink,
And thē he rode to Colbroke, ere time was to wīk ;
And to London on yᵒ morow, & deliuered his letter
Vnto the Draper that was his master.
The letter bad that he sholde resorte
To a Scriuener, take hede what I reporte.
He dwelleth in chepeside, and his name is Rouse.
Byd him deliuer you out of his house,
By such a token, an hole nest of Goblets,
A dosen of spoones, se there be no lets,
A standyng cup with a couer percell gilt.
Now, thoght yᵗ Draper, I haue in my hand the hilt ;
I wyl plede in possessiō, might I yᵗ possed.
To the Scriuener his seruant he sent wᵗ spede
For this foresayd geare, and bid him not tary ;
This seruants name was called Harry.
His errand he sayeth vnto the Scriuener,
And diligently this Rouse gaue an eare :
From the begynnyng markyng his tale well ;
And when the seruant had tolde euery dell,
The Scryuener sayd : I wyl delyuer none to thee ;
Go home, and byd thy Maister come to mee.
I wyll so answere hym, that he shalbe content.
The Seruant in haste to his Master went,
And tolde hym that he must him selfe repayre
For this Plate so costly and so fayre.
A! I see well, quod the Draper, this man is no foole ;

Loe! what it is to put a childe to scoole
To learne wisdome, while he is yong !
Upon his way he walked so long,
Tyll he came thither, and gan to tell his tale.
Neibor, quod y⁶ Scriuener, let vs drynk som ale,
And speake no more in this matter for shame,
For ye are begyled, and I am the same.
Nay, by cockes body, I put you out of doubt,
Sayd the Draper, ye shall not laugh it out
With me after suche maner: for I wyll haue it
    indeed.
Ye shal haue none of me, by Christs crede,
Quod the Scriuener, get it where ye can ;
But harken what I shall tell you, man,
Let me rownd in your eare that nobody·know :
For, and if it be abroade yblow,
We shalbe laughed to scorne both,
Wherfore, Neyghbour, looke ye be not wroth.
She shewed you she had Plate, and so she told me ;
But all the good she hath is not wurth a peny.
I haue it proued ; therfore leaue your sighyng ;
This shall be good I tell you for our learnyng.
Good! quod the Draper, in the Deuylles name !
A vengeance lyght on her and open shame !
By the holy Masse, quod he, I wil haue the quean,
Els it shall cost me the labour of all my men.
For the space I tell you of this fortnyghts daye

She shalbe punyshed truely, as I you say,
To the ensample of all other, & god grant me lyfe ;
Farewel, neighbor, I wyl go dine with my wife.
Sayd the Draper, sith it wyl be non other.
A dieu, neighbor, and farewell, quod the tother.
This Draper went him home in all the haste,
And commanded his seruant to take repaste,
And after to ride, as fast as he can,
To winsor, and demaund for this woman ;
And if it so betyde thou canst her finde,
Take an officer and fast her bynde :
Se her bestowed, and then come and tell me,
And by my thyrst[1] shortly wyl I see,
What the Law wil say to y⁰ hore & theefe both.
I pray thee make spede, and take my boots of
    cloth ;
Draw them on thy legs : for the way is depe.
The seruant in hast vpon his horse lepe,
And rode to winsor, by then it was night,
And at an Inne, where he dyd alight,
He hard tell that the widow was gon,
Where ne whether wist no man.

(1) So old ed. ; but query, *tryst*, for *faith*.

## 𝕿𝖍𝖊 𝖘𝖊𝖚𝖊𝖓𝖙𝖍 𝖒𝖊𝖗𝖞 𝕵𝖊𝖘𝖙

how[1] this wydow Edyth deceiued a seruant of
Syr Thomas Neuelles, who in hope to haue her in
maryage with all her great riches, kepte her
company tyll all his money was spent :
and then she went to seeke
her Freendes.

———❧———

THE seruante to London returned agayne,
And on the next morow she was seene
In Southwark, where she did abyde
The space of iii. dayes, and then a way did ryde
With carryars into Surrey, the sothe to say ;
And at Towton she arryued upon a day,
And there, not farre from a knyghts place,
Nyne dayes her tarying was.
In whiche tyme a seruyng man
Hawnted that House now and than,
With whom she gan to curry fauell ;
His Maister was Sir Thomas Neuell,
She promised hym to be his Spouse,
And desired him to ryde to her house,
To see her treasore and also her store.
I wyll, quod she, sende hym before,

(1) Old ed. has *who.*
(2) Old ed. has *Sussex.*　See *Additional Notes.*

If that ye wyll tell me what tyme ye wyll fare,
Some of my frendes forsoth shal be thare,
And eke my tenantes, as their dutie is.
Then he began her to halse and kysse,
Saying : hart roote, if it please you,
I am all redy, and it were euen now.
I wot well my Maister wyll not say me nay,
And if that I be furth a Monethes day ;
So that I tell hym where aboutes I am,
He wyll not be angry ; but, in Goddes name,
Peraduenture he wil say, where hast thou ben so
  long ?
Than, and I make curtsie, & hold my tong,
He hath done with the twinklyng of an eye.
But after that I haue told hym truely,
That I ryde with you, he wyl be wel content,
Once considering the cause [and] y° fine of our
  intent.
Well then, quod she, on Saterday in y° morning
Let vs ryde forth our way fastyng,
And at Senock¹ there will we bayt.
I feare least my Gerle take some conceyt,
Because that I am so long her fro :
It is xvi. weekes and somwhat mo,
Sinc[e] I garnished her with y° signe of the Crosse.

(1) Sevenoke, in Kent (now Sevenoaks). Lambarde says: *Sennocke*
or *Seven oke.*

3.      F

She learned her boke with the goodman Rosse
In Senock towne, not far from the Church ;
Ye know him wel ynow : for he doth worch
And maketh Carpets now and than.
Trew you say (quod he), I know that man.
Now in sooth I will go, and ask my master leaue,
And here is a Ring, which I you geue
Vpon condition ye wot wel what.
Yes, I warrant you, quod she, I remember that.
Then fare wel, honycombe, til I se you againe.
God be with you, and shield you from the raine,
Sayd the wydow ; but loke that you tell
Vnto your master wisely and well
All our foreward, and leaue nothing behinde.
Yes, yes, quod he, as ye shal wel finde.
To his master he goeth, as fast as he can,
And desired him of licence anon
To ryde wyth this widow a lyttell way,
As far as her house, at S. Mary Skray ;[1]
And I trust in God omnipotent,
My labour in vayne shal not be spent.
His master gaue him leaue for to ride :
Worke wisely (quod he), what so euer betide,
And if that her daughter be borne to land,
Than I aduise thee to fall in hand

---

(1) Now known as *St. Mary Cray.* It is two-and-twenty miles from
Maidstone.

With the child, and let the mother go.
By God, sayd the seruant, and peraduenture so
I wyll yet doe, when I haue seene both.
And vpon the Fryday forth he goth
Toward this widow, ioly and amorous—
She was lodged in an honest man's house.
That night they made mery, with fyl y⁰ cup, fil,
And on the morow they ride forth at their will.
To Senock they come by than it was prime,
And goeth to dinner all by tyme.
They made good cheare, and spared for no cost ;
The wydow of new gan for to bost,
But of her daughter she spake no worde,
And when that taken vp was the borde,
And all payde for that was come in,
Come hether (quod she), swete hart mine,
I requyre you that you wyll take the way,
As fast as ye can, to S. Mary Skray,
And demaunde there for the wydows house,
That lately was both wife and spouse
To such a man, whose soule god pardon !
And when that ye come to the house anone,
Ye shal say vnto my seruant there,
I meane hym that is charged with my gere,
And all my household stuffe in my absence,
That he, ere euer ye depart from thence,
Shew you mine house round all about,

And eke my comodities within and without,
And when you haue viewed everything,
Than bid my seruant without tarying
Leade you fast into my closet ryght,
And doe vp the window to let in the light,
Vnlocke the dore with this same key—
If I trusted you not, I swere by my fay,
Ye should not come so neare my gromelseede—
And take no more than I you bede ;
Within my closet ye shal anon finde
A little Casket, that standeth al behinde
My ship Coffer, downe iust by the wall.
Beare with you the Casket prety and small;
But I charge you take none other thing:
For and you doe, at my returning
I shall know all ; therefore now take heede.
Mary, sayd the yong man, God forbede,
Seing that ye do trust me so wel.
Go your wayes thē, quod she, & here I wyl dwell,
Tyl ye come agayne, but looke ye make haste.
I wyll ride (quod he) euen all as fast,
As my Geldyng can beare me away.
Forth he galopeth to saint Mary Skray,
And there he inquered as she hym bad,
And anon perfect tidings he had
That he was begiled : for there was no man
Could tell any tidings of such a woman.

Then away rideth he as fast as he may,
And came to Senock at the next day.
But he could not come thither so soone,
But ere euer that he came, the wydow was gon,
Nobody could tell whether she was yede.
Master Neuels seruant rid home w^t good spede,
Being in his minde not well content,
For some money he had her lent,
And payd for her cost, I cannot tell what.
Yea, with a mischife, I could not beware that,
Quod he than ; but yet no force, let go ;
I wylbe aduised, agayne or I doe so.


## The eyght mery Jest,

how this wydow Edyth deceiued a seruant
of the Byshop of Rochesters[1] w^t cogging and boastyng of her great Richesse, who likewise
thought to haue had her in mariage.

The Wydow northward tooke her way,
And came to Rochester the next day,
And there, within a little space,
To a yongman that seruant was

(1) The celebrated Fisher.

Vnto the Byshop in the Towne,
She promised him dale and downe,
On that condition he wolde her wed,
And keepe her company at boord & in bed.
This yongman was glad and light :
Now, thought he, I shalbe made a knight
By the meanes of this gentlewomans store;
Gramercy, Fortune I can no more.
He permytted in hast to be assembled
With her at the church, and there resembled
Or ioyned in one flesh that is dying,
And two soules euermore liuyng.
Good cheare he made her in her Inne,
And eke he would not neuer blinne,
Tyl he had brought her to his Lorde,
Before whom they were at accorde
Upon a condition maryed to be,
Which condition was, if that she
Could performe all that she had sayd,
He wolde then marry her, it should not be delayd.
Here vpon they departed and forth went ;
On the morow my Lorde for her sent,
To dyne with him, and to commen further.
Then was she gone ; but when and whether,
No wyght any worde of her could tell ;
But yet she walked to my Lorde of Arundell.

## The nynth mery Jest,

how this wydow Edyth deceyued a Lorde,
sometime Earle of Arundell ;[1] and how he sent fiue
of his men seruantes and a handmayden to
beare her company, and fetch her daughter who, as she boasted, was Heyre
of great Landes.

———◦◦◦———

And there anon she tould the Earle,
That she had a daughter, a little gerle
Which was borne to be Heyre
To great inheritaunce & lands good and fayre,
And mouable substaunce not a lyte,
If it please God her to respyte,
And graunt her lyfe, tyll she succeede
Her elders aliue, of whose lede
She is issued by lyneall dissent.
And eke she sayd, or that she went,
That her daughter should holde land
Heareafter, when it commeth to her hand,
Of that Earle, and pay hym rent.
Wherfore she sayd that she was content,
His Lordship should haue her to dispose

(1) Thomas Fitzalan, 12th Earl of Arundel, of that family, K.G. ;
Ob. 1524.

And mary her, as him best suppose,
Vnto gentylman, Yeman or Grome.
She wold haue her daughter come ;
If it pleased his Lordship it should so be,
She wold fetch her into that contrie.
The Earle was contented it should be so,
And bad his seruants for to go,
That is to say, to the number of fiue,
 nd redy make them bliue,
To wayt on this gentil wōn, & bring her thither,
She herselfe could not tell whether,
Notwithstanding she did say,
That her houshold was at Foots Scray,[1]
Where she retayned great famely,
As they shall well find sykerly
At their repayre, and God before!
And foorth they ride without more.
She was accompayned, as I haue sayd,
With fiue Yemen and a Mayde ;
And all they woed as they rode,
Each to him selfe at large abrode.
One sheweth his lustynes & mastery,
An other taketh vp his horse on hye,
The thyrd sayd that he had treasure in store,

---

(1) In the neighbourhood of St. Mary Cray. Both places derived
their name from the Cray, a well-known trout-stream ; which has also
christened other localities thereabout, particularly the parish of Crayford.

The fourth sayd that he had myckle more,
The fifth was a man of few words ;
At the last he sayd : a straw for your hoords !
Peraduenture he is here that saith not all,
That somewhat could say, if nede should fall.
Be mery, Wydow, then quod he,
And cast a Sheps eye once on me :
For, though that I ride pensiue and styll,
Perhaps yet I could satisefy your wyll
As well as some other, though I cry not out.
But all this while she cast about,
How she might conueniently steale them fro.
But at a woods side it happened so,
A fayre house there was, which she sayd
Her husband bought it, and for it payd,
Two yeares before he let his lyfe,
And she was now in mikell stryfe
For the sayd house and lands withall,
And sued she was in Westmynster hall.
Great thought she toke for a freend,
That in her right wold her defend.
One of the company, that hard this,
Fayned him to light downe to p**,
Purposedly for to go to enquyre
Of this matter, to know yf that it were,
As she had sayd, or els that she lyed.
To the house he goeth, and there he tryed

That she was falce, and a noughty queane,
In all England not worth a beane.
When he hard this, he galoped fast;
His company he ouer toke at the last,
And declared vnto them, from poynt to poynt.
Then all their loue was sodenly quoynt.
They light doune all by one accorde,
Xv. myle when the had rode,
And stripped her out of her array :
Walke, hore, they all gan say.
Home agayne they toke the way;
And yet she repayred to Foots Scray.
There she abode a certayne season,
The next house vnto one master Heron.
A Gowne and a Kyrtle there she dyd hyre
Of a poore woman, to were to a fayre
Kept there besides vpon an holy day.
Fayne she wold haue made her selfe gay,
At the foresayd fayre to haue be solde,
If any man wold be so bolde,
Without examynation for to alight.
And when that she was out of sight,
She got her away a great pace.
Then came she to Croyden, there as she was
Continewing by the space of the wook,
Duryng the which time a poore Cook
There dwellyng she dyd begile,

And borowed of him, in that while,
Fiue shillings in Groats and pence ;
And then priuely she stale away from thence.
Then she came to Eltham the right way,
Where she rested her three weekes & a day,
And dyd nothyng but ay enquere
Of Gentlemen dwelling here and there ;
And when she saw her time, on an holy day,
She walked to a Thorp[1] called Batersay ;[2]
And, on the next day after, she took a Whery,
And ouer Thames she was rowed ful mery.

## The tenth mery Jest,

how this Wydow Edyth deceiued three yong
men of Chelsay,that were seruants to Syr Thomas
More, and were all three suters vnto her for
Maryage, and what mischaunce
happened vnto her.

———⚬———

At Chelsay was her ariuall,
Where she had best cheare of all,
In the house of Syr Thomas More.
After that she had tolde of her store,
And of her hauyour and credence eke,

(1) Village.          2) Battersea, in Surrey.

There was nothing for her to seeke,
That could make her mery other euyn or morow,
I pray to God now geue her sorow !
At Eltham she sayd that she dyd dwell,
And of her substance there she gan to tell :
Two wolsted Lomes she had, by her fay,
And two Mills that went night and day ;
A Beere brewhouse, in which euery week once
Twenty quarters were brewed al at once ;
Fowre Plowes she kept, the earth to cultiue,
And xv. great knaues to help her to thriue ;
Seauen womcn seruants, y$^t$ wull to spin & carde,
And to mylke the kyne abroad in the yarde.
She recounted her famyly & houssholde so great,
That three yong men she cast in a heat,
Which seruants were in the same place,
And alb they woed her a good pace.
By meanes, I tel you, and by brocage,
They sware they wolde be all her owne page.
·One of them had to name Thomas Croxton,
And seruant he was to master Alengton :[1]
A man, I tell you, in whom dame nature
Had[2] don her part as in stature :
He was mighty chyned, with boanes stronge,

(1) Was this Robert Alynton, author of *Libellus Sophistarum*, of which there were several editions from the early English press ?
(2) Old Ed. has *hap*.

Shoulders broade and armes longe,
Very actiue, and apt to euery thyng,
Able to serue any Prynce or Kyng,
As for his person and conditions withall.
But there is a poynt, least that for parciall
I should be holden, because he is my frend ;
Wherfore of his prayse here I make an end,
And som what I will tell of his woyng.
To his master & mistris he was gretly beholdīg :
For busy sute they made night and day
In his cause, if[1] I shall the sooth say ;
And he him şelfe was full seruiseable
To this wydow at dinner and at the table ;
And eke at supper he stoode ay at her back,
So neare that, and if she had let a crack
Neuer so styll, he must haue had knowledge ;
But all is honycombe, he was in such dotage ;
Wherin a little while I let him dwell,
And of the seconde woer I shall you tell ;
Which had to name Thomas Arthur,
And seruant he was to master Roper.[2]
A proper man, neither to hye nor to low ;
But Dame nature sothely, as I trow,

---

d. has *it.*

(2) William Roper, Esq., of Well-hall, in the parish of Eltham, Kent,
Sir T. More's son-in-law.   He married Margaret More.   Roper left
behind him the *Life of Sir Thomas More,* which has passed through
several editions.

Referred his gift vnto Dame grace,
Desiring her to consider the case
Concerning this man, and that she wolde
Indew him with verteous maners manifolde ;
And no doubt she was therin nothing slacke.
Peace, no more ! he standeth at my backe ;
And yf he here me praise him, he wil weue I flatter,
Therfore I wyl resort to former matter,
And tel of his woyng, partly as it was,
And what spechfolke he had by gods grace ;
His owne Master and Mistris also,
With other beside, I cannot tel who, .
That laboured for him incessantly.
And his owne selfe, I tel you truly,
Was not necligent, ne lost no time,
But gaue attendaunce from morning to prime,
And the after none, with part of the night ;
In her chamber the candels he did light,
And tymbred her fyres in the chymney :
And can ye finde in your hart, he wold say,
To loue me, swete hart, best of all ?
Yes, quod she, but I wyll not tell you all,
What my hart thinketh as now ;
But, Thomas, against to morow I pray you,
That you wyll get you leaue to ryde with me
As far as Braynford, and there ye shall se
Some money receyued, els it is yll.

But I wold we had one, that this cup wold fil
With Malmesey, y* we might drink to bedward.
Whip ! quod Thomas, and got him down ward,
And commeth agayne with the cup full.
Drynk, Wydow, quod he, a good pull,
And when ye see your time, get you to rest :
He haue you in his keping y* may keepe you best !
Adew, quod she, and farewell till to morow ;
Here is good Malmesey, els god geue me sorow.
On the next day, Thomas rode w* this wydow
As far as Braynford, and I shall tel you how,
And what chere they made by y° way as they rod.
Thomas right well his horse bestrode,
A full fayre styrop out at the long ;
His horse was a beast goodly and strong,
And beare them both easely away,
And styll wolde stand, while Thomas did say :
Let me kis you, darling, turne your face hether ;
Be it, quod she, ere that we wend farther.
And thus the passe the time, as they ride
To Braynford, where they did not long abyde :
For shortly to Thomas she gan then tell,
Her debtour was gon to Kingston to dwel.
Thomas began for to muse of the matter,
And then priuely he did inquere
Of the goodman of y° house, wher his horse stoode,
Which knew her right well, & sware, by y° roode,

She lied in euery thing that she dyd say.
Then quod Thomas to him selfe : a syra, a syra !
Is this the matter in very deede ?
Homeward he caryed her, with good speede,
To Chelsay againe, where she was vsed
As she was before, and holden excused.
Thomas kept al this within his owne brest,
Because his felows should not at him iest.
And in her chamber, the next night folowing,
There was the reuell and the gossupping :
The general bumming, as Marget Giggs sayde ;
Euery body laughed, and was well apayde.
Two of her woers being there present,
Thomas Arthur, when he saw his time, went,
And sat him downe in a chayre solemply,
And sayd nothing, but now and then an eye
He cast at his loue, as she stoode at the Cubord.
When she perceiued, she spake nere a word,
But stept vnto him, and kissed him sweet,
Sayīg : how is it wᵗ you, I pray you let me weet ?
Thomas answered : on this world, I think.
Tut, a straw ! quod she ; take the cup and drink.
Therwith she imbraced him : be mery, sweet hart ;
She turned her **** in his lap, & let a great ****.
And I loued you not (q. she), I wold not geue you
    this.
Ha, ha, quod Tomas, ye be a mery one, i wis.

They laughed on a row, y$^t$ som of them shoke ;
The Wydow desired y$^e$ court to be broke,
And ech wight to his bed to repayre.
The morow was Sunday, and the wether fayr.
This Wydow determined her selfe to walk
As far as Halywell : for she hard men talke,
That there should be a sister that day professed,
And to offer with her she was disposed,
Desiring the yong Nunne, w$^t$ her sisters all,
To pray for her to the hie God immortall,
That it shal please him of his aboundant grace,
In the end of this world, y$^t$ away from his face
She ne should be seperate in any wise.
To Holywell she walked, and once or twise
She drank, or she came there: for y$^e$ way was long.
The Nuns in y$^e$ quyre had begon their song
ιn the hye masse ; & Bels gyn to ryng,
When the wydow approched to make her offering.
After y$^e$ Gospel, her purse she toke in hand,
And serched therin ; but nothin she fand.
A syde she cast her eye, and anon was ware
Of Thomas Croxton, at Chelsay her first woer,
To whom she sayd : I pray you lend me fast
Some white mony that I might offer in hast,
Or els chaunge me a noble, quod she. Anón,
Thomas Croxton looked her vpon,
And sayd : sweet hart, ye shal chaunge no Golde

**3.** G

At this time : I haue money inough. Holde,
How much wyll steede you ? say on : let's see.
Xii. pence, I pray you, delyuer vnto me,
Quod she than, and see it be in Grotes :
For I wyll offer xl. pence, because of reportes.
And I might once get home, I wold not care for
    money.
When she had offered, the sooth to say,
She romed in the Cloyster too and fro,
Tyll a yong man saw where she dyd go ;
And Wa[l]ter Smyth was this yongmans name,
One of her louers, and I might tell for shame.
A ! thought Wa[l]ter, now here is good place
To speak of my matter, and to show the case,
How it standeth with mee, and also to be playne.
Softly he walketh [to] this wydow agayne,
And fyrst hailed her, as him thought meete ;
Then toke her in his armes, and kissed her swete.
She knew him well inough : for he was one of the
    three,
That I told you before dwelt in Chelsay.
This Wa[l]ter his tale gan for to tell :
Wydow, quod he, take keepe and mark well,
What I shal to you say without dissimulation :
I can no lenger mew mine hartely affection,
Ne inclose the secrets of my trew minde,
But to you I must breke, trustyng ye wilbe kinde,

Syrcūstance voydyng, because I cannot suiurne
Long with you at this time, but I must returne
From whence I come ; therfore to you anon
Among your suters I pretend to be one.
Now, wydow, looke well vpon me, quod he,
And yf ye can finde in your hart to loue me
As wel, sweet darlyng, as I loue you,
Than I trust there shalbe such seeds isow
Betwyxt vs both, that it shalbe principally
To Gods pleasaunce and to our comfort secondly.
Then the Wydow answered w' a smiling chere,
And sayd : goodmā Wa[l]ter, I pray you tel me here,
Whether ye mean good sadnes,[1] or els y' ye iest.
I thinke as I speake, so god my soule rest,
Quod Wa[l]ter ; therfore shew vnto me,
That I shalbe accepted,[2] or els that I am not he.
I am a yong woer, and dare not speake for shame,
But yet to loue unloued ye know it is no gaine.
Troth ye say, quod she, I affyrme the same ;
And if I loue you not agaī, in faith I am to blāe :
Whē I come next to Chelsay, ye shal wel find,
That afore all other I beare you my good mynd.
A Crucifyx, quod she, of the pure Golde,
Which many a day hath remayned in my holde,
Ye shal haue it for a token and a remembrance.
Thā Wa[l]ter stode on tipto, & gan him self avance :

(1) Seriousness.          (2) Old ed. has *excepted.*

G 2

I thank you, quod he, euen with all my hart.
He kissed her deliciously, and then dyd depart.
To Chelsay againe she came the same night,
But thā yᵉ world was chāged; al was cum to light ;
Her substance was knowne & her selfe also :
For Thomas Arthur yᵗ day had ridden to & fro,
And tried her not worth the sleue lace of a gowne
In all England, in Cittie nor yet in towne.
Than well a way her dyet was chaunged;
Her potage & eke her ale were well poudred
With an holsome influence, that surgeons call
Pouder Sinipari ; yᵗ wil make on cast his gall.
It made her stomake vnable to broke any meate,
Now was she cold and forthwith in an heate ;
Her pulses beate, and her collour went and come ;
No morsell dyd she eate, but now and then b**.
She was greatly mistempered, & far out of frame ;
All that sate at Supper had good game
Her to behold, and they laught all aboute.
Quod she:· for Goddes loue let me come out ;
Let me come, let me come, for our Ladies sake ;
My belly rumblyth, and my hart doth ake
In such wise, that I know I am but dead,
If I have non ayre : ah, good Lord, my head !
But she was ay kept in, that she could not start,
Tyll my Lady gan to haue pytie in her hart,
And for womans honestie, bad that she should ryse ;

But ere that tyme I am sure twyse or thryse
It knocked at the doore to have issued out,
But with great payne, she made it walke about.
When that she was vp, she got her foorth apace ;
And er she had walkt xxx. fote, she marked a
    chase,
And ekesones another, thrugh the Hal as she yede.
Her nose burst out also, and gan for to bleede.
Into y⁰ colehouse she goth, & there made a draght;
Held her ay thereon, till she had layde her laght.
And whē she was of her nest, one yᵗ hight Browne
Came rōnyng in his Dublet wᵗout cote or Gowne,
Saying : Madame, Madame, by the mans bones,
I feare me, least there be fyre among your coles ;
Howbeit, I saw no lyght but a stynkyng smoke.
O boni Deus! quod my lady, get thee fast and look :
God sheld, and our lady, that any recheless wight
Bare thyder any Candel this present night.
Go loke, go loke, quod she, in haste get the hence.
Browne went him furth, & by the supplemence
He tryed that there was no materyall fyre.
He laughed, and sware by the sole of his Syre,
That one word more he could not speake for shāe.
Good night, quod he, at the best is this game.
Soone after, the wydow came forth wel eased :
That Cony, yᵗ cony, quod she, was not wel rosted
That I eat at Halywell, but I haue made anoydance

The deuill go w^t all, & a vengaunce.

I shal mend now, I trust; & then she went to bed.

Her lodging was chāged there, y^t rested her hed.[1]

But she was in more honour than euer she was
    afore,

Notw^tstādīg her gown & kyrtle of her gore .

Was taken away, and restored to the owner.

The mastiff[2] chaynes day & night she did were,

And w[h]ere gret Estats[3] were chaynes about theyr
    necks,

She had dis[d]ayne to were thē on her legs.

But whether she be content or displeased,

For the space of three weeks y^e chaynes she wered;

And after, in a day of a gayle deliuery,

She. was discharged, being glad and mery.

---

(1) The widow was now sent to gaol for three weeks.

(2) Massive.    (3) *i.e.* wealthy people or persons of quality.

## 𝕮𝔥𝔢 𝔵𝔦. 𝔪𝔢𝔯𝔭 𝕵𝔢𝔰𝔱

how this wydow Edyth deceyued three yongmen
of the Lorde Legates[1] seruants with her great
lying, crakyng, and boastyng of her great
treasure and Juelles.

———⚭———

To Westminster she walked after, as I trow,
And in the house, wᵗ the pie in yᵉ wyndow,
She was lodged ; but there was no place
Long for to tary, considering her case.
Gon was her money wel neare all ;
She had full sodenly a great fall,
As ye haue hard before ; but yet, nothyng dismaid,
On a day to herself thus she sayd :
What, should I here dwell, and no peny in purse ?
If I tary any lenger, I pray that gods curse
Lyght vpon me euen by and by.
Then away she got her, and that hastely,
And ere she had walked a forlong way or two,
She had bethought her where for to go.
Heauen kyng, quod she, full of grace,
Why remembred not I my Lord Legats place ?

(1) Wolsey, who was appointed Legate a latere in 1516.

By God, I must haue there yet some good cheare.
Alone wyll I go without any feare ;
And furst into the porters lodge full right,
And there demaund for such a knight,
That I know well is not there now.
I shal report, in what maner and how
My landes be kept from me by strength.
Such a tale I wyll tell at length,
That some man wyll geue an eare, I trow,
And desire me further for to know.
To the porters lodge she goeth a great pase,
And, as she had deuised, opened the case.
The porter asked why she went so bare :
In sooth, quod she, I take no great care,
How that I go, whyle my busynes last ;
I trust it shalbe mended now in haste.
Than in came a yoman that was called Shyre,
And stood vpright, and warmed hym by the fyre,
Geuyng an eare alway now and than ;
And at the last, he stept foorth lyke a man,
Saying : fayre mistresse, what is your sute ?
If ye think it best, come tell me without ;
And for the good mind I beare to all wydowes,
I promise you, ere you go out of this house,
Ye shal haue friends, and that without money ;
Wherfore take ye no thought, but be ay mery.
And while they were comonyng of this warke,

A Yeman approched y^t was called John Clarke :
And he demaunded what the matter was.
Gentleman, quod she, thus standeth the case :
I am a poore wydow left all alone,
And hether I am come to make my mone.
Great wrong I haue, as God well knoweth :
For in all this world I ne oweth
Pound nor Noble that ought to be payd,
But of ten times so much I am delayd.
I pray to God once to send me an hed,
That I may sleep at home in my bed :
For I am wery of this renning about,
And yet alway I stand in great doubt,
Least that the bigger wyll eate the Been :
Gentylmen, quod she, ye wot what I meane ;
Therfore help me for your mothers blessyng,
And ye shal haue golde, & golde good sterlyng.
Further, she saw comming to her ward
The thyrd Yeman, called Thomas Ap-richard,
Which anon demanded what y^e matter ment.
Iohn Clarke quickly by the hand him hent,
Led him apart, and tolde in his eare :
Seest thou, quod he, this homely gere ?
By gods sids, she is a wydow, and y^t of gret sub-
    stance,
And mary she would, I know by her daliance.
Peace, quod Thomas, haue her to the wyne,

And let us drawe cuttes, eyther thyne or myne.
So be it, sayd Clark, and let vs no more talk.
Misteris, sayd he, wil it please you to walk
In to the towne, and drink a pynt of wine ?
And doubt ye not ye shal do wel and fine :
For, and if that ye pretend title of right,
Ye shal haue them y$^t$ in your quarrell wil fight,
And nede be ; but it shal not come therto.
Gentlemen, quod she, I am pleased to go
With you at this time, trusting of your ayde,
And one of you three I shal make wel apayde,
Who so ever he be, and God before !
Master Clark, tell me where ye were bore,
And yf ye wylbe a good husband, so god me spede,
And folow my counsell, ye shal haue no neede
To none of your kyn, but ye shalbe able
To lend vnto him Hall, Chamber and stable,
As he shalbe able to lend vnto you.
God thank you, sayd Clark, but here is y$^e$ house,
Wherin we wyl drink, and make good chere.
Hostes, quod he, fetch vs bread, ale and beere,
And eke wine, and that of the best,
Said Thomas Aprichard : for, so god my soule rest,
This night I am disposed to laugh it euen out.
Be mery, wydow, and nothing doubt :
For he dwelleth not vnder our king's obeysance,
Shal do you wrong in England, nor in Fraunce.

But all Thomas words little she did regard ;
Her eye was euer to John Clark ward,
To whome she sayd the selfe same tide :
Master Clark, quod she, wyll ye to morow ride
As far as Barking? ye shal haue horse of me,
And eke a noble in your purse, so mot I thee ;
And there nothing else shal ye do,
But se my folks and cattels also ;
And then returne, when ye shal se it good.
Quod John Clarke : I shal, by the rood ;
But where standeth your horse, let me y$^t$ know ?
He is not far hence, as I trow.
Quod she : I shal tel you in the morning.
Well then, let us drink in the euening,
Quod John Clark : for here is good drink indeede,
And good meat also ; I pray you, widow, feede.
The time they pas merely til ten of the clok,
Yea, and I shal not lye, till after the first cok ;
Then they departed, and to their beds went ;
Thomas ap-richard payd for all that was spent.
John Clark in the morning made him yare ;
Thought he : now I wyll yander away fare ;
I lyke this gere euen very well.
He inquered for y$^e$ wydow ; but no man can tel,
Where she is become, with walk queane walk.
Jhon Clark then fell into other talk,
And let her go, the feend be her gyde !

But here now I can not long abyde,
Considering her pastime in euery place :
For, if I shuld leaue off, it shuld deface
In a maner her booke, which were great pitie,
And ruth also, I swere by Saint Dauye ;
Wherfore some what further of her I wyl wryte,
And without addition truely to indyte

## Finis

∴

## The xii. mery Jest,

how this wydow Edyth deceyued the goodman of
the Three Cuppes in Holburne, and one John Cotes,
that ryd with her to Saint Albans to ouer see
her lands and tenements, and how they
were rewarded.

————⸕⸕————

From Westmīster to Holburne she flew at one flight,
And at the signe of yᵉ Three Cups she did alight,
Trustyng there to season[1] on her pray,
For she had eaten no meat of all that day.
Fyrst she asked for the goodman of the Inne,
And as soone as she saw him, anon she did begin

(1) Seize.

To tell him a tale, and neuer a true worde.
Host, quod she, might I be with you at borde
For the space of eyght or els nine dayes?
And ye shal finde me honest at all assayes :
Ful well I shall pay for all that I take ;
O blessed Lady, so mine head doth ake !
I haue ron so fast that my winde is neare gone.
Mayd, I pray you step to the dore anone,
And looke yf ye may se fowr tall men,
With swords & buklers, as fast as they may ren ;
They have chased me all this long day,
And wyll not be answered for ought y$^t$ I can say.
I see well that she is best at ease,
That hath little or nought in this world to lese.
All my trouble I may wyt a little substance,
Which is my owne, it procureth me greuance.
But, my Hoste, quod she, help me now ;
I shall tell you in what maner and how
The case standeth, and remedy is none,
But and if I be taken, I must needes begon.
What betwixt y$^e$ kings seruāts & my lord Legats,
I am so asayled y$^t$ I wot not whither to go ;
Diuers wold have me, but I am determined this also,
Neuer to be coupled to a Courtier iwis,
While that I liue, and god be my good Lorde.
Her hoste desired her to sit downe at the borde :
Ye shal, quod he, haue the best help that I can,

And, for your sake, I wold I were a single man.
Therwith he twinkled, and loked ful narrow,
And kissed her twise, & chirked like a Sparow.
In sooth, sayd she, if there were an honest man,
Wise and toward, I may say to you now,
I could finde in my hart to make him a man ;
And if euer I marry, he shalbe such a one.
As to loke for great goods I wyll not in soth :
For I have inow for him and me both,
And if that he be not to great a waster.
But I wyl none that shalbe called master ;
These Roysters of the court no poynt towchon ;
My nebors, when they com to make their mone,
Desiring of reformation of things misused,
Shal not stand caples vn[1] to him that is vsed
To lyg by my side, and to kis me in the night.
Nay, nay, I wil none such, by god almight.
But, hoste, quod she, against the next saterday,
I pray you prouide me, and if that ye may,
Whatsoeuer they cost, two men and two hors :
For I must ride to S. Albons in maner perforce.
I have ben long thence—the worse huswife am I—
But I trust I haue them there, y[t] wil loke and espy,
If any fault be, and se it amended.
Mine houses there be merely[2] wel defended.
I meane this : they stand in good reperation ;

(1) Old ed. has *i*.          (2) *i.e.* entirely, altogether.

And my house at y⁰ Crosse Keyes is lyke yᵉ facion
Of your house here ; but yᵗ it is much bigger.
God haue mercy on the soule of my good father !
He had great pleasure there to lye.
And is the Crosse Keyes yours, say ye truely ?
Quod her host.  Mary, there is a fayre lodgyng
And a goodly backside thervnto belonging.
Yea, quod she, I haue ther housing, & also grōud
In yᵉ towne & nere, by worth v. hundred pound,
And if it should be solde to the valew ;  ′
And in Barnet the Inne repayred new,
With the signe of yᵉ Lyon, is mine own right ;
My father bought it of a good Knight—-
God remit their trespas both twayne !
But I pray Christ graunt we haue no rayne
Against we ride : for the way wylbe foule.
Her host answered, and sware, by his soule :
I shal man you, quod he, and against that tyde
Eke puruey an other, that gladly will ryde
Wayting vpon you, and if that nede bee,
He shal stand in a mans stede, so mot I thee.
Also ye shal haue to your handmayd
Mine owne deare doughter, as my wife sayd ;
Ride when please you, al things shalbe redy ;
I lack no more but a payre of Bootes truelɏ.
Mine host, quod she, care ye not for that ;
Take ye payne, tyl ye come to Barnat,

And there ye shal haue choyce of twelue payre,
Which I distrained for mine house there.
A tenauntry I haue there, in which did dwell
A Sowter y‍ᵗ made Boots for to sell,
And shoes also, full good and strong.
I may say to you he dwelled there so long,
Tyll his haire gan to grow throw his hoode;[1]
And than when the falce knaue vnderstoode,
That I was at Otford,[2] away in Kent,
Besy there prouing my husbands testament,
He wolde haue stolne away by night;
But yet his purpose came to light.
It hapned so, that a tenaunt of mine
Was late in the euening milking of kine,
And saw mine horeson, when he busked him fore-
        ward
With such trash as he had, and then hōward
She her hied as fast as she may,
And told her husband : to morow or day,
Twyfeld wyl fleet, and the rent is vnpayd.
Go & distrayne him, in hast she sayd,
In my masters name ; and so he dyd indede.
Boots and shoes I haue inow, so God me spede,
And other trumpery, I cannot tel what ;

(1) *i.e.* until he fell into bad circumstances. The same expression occurs in Bansley's *Treatyse*, circa 1550, and in Deloney's *History of Thomas of Reading*, circa 1597.
(2) Three miles from Sevenoaks.

But I wyl se when I com to Barnat.

Host, quod she, I pray you let vs wel be horsed :

For I haue been many times trobled

By the way as I haue ridden, for lack of hors.

Her host answered: geue ye no force ;

Ye shal haue such that shal beare ye thorow.

Wel then, quod she, al is good inow ;

At S. Albons I haue horse of mine owne.

The goodman then walked into the towne,

And prouided her a seruant, that was called

John Cotes, a man that neuer fayled

His mayster nor[1] maystresse in tyme of neede.

On the day appointed they ryde forth w$^t$ speed,

And at their departyng this wydow borowed

Vpon her Hostesse, which she hartely desired,

A Cap, an Hat, and three kerchieues therto,

A cople of syluer pinnes, a payr of Hokes, and no

    mo.

Apace they rydе, tyll they come to Whetston,[2]

And there [she] gan to speake to them anon :

My friendes, quod she, take keepe what I say ;

I haue bethought me, rydyng by the way,

That it is not best for vs this day

To ride through Barnet, and I shal tel you why :

(1) Old ed. has *not.*

*(2)* Wheston, in the parish of Friarn-Barnet, between the latter and East-Barnet.

One knaue or other wyll vs there espy ;
I know that I am wayted for in the towne ;
Wherfore, by myne aduise, let vs light downe,
And bayt here, and rest a lytell whyle,
And then ye shall see vs them all begyle :
For, when that we come to Barnet townes ende,
We shall there then, spyte of the feende,
Ryde in the Lane on the backside ;
I know the way, we shal neede no guyde ;
And at the wyndmyl we shal come in owr way
        agayne,
And that furthryght fayre and playne,
Tyll that we come to Hatfeld Parkepale,
And there I haue a Tenant that selleth Ale,
And a Farme besides, which yelds me by the yere
Thirteen pound, and when I come, good chere,
Mine horsemeat & mans meat, & cost me nought.
Mine husband, when he died, for y$^t$ Farme ought
Fortie Markes ; but, I thank God, now
My Farmer may go both to Cart and Plow
At his owne pleasure, and no man him warne.
Wel then, sayd Cotes, beside this barne
Let vs now lyght, and walk to our Inne ;
This Mayde here shal fyrst beginne :
Lepe downe, quod he, & let me helpe your Misteris.
Nay, sayd the wydow, I wil none of your seruice
At this time ; I shal descend without assistance.

The place wher they baited was not far thence,
To the which they romed, & made good chere ;
And when they had payd for bread, ale & beere,
And for other things, I cannot tell what,
The wydow departed from yᵗ place there she sate,
And called for horse. Let us ride now, quod she.
I am well contented, so mote I thee,
Sayd her host ; and Cotes agreed therto.
But hostes, quod she, or euer that we go,
Whan we be on horsback, fyl a pint wᵗ Malmsay,
And, syrs, betwene you, looke that ye wel pay
For euery thing, and that with the most.
I haue done, sayd Cotes, whatsoeuer it cost ;
She is allowed after her owne price.
To horsback than they yede at a trice,
And ridden forth, tyl they come to Barnat.
Now friends, quod she, I wyl algate
Leaue the towne, as I told you before.
Cotes answered, and a great oth swore,
That he wold not ride out of his way :
Care ye not, quod he, what folks say,
And if that ye be knowne, what for that ?
Put on your head this hood and your hat,
And eke this cloke about you ; & if you doubt
Than, and they gawren round about,
Ye shal not be knowne of any maner wight ;
I pray you let vs ride : for it draweth vnto night.

Tut! quod she, ye be a mery man;
Trow ye that my owne folk ne can
Know me, and if I be disgused?
Yes, I warrant you ye shal heare it cryed,
If we ride through y* towne : for I shall tell thee
    Cotes,
I haue them in my Inne [that,] and they se but my
    fote,
They wil know me, and what remedy then?
I know you wyll defend me, lyke prety men,
Vnto your power; but what is one or tway
In comparison to sixe, if they mete in the way?
But, seing ye wyll ieopard it, geue me my cloke;
Ride forth a pace, and not once aside loke.
Whē we com agaīst y* Lyon, but hang down your
    heads,
And geue me in my hands your beades;
I wyll occupy both my hart and eke my minde;
The better assystance I trust we shal finde.
Ye, but, quod her host, how shal I do for my boots
I pray you that eyther I or els Cotes
May ride for them, and gallop after in hast.
I say, quod she, tyll we be this towne past,
We wyl not tarry for ought that may fall.
Worce arayed then you are, ye cannot be at all;
At S. Albons we shal amend al fawtes,
And I trust arme vs for al assautes.

Wel then let vs ride, in Christes holy name,
Yf ye think it best : for I am yet the same
Man that I was yerst for al the myre.
They rode through y<sup>e</sup> towne, lyke as wylde fyre
Had ben new put in euery horse tayle ;
And when y<sup>t</sup> they came to y<sup>e</sup> wyndmyl w<sup>t</sup> y<sup>e</sup> sayle,
There Cotis gan for to speake anon :
What way, quod he, shal we ride vpon ?
Misteris, where is your Farme y<sup>t</sup> ye told of before ?
Alas ! sayd she, that euer I was bore !
It maketh me sick to think on the foule way,
That we must pas throw ; what shuld I more say ?
A lane there is betwene vs and that ;
The Porter of hel, I dare say, with his bat
Cannot escape, but he must ligge in the myre.
But we wyl doe well. I wot what is our hyre.
To Hatfeld we shal ride this same night,
And to morow, when we haue the day light,
We shal yede to S. Albons by than it is noone,
And my besynes there wil not be don soone.
It wyll cost vs two or three dayes wark.
But, Syrs, quod she, is none of you a clark ?
I must haue a quytance made for my rent
To a knaue, which me sore repent,
That euer he occupyed any ground of mine.
I am sure he hath of Oxen and kyne
An hundred heds, and much stuffe besyde ;

And y° arrand knaue, whē I com, he wil him hyde,
Makyng him as bare as a byrds tayle ;
And when I speake with hym, he wyl not fayle
To tel me a tale, hinching and pinching,
And in faith, Mysteris, I haue no good thing
To make you there, but it doth me good to se you.
But if I could tell in what wise and how
.To anoyd the heynard, he should not long abyde.
Well, sayd Cotes, what so euer betyde,
This same present night I wyll ryde
To S. Albons.   I lyke not this tittell tattel.
Why, quod she, and ye think your horse be able
To beare you through, than do as ye lyst ;
But I pray you that you bring me first
To Hatfelde, and than ye shal haue a token
To my seruant, that dwelleth in my Inne
With the Crosse Keyes, in S. Albones towne ;
And to morow in the morning, vp and downe,
Ye may se mine house and my easment there,
And afterwards trusse together al my gere.
You shal haue in y° parlour next to the strete
A Cofer, standyng at my beds feete,
In which Cofer all my money is.
Three hundred Marks I haue therein, I wys,
In six bags ; but loke that ye beare
But two of y° lest w^t you : for I haue certain geare
In the tother fower, which shal not as yet

Be seene of any body, I let you wyt ;
Ye may say that I trust ye to let you come so nere.
Show Thomas Edwards, my seruant there,
Where I am, and that I sent you thither,
Commandyng him for to delyuer
My keyes to you by such a token,
The which keyes were made to open
The new chest at mine owne beds feete,
And eke my Whuch that is fast ishyt,
Wherin remayneth all my plate.
Trusse it surely ; and yet, beside al that,
I pray ye that ye wyll take so much payne,
If that ye se no lykelyhood of rayne,
As to bring with you vnto this towne
A Kyrtle of chamblet[1] and my tawny gowne.
They ly on the presse in my owne chamber :
My purse also, with my Beades of amber.
Take these things, I pray you, as fast as ye may,
Make a fardle therof, and send them away
By Thomas Edwards to the Lyon in Barnet.
And when ye haue thus don, remember this yet :
Take two fresh Geldings out of my stable,
And leaue yours there, till they be better able
To iornay on the way.   Syrs, say I not well ?
Yes, sayd Cotes, if it be as you tell.
At the Checker in Hatfelde she toke her lodgeing,

(1) Camlet.

When it was ful late in the euening.
There her Host and Cotes departed her fro,
And also, as fast as their horses can go,
They ryde, tyl they come to S. Albons towne,
And there demaunded vp and downe
For the Crosse Keyes, and found it at last.
Thomas Edwards there they asked for in hast,
And than was none such in all the throufare.
That hore, quod Cotes, euyll mote she fare !
Hath begiled vs, and what remedy now ?
His felow answered : I shal tel thee how ;
Peraduenture ther ar more Crosse Keyes then
       one ;
Aske ye som body, and ye shal know anone.
The hostler told them y$^t$ there was yet another ;
I thank you, sayd Cotes, my owne good brother.
There they demaunded, as they dyd before ;
The good man asked where they were bore,
And what they wolde haue that time of night.
Quod Cotes to his felow : let vs downe light ;
This is the house, I wot well inow.
A, master Edwards, I pray you tel vs, how
That ye liue here in your mistris absence.
Mistris !$^1$ quod he ; Syrs, get you fast hence :
For by our Lady ye be falce knaues both ;
And then he gan to sweare many an oth.

(1) Old ed. has *masters*.

Soft & fayre, sayd Coates, breake not your pa-
cience.
We shal tel you, what we ar & whence.
Such a gentilwoman sent vs, & she her selfe sayd,
That this house is her own; her husband for it paid.
A ha! I wot now, wher abouts yᵗ ye be ;
By coks wounds, she is an arrant hore, quod he.
She sent hether, wᵗin xii. monthes & little more,
After this same facion, I am sure halfe a score.
But, syrs, I shal tel you, it is wisdom ye take heed.
Cotes in all the hast raght to him his steed,
His Jade, I would say, & his felow his also,
And forth they ryd, wᵗout words mo,
To Hatfeld agayne by one of the clock,
And at the Checker dore they gan for to knock.
The goodman was yet vp, & the wydow also :
What, quod she, how happeneth that you two
Com agayne so late ? had you no better chere ?
Hore, hore ! by coks blood, euen here,
Sayd Cotes, and it were not for shame,
I should canvas thee, and make thee lame.
Peace, quod his felow, art yᵘ wel in thy wit ?
Thou wilt mar al ; I pray thee downe sitt,
And hold thy tong, the deuyll pul it out !
The wydow answerd : nay, I put you out of dout,
My seruant is subtil, yᵗ kepeth there my house.
By gods foote, quod Cotes, not a poor louse

Thou art not able to foster in all the towne.

Tut ! sayd she, haue ye brought w$^t$ you my gown,

And mine other geare, tell me truely?

Than her host answered soberly,

And told her all how they had sped.

Well, then, quod she, let vs go to bed,

And to morow I wil my selfe thither,

And eke you two shall ride together.

I trow ye shal heare an other maner of tale.

Goodman of the house, borow me a male

Against to morow, I pray you hartely ;

And, mayden, make redy my breakfast early ;

I se wel that my men be halfe in dispayre.

Then to bed they got them wel and fayre.

Cotes and his felow gave in charge

To the goodman of the house, y$^t$ ne at large

He should suffer in any wise that night

The wydow to walke, til it be day light :

For we doubt, quod they, y$^t$ she wil make a start.

Theyr host bad them be mery in hart,

And take no thought for ought that may fall.

I will se you, quod he, agreed all,

Or euer ye depart this house fro,

If ye wylbe resonable, I can no mo.

Then imediatly they yede to rest ;

The wydow thought she would do her best,

Once yet to begile them both twayne.

To her hoste she gan for to complaine ;
With weping eyne she sayd : alas !
Help, host, now ; thus standeth the case.
One of these knaues wold haue me to wyfe,
And in sorow with hym to lead my lyfe.
I haue deuised all the wayes that I may
To scape from them, and to go a way,
But I cannot, and I should dye therfore ;
The blessed Jesu, that of a mayd was bore,
By[1] myne ayde ! as I entend well.
Therwith she wept, and on her knees fell.
Than her host asked what she wolde geue,
On that condition she might have leve
To walk at her wyll, whether[2] she wolde.
Three Grots, quod she, in fayre pence itolde,
And that is all that euer I haue
At this tyme vpon me, so god me saue !
The money he receyued, and then bad her goe,
Whether she wold, but doe no more soe.
At three of the clocke in the dark mornyng,
Away she yed before the dawning,
And where she become then that tyde,
I cannot tell you, in al this world so wyde.
But fare well, troll, syth that she be gon.
Cotes and his felow in the morning, whan
They were vp rysen, and [had] kempt their heaire,

(1) *i.e.* Be.          (2) *i.e.* whither.

For the wydow they asked ; & than was there
No body could tel, whither she was yede.
Their host they demanded, and he sayd, by crede,
He wyst not where she was.   Let her go,
Quod he then : it is well ye skaped[1] so.
One loked on an other, & wist not what to say ;
And, in conclusion, euen the right way
To London they tooke in all the haste ;
They wolde not once tarry, to breake their faste :
And of these poses[2] I make an ende,
God saue the Wydow, where [so][3] euer she wende.


**Finis.   by Walter Smith.[4]**


**Imprinted at London in Fleet-lane :
By Richard Johnes.**


(1) Old ed. has *shaped.*
(2) So ed. 1525.   Ed. 1573 has *this prosses.*
(3) So ed. 1525.   Ed. 1513 has *where euer.*
(4) Ed. 1525 has *Quod Waterius Smyth.*

# PASQUILS JESTS

## mixed with

# MOTHER BUNCH'S MERRIMENTS.

-

" *Barabas.* Now I remember those old women's words,
Who in my wealth would tell me winter's tales."
Marlowe's *Rich Jew of Malta*, 1633.

Pasquils Iests, mixed with Mother Bunches Merriments. Whereunto is added a doozen of Gulles.
Pretty and pleasant to drive away the tediousnesse
of a Winters Evening. *Imprinted at London for
John Browne, and are to be sold at* his shop in Saint
Dunstones Church yard in Fleet Street. 1604. 4°,
black letter.

*₊* This edition, of which there is a very indifferent
copy in the British Museum, contains twenty-four leaves,
including the title, and fifty-two tales, besides the
" doozen of Gulles."

Pasquils iests, with the merriments of Mother Bunch.
Wittie, pleasant, and delightfull. London, Printed
by M. F[lesher], and are to be sold by Francis
Grove, ouer against Saint Sepulchers Church without
Newgate, 1629. 4°, black letter, 31 leaves, including
title.

*₊* According to the *Bibliographer's Manual*, which
is of course known to be of no authority, there were
editions in 1608-9, and in 1627. Of these, at all events,
I have been unable to procure particulars. The edition
of 1629 does not possess the *Gulles;* an Epistle to the
Reader is substituted.

Pasqvils Iests : with the Merriments of Mother Bunch.
Wittie, pleasant, and delightfull. London : Printed

by M. F[lesher], and are to be sold by Andrew
Kembe, dwelling at Saint Margarets hill in Southwark. 1635. 4°, black letter.

*₊* In this edition, a copy of which is in the Capel
Collection at Cambridge, the *Gulles* are also missing.
The " Address to the Reader " occupies three pages.
The work consists altogether of 60 pp. unnumbered.

Pasquils Jests, with the Merriments of Mother Bunch.
Wittie, pleasant, and delightful. London, Printed
by M. F[lesher], n. d. [circa 1635]. 4°, black letter.

*₊* This impression contains seventy-six stories, but
has not the *Gulles.* There is, however, the *Epistle to
the Reader.*

Pasqvils Jests : with the Merriments of Mother Bunch.
Wittie, pleasant, and delightfull. London, Printed
by J[ames] F[lesher ?], and are to be sold by William
Gilbertson at the signe of the Bible in Giltspur-street,
n. d. [circa 1650]. 4°, black letter.

*₊* This edition contains seventy-eight tales, and
consists altogether of thirty-one leaves. It has not the
*Gulles;* but there is an Epistle to the Reader, similar
to that in the preceding editions, accompanied by the
same verses. On the reverse of the title is the following injunction within a woodcut border :—

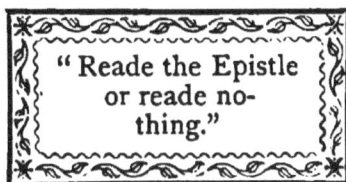

> " Reade the Epistle
> or reade no-
> thing."

This is also found in the editions printed by M. F. in 1629, in 1635, and without date.

Pasquils Iests, with the Merriments of Mother Bunch. Witty, Pleasant, and delightfull. London, Printed by J[ames] F[lesher?], and are to be sold by F. Coles, T. Vere, and J. Wright. 1669. 4°, black letter, 31 leaves, including title and preface.

\*\*\* This edition almost exactly corresponds to those of 1629 and 1635.

The present republication of *Pasquils Jests* is from a transcript of the first edition, 1604, 4°, which I owe to the kindness of J. O. Halliwell, Esq. who, on my application to him, at once in the most obliging manner placed it at my disposal. Aware, however, how liable the most careful copyists are to error, I have compared this reprint, in its progress through the press, word for word with the original ; and I have added the " Epistle to the Reader," only found in the later impressions. This address seemed worth preserving on account of its curious allusions, if not for the sake of the ludicrously extravagant vein in which it is written. *Pasquils Jests* may perhaps be added to the list of the publications of Nicholas Breton ; but there is no certainty on this subject, and the work has always been regarded as anonymous. It was at first my intention to have incorporated the twenty-six additional stories, which occur in the edition printed for W. Gilbertson, a copy of which is in the British Museum ; but it seemed, on the whole, better to present the book to the reader in

its genuine state, merely supplementing the prefatory
address. The additions, which were subsequently
made, were very probably not by the original editor,
and were merely anecdotes introduced from other collections to impart an air of novelty to the publication
on its reappearance. It is a curious circumstance,
that the GULLES were omitted in all but the very early
impressions.

Mother Bunch, under whose name these humorous
tales were ushered into the world, appears to have
been a sort of second ELINOUR RUMMING, or LONG
MEG OF WESTMINSTER ; and, if we may believe all
that we are told, was a still more formidable virago
than the two latter. It is probable enough that the
lady in question was some well known ale-wife of the
time, whose facetious and popular character suggested
to the compiler of *Pasquils Jests* the notion of assisting
the sale of his work by introducing her on the title-
page under what may have been her common nick-
name. Her celebrity was, doubtless, extreme, and
subsequent book-makers did not scruple to trade upon
it. Hence we have *pseudo-Bunchiana*, to wit: " Mother
Bunch's Golden Fortune-Teller," " Mother Bunch's
Closet Newly Broken Open," and the like, the chrono-
logy of which publications is rather dubious, from the
persistent absence of dates.

The bibliography of Jest-books can seldom be complete or satisfactory, as books of this class are peculiarly
difficult of access, and as unknown and undescribed
editions present themselves at intervals. Two editions

3· I

only are in the British Museum, that of 1604 and the one printed for W. Gilbertson; and both are recent acquisitions. The Bodleian possesses the impressions of 1629 and 1669.

The reader will easily recognise in the following pages stories which have already occurred in a slightly varied form, in some cases with the change only of names and places, in *A C. Mery Talys, Mery Tales & Quick Answeres*,[1] &c.; but this class of literature has never done anything but repeat itself over and over again since the days of Hierocles, and in the whole circle of modern jest-books there is not probably a single anecdote, or a single witticism which has the slenderest pretension to originality. A good deal of the *Sheridaniana* is merely a reproduction of old material for the nonce.

" Pasquil's Jests " was one of the revivals of our early literature projected, but eventually abandoned, by the Shakespeare Society. In some of the original editions there is a Table of Contents.

---

(1) It has not been thought necessary to indicate, in each instance, where a story is common to other collections forming part of the present series of old English jest-books, as the reader is now enabled to compare the various versions in which the same anecdote has appeared from time to time.

# ℭo tɦe ℳerrie ℜeaðer.

## ℭɦe ðescription of ℘asquil anð ℳotɦer ℬuncɦ.

MOST pleasant Reader, my onely ayme in writing this Booke, is but to make thee laugh, and to shorten the tediousnesse of a long Winters Evening. Know then, that noble *Pasquil*, the Author of these Jests, was in his time the onely merry companion, who for Wit, Mirth, Eloquence, and Joviality, was the merriest Grigg (as saith the Story) that I ever read of. Now for *Mother Bunch*,[1] the onely dainty, wel favored, well proportioned, sweet coomplexioned, and most delightful Hostesse of *England*, she was squared into inches, being in height twenty thousand and a halfe, wanting a fingers bredth jump, in bredth eleven thousand and two inches and a nayles bredth just ; she spent most of her time in telling of tales, and when she laughed, she was heard from Algate to the Monuments at Westminster, and all Southwarke stood in amazement, the

---

(1) In the play of *The Weakest Goeth to the Wall*, 1600, one of the *dramatis personæ* is BARNABY BUNCH the Botcher, who alleges that he is the son of the redoubted lady of the same name, the matured fruits of whose prodigious faculty as a storyteller were given to the world in 1604. In Act I. sc. 2 of *The Weakest Goeth to the Wall*, we are told by Master Bunch himself, who is of course the best authority on such a point, that he had been originally in the same line as Mrs. B. viz. an *ale-draper*, somewhere near Thames Street ; but adverse circumstances, it seems, compelled honest Barnaby to change his views in life, and to settle down into a repairer of gentlemen's apparel, or, more briefly speaking, a *Botcher*.

Lyons in the Tower,[1] and the Bulls and Beares of
Parish-Garden roar'd (with terrour of her laughter)
lowder then the great roaring Megge. Shee was once
wrung with wind in her belly, and with one blast of
her taile, she blew downe Charing-Crosse, with Pauls
aspiring steeple ; she danced a Galliard on towerhill,
and all the great Ordnance leapt for joy, and London
shooke as it had been an earthquake ; her quotidian
or daily diet was three fat oxen,[2] two boyled and one
roasted, with the Intralls : twenty three fat Muttons
and a quarter, with the Heads and Gethers parboyl'd :
fifteen dozen of fat Capons, with the wings and leggs
of seven dozen of yong Chikens, and to close up her
stomack, ninety and nine dozen of Larks wel roasted,
and forty seven dozen of two penny wheaten bread,
and to every loafe shee drank a tun of her strongest
May. Ale,[3] with Nutmeg and Sugar : yet shee never

---

(1) In the *Guls Horn Book*, 1609, by T. Decker, the *Monuments at
Westminster* and the *Lions in the Tower* are also enumerated among
the chief attractions of the metropolis at this period.

(2) The appetite of Mother Bunch far exceeded that of *Gluttony* in the
Vision of the *Seven Deadly Sins*, introduced into Marlowe's *Faustus :*—
" *Glut.* . . . . . I am Gluttony. My parents are all dead and the
devil a penny they have left me, but a bare pension, and that is thirty
meales a day and ten bevers, a small trifle to suffice nature."
Her ladyship's digestive powers must have surpassed those of the
"Great Eater of Kent," whom Taylor the Water Poet has immortalized
in a tract printed in 1630.

(3) [*Bar. Bunch*]. O, for one pot of Mother Bunche's ale, my own
mother's ale, to wash my throat this misty morning ! It would clear my
sight, comfort my heart, and stuff my veins, that I should not smell the
savour of these stockings."—*The Weakest Goeth to the Wall*, Act I.
scene 2.

did rise from the table (as saith the story) but with a
good appetite. For her signe shee perk't up her red
nose, that ushered her face, red as Skarlet, which when
shee stood upright, looked over the City like a blazing
star ; and when it appeared, Bakers made hast, and
Cookes came running, with whole Ovens ful of Pies,
to bake at the sweltering heat which proceeeded from
her jolly red nose. A most pretious and rich nose it
was, set with Rubies of all sorts, and hung in clusters
like your French Grapes, which being well prest,
yeelded from the abundant goodnesse five tun of well
clarified liquor. Shee dwelt (as saith the Auther) in

Nash, in his *Pierce Penilesse his Supplication to the Deuill,* 1592, has
the ensuing passage :—"The next obiect that encounters my eyes, is
some such obscure vpstart gallants, as, without desert or seruice, are
raised from the plough to be checkmate with princes ; and these I can
no better compare than to creatures that are bred *sine coitu,* as crickets
in chimnyes ; to which I resemble poore scullians, that, from turning
spit in the chimney corner, are on the sodayne hoysed vp, from the
kitchen into the wayting chamber, or made barons of the beanes, and
marquesses of the mary-boanes ; some by corrupt water, as gnats, to
which we may liken brewers, that, by retayling filthie Thames water,
come in few yeres to be worth fortie or fiftie thousand pound ; others, by
dead wine, as little flying worms ; and so the vintners in like case ; others
by slime, as frogs, which may be alluded to Mother Bunches slymie ale,
that hath made her, and some other of her fil pot familie so wealthie—"
    Coeval with Mother Bunch, and a rival dealer in strong ale, was one
MOTHER WATKYN, whose beverage appears to have enjoyed a celebrity
almost equal to that of her contemporary. See Chappell's *Popular
Music of the Olden Time,* p. 136-7, and *An Elizabethan Garland,* 1856,
p. 30. "Watkins ale" was formerly a favourite dance-tune. It is mentioned by Chettle in *Kind Harts Dreme* (1592), and by other writers of
the Elizabethan era. The virtues of Mother Watkin's ale were commemorated in a ballad of the time (still extant) entitled :—
        " A ditty delightful of Mother Watkin's ale,
        A warning well weighed, though counted a tale."

Cornehill (neere the Exchange) and sold strong Ale,
whose health to this day all joviall drunkards never do
forget ; the many vertues of her Ale [it] is impossible
for one penne to write. The Dutchmen were her best
customers for a long time, untill the report of her Ale
had spread it all England over. Young men and
maides frequented her house, more than either *Pymlico*
or the now flourishing *Totenan* [sic] *court.*

She raised the spirits of her spiggot to such a height,
that Maids grew proud, and many proved with childe
after it, and being asked who got the childe, they
answered, they knew not, onely they thought Mother
*Bunches Ale,* and another thing had done the deed ;
but whosoever was the father, Mother *Bunches* Ale had
all the blame.

Shee was an excellent companion, and sociable ; she
was very pleasant and witty, and would tell a tale, let
a ****, drink her draught, scratch her ****, pay her
groat as well as any Chymist of Ale whatsoever. From
this noble Mother *Bunch* proceeded all our great
greasie Tapsters, and fat swelling Ale wives, whose
faces are blowne as bigge as the froth of their bottle-
Ale, and their complexion imitating the out side of a
Cookes greasie dripping-pan, and you could hardly
goe round about her in a Summer after-noone. Mother
*Bunch* lived an hundreth, seventy and five yeares, two
dayes and a quarter, and halfe a minute, and died in
the prime of her charity : for, had she lived but two
moneths longer, she had knit Pauls a night-cap, and
bought London-bridge a payre of Pantoffles to keepe

his feet out of the cold swelling water. But shee died, and left behind her these pleasant tales following, which she used to tell those nimble spirits, which drank deepe of her Ale, and as she changed their money, as was generally related.

" These[1] harmlesse lines that have no ill intent,
I hope shall passe in mirth as they were meant.
What I intend, is but to make you sport,
By telling truth to please the better sort :
    And what it is, that I have aym'd at now,
The Wise may judge, for Fooles I care not how."

(1) These verses are here printed on the verso of the last page of the Epistle to the Reader, just as they occur in Gilbertson's ed. and in that printed by M. Flesher.

# Pasquils Jests and Mother Bunches Merriments.

## A tale of a Scriuener of London and a Countreyman.

IT fell out upon a Satterday, being market day, that a Countrie fellow of the better sort of husbandrie, came to London to lay out a little money upō some necessary trinkets : and hauing dispatched his businesse, after hee had pretily refreshed his spirits with a pot of the best that the Alehouse could afford him, made homewards very merily ; but by the way, casting his eye, by chance, upon a kind of Writers, that would haue bin a Scriveners shop, and seeing the master of the poore house, or the poore master of the house, sitting alone in a rugge gowne, wrapping in his armes, to auoyd the bitternesse of the weather, minding to make himselfe a little sport, fell thus to salute the poore Pen-man : I pray you, master, what might you sel in your shop, that you haue so many ding-dōgs hang at your doore ! Why, my friend, quoth the Obligation-maker, I sell nothing but Logger-heads. By my fay, master, quoth the Country man, you haue made a faire market with them, for you haue left but one in your shop, that I see : and so laughing, went his way, leauing much good sport to them that heard him.

## A pretty tale of a poore man and a Lawyer.

A POORE man hauing bin much injured by an unkinde neighbour, who by the power of his purse would haue put him by the right of his land, went to a Lawyer dwelling not farre off, to whom hauing deliuered his griefe, he gaue little for his counsell, but a great many thāks, and countrie curtsies, with God saue his life, and so forth ; entreating him to let him know when he should againe wait upon him for his further advice. Who answered him somewhat short : When you will, neighbour, when you will. The poore man, upon this when you will, came oftentimes afterward to him, but found no will in him to speake with him. Whereupon the poore man telling his wife of his ill hap, was aduised by her to take one of his best lambes, and present it unto him, and then he should see what would follow : her counsell he followed, tooke his lambe, and went to the Lawyer : to whose gate he was no sooner come, but the

Lawyer hearing the bleating of his lamb, opening his window, called him up, and within two words told him he understood his case, and all should bee well : where with hee departed, meeting with his wife going to the market, After they had beene at the Alehouse, and taken a pot or two, the poore man got him up into the market place, and there hauing his throat wel cleared, made this mad out-crie : All ye that haue any matters to trie in law, get ye euerie one a fat lambe, and carry to your Lawyer ; for one word of a lambes mouth will bee better understood of the Lawyer, and doe more good, then twentie of your owne. Probatum.

## Of a Citizen of London that rid out of the City fibe myles.

A CITIZEN riding to Edmonton had his man following him on foote, who came so neere that the horse strake him a great blowe on the thigh. The fellow, thinking to be reuenged, tooke up a great stone to throw at the horse, and hit his master on the raynes of the backe. Within a while his master looked backe, and seeing his man come halting so farre behind, chid him. Sir, your horse hath giuen me such a blow, quoth his man, on the thigh, that I can go no faster. Truely, sayd his master, the

horse is a great kicker, for likewise with his heele
right now, hee gaue me a great stroke on the
reynes of my backe : when it was his man that
threw the stone.

### A pretty tale of a Complaynant that cryed to a Judge for Justice, yet refused it when it was offered him.

ONE Dromo, a certayne Tiler, sitting upon the
ridge of a house, laying on certayne roofe tiles,
looking back, and reaching somewhat too farre for
a little morter that lay by him, fell backeward, and
by good hap fell upon a man that was sitting under
the house, whom with his fall he bruised to death,
but thereby saued his owne life.   Not many dayes
after, a sonne of the dead mans caused this man
to bee apprehended for murther, and hauing him
before the Judge, cried unto him for Justice : who
asking of the prisoner what he could say for himselfe, receiued this answer : Truly, sir, I neuer
thought the man any hurt, neither did I thinke to
fall ; but since it was my hap to hit upon him to
saue my life, if it please your Lordship, I am contented that hee shall haue justice ; for myselfe, I
had no malice to his father, though I see he hath
a great deale to me ; but let him do his worst, I
care not, I aske no fauour : let him goe up to the

top of the house where I sate, and I will sit where
his father sate ; let him fall from the place as cunningly as hee can, and fall upon me to saue his
life, I will be contented. The Judge, seeing the
mans Innocency in intent of any euill to the man
whome hee had slayne, willed the Complaynant to
take this course for his contentment ; which hee
refusing was dismissed the Court, and the Prisoner
thus by his wit released.

## 𝔥𝔬𝔴 𝔞 𝔐𝔞𝔯𝔠𝔥𝔞𝔫𝔱 𝔩𝔬𝔰𝔱 𝔥𝔦𝔰 𝔭𝔲𝔯𝔰𝔢 𝔟𝔢𝔱𝔴𝔢𝔢𝔫 𝔚𝔞𝔩𝔱𝔥𝔞𝔪 𝔞𝔫𝔡 𝔏𝔬𝔫𝔡𝔬𝔫.

A MARCHANT that trauailed betweene Ware
and London, lost his budget, wherein was
a hūdred pound, who caused to proclayme in all
villages and market townes, that who so had found
the same, and would restore it againe, should haue
twenty pounds for his paynes. An honest husbandman that chaunced to finde it, brought it to
the Baylife of Ware, and required his twenty pounds
for his paynes, when he deliuered it. When the
couetous Marchant understood this, and that he
must needes pay twenty pound for the finding of
it, he sayd there was an hundred and twenty pound
in the budget, and so would haue had his owne
money and twenty pound ouer. So long they

stroue, that the matter was brought before a
Justice. When the Justice understood by the
Baylife that the cry was made for a budget with
an hundred pound in it, he demaunded where it
was? Heere (quoth the Baylife), and gaue it him.
Is it just an hundred pound (quoth the Justice)?
Yes (quoth the Baylife). Hold (quoth the Justice
to him that found the budget), take thou this money
to thy use, and if thou happen to find a budget
with a hundred and twenty pound, bring it to this
honest Marchant man. It is mine, I lost no more
but a hundreth pound (quoth the Marchant). You
speake now too late (quoth the Justice), for your
couetousnesse hath beguiled your selfe.

## A Jest, sabing your reberence, worth the laughing at.

IN a City, I find not where, met a company, I know
not who, and about I know not what : but after
that they had layd their heads together to conclude
upon a thing of nothing, as the use is of such kind
of people, fearing to surfet of fasting, they got them
to dinner, where, when their bellies were full of
wine, their braynes set their tongues to worke about
wonders : and hauing made a great noyse to little
purpose, they fell to questioning among themselues,
what was the rarest thing in the world. One he

sayd, the Phenix, because there was but one, and she killed herselfe, and liued againe of her owne ashes. Another sayd, a Diamond, because it would write in glasse. Another sayd, a Parrat, because it would speak like a man. Another sayd, a true friend, [because] the world was so full of falshood. Another said, Gold, for that it wrought wonders in y^e world. And another said, Loue, because it robbed wise men of their wits. But while they did thus differ in their opinions, one plaine, Asse-headed foole, being willing to say his mind, upon a sudden falling into a laughing, told them they were all wide: for he knew a rarer thing then all they: which they desiring to know, hee told them it was a sweet ********. Whereat euery one holding themselues by the nose, left off their talke, and laughing at the foole, rose from the table.

### How cunningly a knabe deuised to get money by his wit for himselfe and his three companions.

THREE loytring companions that fell in company together, domineerd so long, that all their money was consumed and gone. So being penny-lesse, sayd one of them: By my fayth, we are now in a faire taking: for we may, if we will, seeke our dinner with Duke Humphrey. Nay, zounds (quoth the second), If I come where any presse of people be, I can get money enough for us all. Sblood, and I (quoth the third) can lightly assemble people. They were at that time not passing two miles from a small towne in Barkshire where, when they came, there was a new Pillory set up, where the third of them steps to the Baylife, and desires him to haue the mayden-head of their new pillory. The Bayliffe being a butcher was halfe amazed, and standing musing, at last he asked counsel of his neighbours, and they bade him set up the knaue and spare not. So up he went, and when he was up, he looked about and saw his two fellowes busie in the holes of the Butchers aprons, where they put all their money. To it, to it (quoth he), apace. The people laughed hartily to see him stand there. At last, when he saw that his fellowes had sped their matters, and were going away, he said to the Bayliffe : Turne the pillory about, and now I will come downe. So he, laughing hartily, did. And when he was come downe, the Bayliffe sayd : Now by my fayth thou art a good fellow, and because thou hast made us some sport, I will giue thee a Tester to drinke : and so, thinking to take some money out of the hole of his apron, hee found there neuer a penny. Cockes armes (quoth the bayliffe), my money is picked out of my apron :

and then the rest of the butchers beside swore they had lost theirs also. I hope (quoth the fellow), you do not think that I haue it. No, by my troth (quoth the Bayliffe), I know well enough thou hast it not, for thou wert on the Pillory all the while. Why then, no harme, no force (quoth the fellow), and so went his wayes.

## How one at Kingston fayned himselfe dead, to trye what his wife would doe.

IN Kingston dwelt one Rawlins, newly maried, which to prooue what his wife would doe, fayned himselfe dead, while she was in the backside washing of her clothes, and layd himselfe all along the floore. Whereupon his wife comming suddenly in, thought that he had bin dead indeed : but hauing laboured hard all the day, and being sore an hungred, shee stood musing with her selfe, whether it were best to lament his death, or to dine first : which motion of eating liked her best : whereupon shee cut two or three collops of salt Bacon, and broyled them on the coales, and ate them up : and being very hungry, shee forgot to drinke, but the saltnesse of the meat at last made her throat so harsh that shee tooke a pot and went to draw some drinke : but one of her neighbours

3.        K

comming suddenly in, made her set down her pot,
and as if her husband had but new falne downe,
shee began to lament so heauily, and with such a
noyse, that all the neighbours came running in,
where they found her most pitifully bewayling the
sudden death of her husband. Whereupon they
began to comfort her, and told her, she must be
content, for there was now no remedie. Alas! sayd
she, Oh, my sweet husband! what shall I doe? At
which words, her husband lift up his head, and
sayd: Full ill, my sweet wife, except you goe quickly
and drinke: for the salt Bacon I am sure hath
almost choked you.

## 𝕬 knabish answere of an unhappy countrey wench to a foolish yong fellow.

A CERTAYNE idle headed young man, that
loued to heare himselfe speake, though it were
of matter to little purpose, riding upon a fayre day
to a market towne, ouertooke by chance, among
other creatures of her own kind, an indifferent well
fauored and well growne countrey wench, whom
singling by her selfe as much as he could, he fel to
commune with, in an odde maner of loue-making,
when beginning very low, marking her new shod
feete, hanging ouer her dossers, beganne with this

commendation : Truly, sister, you haue a very fine
foot there. Yea, sir (quoth yᵉ wench), that I haue ;
a couple. The yong man thinking to shew some
little wit, in a scoffe replyed with this speech :
But are they twinnes, sister ? were they both borne
at one time ? No, indeed, sir (quoth the wench) ;
there hath beene a man borne betwixt them. Wherewith her neighbours that rode by her, falling into a
laughing, made him find that she was a married
wife : which being contrary to his expectation,
being much troubled with her answere, with lacke
of wit to reply, galloped away with a flea in his
eare.

## A flowting answere to a flowting question.

A POORE man, upon a time comming into a
market with a very leane horse, setting him
neere unto a company of fat and fayre Geldings
to be sold, was asked of a scoffing companion, how
he sold his horse by the ell ; which the poore man
taking something discontentedly, and yet not willing to quarrel with him, made him an answere fit
for his question, when holding up his horses taile :
I pray you, sir (quoth he), come into the shop
and you shall see.

## A warning for tale-tellers.

I READ in the records of a certayne schoole, where faultes were reckoned up all the week, to be payd upon the Satterday, that an unhappy boy, willing to haue one of his fellowes taste of such schoole-butter as hee had often broke his fast with, one morning came to his master with this speech : Truly, sir, you haue often beaten me for looking off from my booke, and such a one scapeth without rebuke. Yea! (quoth he) call him to me. Who no sooner came to him, but [hee] heard him his lesson. Which perfectly repeated : How now, Sirra (quoth he to his accuser), how like you this geare? How did he looke from his booke, and say his lesson so well? Let me heare you; who was imperfect in many poynts. Well, sir (quoth hee), how doe you know that your fellow did not looke upon his booke? Marry, sir (quoth he), I did watch him all the while. Then, sir (quoth his fellow), I beseech you aske him who looked on his booke while he watched mee. Whereat his master smiling, tooke the accuser, and openly in the schoole whipped him well, first for his lesson, and after for his accusation.

## ©f a worshipfull gentleman in Lincolnshire and his man.

A CERTAYNE gentleman in Lincolnshire, being also a Justice of Peace, had an olde servant many yeres, called Adam Milford, who upon a time came unto his master, and desired him, in regard he had bene his servant so many yeeres, hee would now giue him something to helpe him in his old age. Thou sayest true (quoth his master), and I will tell thee what I will doe. Now shortly I am to ride up to London; if thou wilt pay my costs and charges by the way, I will giue thee shortly such a thing as shall be worth to thee an hundred pound. I am content (quoth Adam); and so payd for all their reckoning by the way. So being come to London, he put his master in mind of his former promise that he had made to him. What, did I promise thee anything? I (quoth Adam), y$^t$ you did : for you said you would giue mee that that should bee worth to me a hundred pound, for paying your charges to London. Let me see your writing (quoth his master). I haue none (quoth Adam). Then thou art like to haue nothing (quoth his master); and learne this of mee, that when thou makest a bargayne with any man, looke thou take a writing, and beware how thou makest a writing to any man. This hath auayled mee an hundred pounds in my dayes. When Adam saw there was no remedy, he was content; but when they should depart, Adam stayed behind his master to reckon with his hostis; and on his masters scarlet cloake borrowed so much money as came to all their charges that hee had layd out by the way. His master had not ridden past two myles, but it began to rayne apace; wherefore he called for his cloake. His other men made answere, that Adam was behind, and had it with him. So they shrowded them under a tree till Adam came. When he came, his master sayd all angerly : Thou knaue, come give me my cloake; hast thou not serued me well, to let me be thus wet? Truely, sir (quoth Adam), I haue layd it to pawne for all your charges by the way. Why, knaue, quoth he, didst thou not promise to beare my charges to London? Did I? quoth Adam. I, quoth his master, that thou didst. Lets see, shew me your writing of it, quoth Adam. Whereupon his master, perceiuing he was ouerreacht by his man, was fayne to send for his cloake againe, and pay the money.

## 𝕳𝖔𝖜 𝖒𝖆𝖉𝖉𝖊 𝕮𝖔𝖔𝖒𝖊𝖘, 𝖜𝖍𝖊𝖓 𝖍𝖎𝖘 𝖜𝖎𝖋𝖊 𝖜𝖆𝖘 𝖉𝖗𝖔𝖜𝖓𝖊𝖉, 𝖘𝖔𝖚𝖌𝖍𝖙 𝖍𝖊𝖗 𝖆𝖌𝖆𝖎𝖓𝖘𝖙 𝖙𝖍𝖊 𝖘𝖙𝖗𝖊𝖆𝖒𝖊.

COOMES of Stapforth, hearing that his wife was drowned comming from market, went with certayne of his friends to see if they could find her in the riuer. He, contrary to all the rest, sought his wife against the streame; which they perceyuing, sayd he lookt the wrong way. And why so? (quoth he.) Because (quoth they) you should looke downe the streame, and not against it. Nay, zounds (quoth hee), I shall neuer find her that way: for shee did all things so contrary in her life time, that now she is dead, I am sure she will goe against the streame.

## 𝕺𝖋 𝖙𝖍𝖊 𝕱𝖆𝖗𝖒𝖊𝖗 𝖎𝖓 𝕹𝖔𝖗𝖋𝖔𝖑𝖐, 𝖆𝖓𝖉 𝖍𝖎𝖘 𝕻𝖍𝖎𝖘𝖎𝖈𝖎𝖔𝖓.

A CERTAYNE rich Farmer, hauing layne long sicke in Norfolke, at last sent for a Phisicion from the next market towne, who, when he came, hee felt his pulses, and viewed his water, and then told him[1] that he could by no meanes nor phisike escape, the disease had so much power in his body; and so went his way. Within a while after, by God's good helpe who is the onely giuer of all

(1) Orig. has *them.*

health, the man escaped, and was well againe ; and,
walking abroad, being still very weake and feeble,
hee met with his Phisicion who, being very sore
affrayd to see him, asked him if he were not such
a Farmer. Yes, truly (quoth he), I am. Art thou
aliue or dead ? (quoth hee) Dead(quoth he) I am,
and, because I haue experiēce of many things,
God hath sent mee to take up all Phisicions I
can get ; which made the Phisicion to looke as
pale as ashes for feare. Nay, feare not (quoth the
Farmer); though I named all Phisicions, yet I meant
thee for none : for I am sure a veryer Dunce liues
not this day then thou art ; and then I should bee
a foole to take thee for one, that art not fit to come
to any man, but to the dogges with thy phisike.
And so he left him. But the Phisicion neuer left
quaking, till hee was out of the sight of him.

## 𝕳𝖔𝖜 𝖒𝖊𝖗𝖗𝖞 𝕬𝖓𝖉𝖗𝖊𝖜 𝖔𝖋 𝕸𝖆𝖓𝖈𝖍𝖊𝖘𝖙𝖊𝖗 𝖘𝖊𝖗𝖚𝖊𝖉 𝖆𝖓 𝖀𝖘𝖚𝖗𝖊𝖗.

M ERRY ANDREW of Manchester who is well
knowne, meeting with three or foure of his
companions on a Sunday, presently hee bade them
home to dinner, yet hee neyther had meate nor
money in his house. Well, but to his shifts he
goeth, and went into an olde Usurers kitchin, where

he was very familiar, and priuily, under his gowne, he brought away the pot of meat that was sodden for the old misers dinner. When he came home, hee put out the meat, and made his boy scoure the pot, and sent him with it to the Usurer, to borrow two groats on it, and bade the boy take a bill of his hand : which the boy did, and with the money bought beere and bread for their dinner. When the Usurer should goe to dinner, his meat was gone; wherefore he all to beat his mayd, calling her whoore. She sayd there came nobody but Andrew there all that day. Then they asked him ; and he sayd, hee had none ; but at last they sayd, that he and no body else had the pot. By my fayth (quoth Andrew), I borrowed such a pot on a time, but I sent it home agayne ; and so called his witnesse, and sayd: It is perilous to deal with men now adayes without writing; they would lay theft to my charge, if I had not his owne hand to shew ; and so he shewes the Usurers bill, whereat the Usurer storms, and all the rest fell a laughing.

### How hee serued another that would haue put him downe in his merry sayings.

ANDREW once was at supper with his friends, and among the company there was one that

spited at his iests and merry conceits. After supper
they fell to reasoning among themselues which was
the most reuerent part of mans body. One said,
the eye; another, the nose; a third sayd, the leg :
but Andrew, knowing that he that spited him
would name the contrary, sayd, the mouth was most
reuerent of all. Nay (quoth the other), the part
that we sit on is the most reuerent; and because
they all maruayled why he should say so, he made
this reason, that he was most honorable that
was first set, and the part that he named was first
set. Which saying contented them all, and grieued
Andrew. The next day they all met againe, and
Andrew, comming last, found them sitting all together ; and when he had saluted them all but his
enemy, hee turned his back-side to him, and let a
great **** in his face. At which the fellow being
mightily angry, sayd: Walk, knaue, with a mischiefe,
where hast thou bin brought up ? Why, disdaynest
thou ? quoth Andrew. If I had saluted thee with
my mouth, thou wouldest haue saluted meé againe,
and now, when I salute thee with that part that
by thy owne saying is most honourable, thou
callest me knaue. Then the company fell a laughing at this jest hartily.

## 𝔗𝔥𝔢 𝔱𝔞𝔩𝔢 𝔬𝔣 𝔱𝔥𝔢 𝔅𝔩𝔞𝔠𝔨𝔢 𝔐𝔬𝔬𝔯𝔢.

I N the yere when fresh wits began to season themselues to abide weathers, it fel out, it is no matter
where, that a certayne yong fellow, next neighbour
to a foole, hauing more money in his purse then
he knew well how to use, and yet willing to ad-
uēture a little to gaine more, light into the acquaintance of a notable crafty companion who,
finding his humour was not to learne how to fit it,
and noting his foolish kind of fleering when he
came among the feminine gender, and how farre he
would be in loue with mayd Marian upon the first
measure of a Morris daunce, came one day to him
very closely, and getting him to beare him company
alone into the fields, there very soberly, in the way
of much affection (as he seemed to make shew of),
told him, that it grieued him to see so proper a
man spend his time so, without a companion fit
for his person, meaning a wife, of which, if an
owle would not serue his turne, it had bin pity any
better creature should haue bin bestowed upon
him. Yet, forsooth, in great secret he told him,
and looked about as though somebody had heard
him, that if he would be ruled by him, he would
helpe him to such a wife as all the world should

not find a better for his purpose : for she should be fayre, and wealthy, and wise, and what more I know not ; but she should be such a one as he should haue cause to giue him thanks for. The young greene Goose, somewhat shamefast, and yet foolish enough to harken to an idle tale, answered him, that though hee was not determined to marry, yet, if he liked her, and she him, hee did not know what would come to passe ; but hee would bestow a quart of wine to haue a sight of her. Not to make a long tale of a little or nothing, without many hummes or haes, it was agreed betwixt them that a day should be set downe when the meeting should be. The place was appoynted, the parties were acquainted, the plot was layd, and the matter performed. But while the goose was gaping for one bayt, he was catcht with another. For the cunning rascall, intending to make himselfe merry with his money, told him he must be finely apparrelled, and bestow a supper or two, in shew of a franke minde ; but when he had her once, then let him do as he list. The foole, already in a net, began to tangle himselfe brauely, made himself new apparel according to the fashion, gaue money to bestow upon a supper or two, where met him a fine boy, drest woman-like, to whom he made such loue that a Dog would not abide to beare it. The counterfeit young mistris with kind words and knauish wiles, finding the length of his foot, gate many tokens of his loue, as Gloues, Skarfes, and such like, besides a Ring or two, and a bracelet; all which he did bestow so louingly, that he must needes be used like himselfe, and so he was : for nothing was refused that came so gently to passe. But after many kind meetings, in the end it was agreed betwixt them that, in a friends house of his, the matter should be made up; which, being little better then a bawdy house, it serued the turn as well as could be. There they met, and being both agreed, upon assurance of eche others loue, to bed they should go that night, and be maried shortly after. Wel, that night there lacked no good cheere, nor wine to make the heart merry; which, being taken in full cups, wrought the matter as they would haue it; for after they had well supped and sate awhile by a good fire, the good Asse fell asleepe; in which, being layd in his bed, instead of the fayre boy, they had layd a blacke Moore wench by him, with whom I know not how he handled the matter; but in the morning, seeing what a sweet bed-fellow he had gotten, suddenly starting out of the bed, [hee] ran to his clothes, and taking them in his hand, ran out into another chamber, crying that he was undone, for he had lien with the ugliest thing that euer was, and he feared it was the deuill. In which feare [he], blessing himselfe as from sprites, running out of the house, with the expence of his money, almost losse of wits, and laught at of all that knew him, like a good Woodcocke, fled away so farre, that I neuer heard more what became of him.

### Of a Doctor and his Man.

A DOCTOR that was newly commenst at Cambridge charged his seruant, that he had not to say anything but that he should aske of him. Within a while after, he inuited diuers of his friends to dinner, and sent his man to desire another Doctor to come and dine with him. The fellow went, and the Doctor told him that he could not come, for he had great busines to dispatch that day. So home he comes, and sayes nothing. When the guests were all come, they stayd from going to dinner till the other Doctor came. When they had stayd till two of the clock, he asked his man if he had bidden him come to dinner. Yes (quoth his man), that I did. And why doth he not then come ? Marry, he sayd that he had other businesse, and he could not come. Why didst thou not tell me this before ? (quoth his master.) Why, sir (quoth he), because you did not aske me.

### 𝔒𝔣 one that beleeued his wife better then others.

A MAN whose wife was no better then she should
be, nor so [well] neither, his friends counselled
him to looke better unto her. The man went home,
and sharply rebuked his wife, and told her what
his friends sayd of her. She, knowing that periury
was no worse then adultery, with weeping and
swearing denyed the same, and told her husband
that they deuised those tales in enuy, because they
saw them liue so quietly. With these words her
husband was content and well pleased. Yet another of his friends was at him agayne, and sayd,
that he did not well to let her haue her liberty so
much. To whome hee answered: I pray you, tell
mee whether knoweth my wiues faults best, she or
you? They sayd, she. And she, that I beleeue
better then you all, sayth you lye all like knaues.

### The Hartfordshire mans answere to the Abbot of London.

THE Abbot, riding in visitation, came to a place
where they had newly builded their steeple, and
put out their belles to be new cast. The abbot,
comming neere the townes end, and hearing no
belles to ring, in a chafe sayd to one of the towns-

men : haue you no belles in your steeple ?   No, my
Lord, quoth he.   Then sayd the Abbot : sell away
your steeple.   Why so, and please your Lordship ?
Quoth he : because it standeth voyd.   Marry, sayd
the man, we may well also sell away another
thing in our Church as well as that, and better
too.   What is that? (quoth the Abbot)   Mary, our
Pulpit (quoth he), for 'this seuen yeere haue we not
had a Sermon in it, nor I thinke neuer shall, but
belles I am sure we shall haue shortly.          ·

### ⨁f one that lost his purse.

A COUNTRYMAN comming up to the Tearme,
by misfortune, lost his purse; and, because the
summe was great, hé set up billes in diuers places
of London, that if any man had found such a purse,
and would restore it againe, he should haue very well
for his paynes.   A Gentleman of the Inner Temple
wrote under one of his billes that hee should come
to his chamber, and did write where.   So, when
hee came to the place, the Gentleman asked him,
first, what was in his purse ; secondly, what coun-
treyman he was ; and, thirdly, what was his name.
Sir (quoth he), twenty pound was in my purse ; I
am halfe a Welshman ; and John vp Janken is
my name.   John vp Janken (quoth the Gentle-

man), I am glad I know thy name : for, so long as
I liue, thou, nor none of thy name, shall haue my
purse to keepe. And so farewell, gentle John vp
Janken.

## Of madde conceited Bulkin.

BVLKIN, well knowne in diuers places for his
mad conceits and his couzenage, upon a time
came in to Kent, to Sittingborne, and there, in diuers
villeges thereabout, set up billes, that all sorts of
people, young and olde, that would come to Sittingborne on such a day, they should find a man there
that would giue a remedy for all diseases, and
also would tell them what would happen unto
any of them in fiue or sixe yeeres after ; and he
would desire but two pence apiece of any of them.
Whereupon people came of all sorts, and from all
places ; so that he gathered of the people that
came, to the value of twenty pounds ; and hee had
prouided a Stage, and set it up, and placed a
chayre where he would sit ; and so they, being all
come in, and euery one set in order, he comes to
the gate, and takes the money from them that
gathered it, and bids them looke that good rule be
kept, and so they did. Also, he bid them by and
by sound the drumme, and then he would begin

3.                           L

his Orations. Hee, when they were gone, with al haste gets him to the backside, and there hauing his gelding, gets upon his backe, and away towards Rochester rides he, as fast as euer he could gallop. Now they, thinking hee had beene preparing of things in a readinesse, sounded the drumme. The Audience looked still when he would come ; and staying one, two, three howres, nay more, thought sure they were couzened. Whereupon one of the company, seeing a paper in the chayre on the stage, tooke it, wherein was written :—

𝔑𝔬𝔴 𝔭𝔬𝔲 𝔥𝔞𝔲𝔢 𝔥𝔢𝔞𝔯𝔡 𝔱𝔥𝔢 𝔰𝔬𝔲𝔫𝔡 𝔬𝔣 𝔱𝔥𝔢 𝔡𝔯𝔲𝔪𝔪𝔢,
𝔜𝔬𝔲 𝔪𝔞𝔭 𝔞𝔩𝔩 𝔡𝔢𝔭𝔞𝔯𝔱 𝔩𝔦𝔨𝔢 𝔣𝔬𝔬𝔩𝔢𝔰, 𝔞𝔰 𝔭𝔬𝔲 𝔠𝔬𝔪𝔢.

Whereupon all of them, falling to cursing and swearing, were fayne to depart, like fooles indeed.

## 𝔒𝔣 𝔱𝔥𝔢 𝔯𝔦𝔠𝔥 𝔴𝔦𝔡𝔡𝔬𝔴 𝔬𝔣 𝔄𝔟𝔦𝔫𝔤𝔱𝔬𝔫.

THIS widdow desired a gossip of hers that shee would helpe her to a husband, not for any carnall desire shee had, but onely to keepe her goods, and see to her lands, which is hard (sayth she) for me to doe my selfe. The woman, for all her talke, yet knew shee spake against her mind ; and therefore, three or foure dayes after, shee came to her and sayd : Gossip, I haue found an husband for you, that is very wise and worldly giuen, but he lacks the thing you wot of, whereof I am sure you care not at all. Marry, quoth the widow, let the deuill take that husband, if he will ; for though I desire not the bodily pleasure, yet I would not haue him lack that thing which, if we should fall out, should make us friends agayne.

## ⅌f a 𝔏awper anⅾ ꜧis 𝔐an.

A WORSHIPFUL gentleman, being a Counseller, keeping a very good house, kept a Gentlemans sonne to be his Clarke, and to wayt upon his table. So one day hauing store of guests, there wanted bread on the table. Hee beckened to his man to fetch some, who, not understanding him, came to him and sayd : Sir, what would you haue? Seest not, knaue (quoth hee), there is no bread on the table? therefore fetch some. There was enough euen now (quoth his man), if they would haue let it alone, and not haue eaten it up. Another time, his guests hauing supt, and ready to depart, hee bade his man draw a cup of wine, to make them drinke before they went. The fellow comming up with the gilt cup couered, his master beckened him to take off the couer. He not understanding, sayd : Master, what would you haue? Why, knaue, take

off the couer, quoth he, off the cup. Then hold
you the candle, sayd his man ; for I cannot do two
things at once.

## 𝕳𝖔𝖜 𝖋𝖎𝖓𝖊𝖑𝖞 𝖔𝖓𝖊 𝖘𝖔𝖑𝖉 𝖙𝖜𝖔 𝖑𝖔𝖆𝖉𝖊𝖘 𝖔𝖋 𝖍𝖆𝖞.

IN London dwelt a mad conceited fellow, which
with his witte liued with Gallants, and domineerd
with good fellowes. Not long agoe, in hay haruest,
he gets a pitchforke on his necke, went forth towards Islington in the morning, and meetes with
two loads of hay comming towards the City to be
sold ; for the which he bargayned with them that
owed the same for thirty shillings. Whither shall
we bring them? quoth they. To the Swan by
Smithfield, sayd he. And so went his way and
left them, and to the Swan he went, to the goodman of the house, and asked if hee would buy two
loads of hay? Yes, quoth the In-keeper, where
bee they? Heere they come, quoth he. What
shall I pay? quoth the In-keeper. Four Nobles,
quoth makeshift. But at last they were agreede
for twenty shillings. When they were come, hee
bade them unload the hay. So while they were
unloading, he came to the Inne-holder, and sayd :
I pray you let me haue my money ; for while my
men unload, I will buy some stuffe to haue home

with mee. The Inneholder was content, and gaue him his money. And so he went his way. When the men had unloaded their hay, they came and demaunded their money. I haue payd your master, quoth the Inne-keeper. What master? quoth they. Marry, quoth he, he that bade you bring the hay hither. We know him not (quoth they). Nor I (quoth hee), but with him I bargayned, and him haue I payd; with you I medled not; and therefore goe seeke him if you will. And so the poore men were couzened of their hay.

### Of a yong Gentleman that would haue kissed a mayd with a long nose.[1]

A YOUNG Gentleman, none of the wisest, would haue kissed a fair maid that had something a long nose, who sayd: How should I kisse you? your nose is so long that our lips cannot meet. The mayd waxing angry in mind sayd: If you cannot kisse my mouth, sir, for my nose, you may kisse me there whereas I haue neuer a nose.

(1) This story is borrowed from *Mery Tales and Quicke Answers,* No. xi.

In *Love's Maistresse, or, the Queen's Masque,* by T. Heywood, 1636, act iv. sc. 2, the 1st Swain says:—

"Besides she hath a horrible long nose."

To which the Clown replies:—

"That's to defend her lips."

## ⍟f one that fell off a tree at Greenested.

THERE was a Husbandman that dwelt at Greenested that was gathering his fruit, and being hard at work, forgot his footing, and downe he comes tumbling, and with his fall brake one of his ribs. To comfort him came a merry man, his neighbour, who sayd hee would teach him such a rule, that if he would follow it, he would neuer fall off a tree agayne. Marry, sayd the hurt man, I would you had taught me that rule before I fel; neuerthelesse, because it may happen to profit me another time, let mee heare it. Then sayd the other : Take heed that you neuer goe faster downe then you go up, but descend as softly, and you shall neuer fall.

## ⍟f a scholer and a ploughman.

A CERTAYNE scholler beeing in Bedfordshire, a rude ploughswayne reprooued him for something, saying, that he could say all his prayers with a whole minde and stedfast intention, not thinking on anything else. Goe to, sayd the scholler ; say one Pater noster to the end, and thinke on no other thing, and I will giue thee my horse. That shall I doe, quoth the ploughman. And so

he began to say : Our Father which art in heauen,
till he came to Hallowed be thy name, and then
his thought mooued him to aske this question :
Yea, but shall I haue the brydle and saddle to ?
And so he lost his bargayne.

## 𝔥𝔬𝔴 𝔡𝔯𝔲𝔫𝔨𝔢𝔫 𝔐𝔲𝔩𝔩𝔦𝔫𝔰 𝔬𝔣 𝔖𝔱𝔯𝔞𝔱𝔣𝔬𝔯𝔡 𝔡𝔯𝔢𝔞𝔪𝔢𝔡 𝔥𝔢 𝔣𝔬𝔲𝔫𝔡 𝔤𝔬𝔩𝔡.

M ULLINS being drunke, and lying in his bed
dreamed that the Deuill led him into a field
to digge for Gold, and when he had found the
gold, the Deuill sayd : Thou canst not carry it away
now, but marke the place, that thou mayst fetch
it another time. What mark shal I make ? qd.
Mullins. With Pilgrime salue (quoth the Deuill),
for that shall cause euery man to shun the place,
and for thee it shall be a speciall marke. Where
he did so, and when he awaked, he perceiued he
had fouly berayed his bed. Thus betweene stinke
and dirt up he rose, and made him ready to go
forth. And last of all, he put on his hat, wherein
also the cat had **** : so for great stink hee threwe
away his hat, and was fayne to wash his head.
Thus all his golden dreame was turned to dirt.

## Of a young woman at Barnet, that sorrowed for her husbands death.

IN Barnet was a young woman that, when her
husband lay a dying, sorrowed out of all measure, for feare that shee should lose him. Her father
came to her, willing her to be contented; for he
had prouided her another husband, a far more
goodly man. But she did not onely continue in
her sorrow, but was also greatly displeased, that
her father made any motion to her of any other
husband. As soone as her other husband was
buried, and the Sermon was done, and they were
at dinner, betweene sobbing and weeping, she
rounded her father in the eare, and sayd : Father,
where is the young man that you told me should
be my husband ? Whereat her father suddenly fell
a laughing.

## A poore beggers answer to a rich Citizen.

A POORE begger, that was foule, blacke, and
lothsome to behold, came to a rich Citizen
and asked his almes. To whom the Citizen sayd : I
pray thee get thee hence from mee, for thou lookest
as though thou camest out of hell. The poore man

perceyuing hee could get nothing, answered : Forsooth, sir, you say troth, I came out of hell indeed.
Why diddest thou not tarry there still ? quoth the
Citizen. Marry, sir (quoth the begger), there is no
roome for such poore beggers as I am ; all is kept
for such Gentlemen as you are.

## The subtilty of a Lawyer repayd with the like subtilty.

THERE was an unthrift in London that had
receiued of a Marchant certayne wares which
came to fifty pounds, to pay at three moneths, but
when he had it, he consumed and spent it all ; so that
at the sixe moneths end there was not any left to
pay the Marchant : wherefore the Marchant arrested
him. When he saw there was no other remedy but
either to pay the debt or goe to prison, he sent to
a subtill Lawyer, and asked his counsell, how he
might cleare himselfe of that debt. What wilt
thou giue me (quoth he), if I doe ? Fiue markes
(quoth the other), and heere it is ; and as soone as
you haue done you shall haue it. Well, sayd the
Lawyer, but thou must be ruled by my counsell
and doe thus : When thou commest before the,
Judge, whatsoeuer he sayeth unto thee, answere
thou nothing, but cry Bea still, and let me alone

with the rest. So when he came before the Judge,
he sayd to the Debter: Doest thou owe this Marchant
so much money? Bea (quoth he). What, beast,
(quoth he) answere to that I aske thee. Bea!
(quoth hee againe.) Why, how now? quoth the
Judge, I thinke this fellow hath gotten a sheepes
tongue in his head : for he answeres in the sheepes
language. Why, sir, quoth the Lawyer, doe you
thinke this Marchant that is so wise a man would
bee so foolish as to trust this Ideot with fifty pounds'
worth of ware, that can speake neuer a word? no,
sir, I warrant you ; and so perswaded the Judge
to cast the Merchant in his owne suite. And so
the Judge departed, and the Court brake up. Then
the Lawyer came to his Clyent and asked him his
money, since his promise was performed and his
debt discharged. Bea (quoth he). Why, thou
needst not cry Bea any longer, but pay me my
money. . Bea (quoth he agayne). Why, thou wilt
not serue me so, I hope (quoth the Lawyer), now
I haue used thee so kindly. But nothing but
Bea could master Lawyer get for his paynes, and
so was fayne to depart.

# A tale of a merry Christmas Carroll, sung by women.

THERE was sometime an olde Knight, who being disposed to make himselfe merry in a Christmas time, sent for many of his Tenants and poor neighbours, with their wiues, to dinner; when hauing made meat to be set on the table, [he] would suffer no man to drinke till hee that was master ouer his wife should sing a Carroll to excuse all the company. Great nicenesse there was who should be the Musician, now the Cuckow time was so farre off.[1] Yet with much adoe, looking one upon another, after a dry hemme or two, a dreaming companion drew out as much as hee durst towards an ill-fashioned ditty. When hauing made an end, to the great comfort of the beholders, at last it came to the womens table, where likewise commaundement was giuen that there should no drinke be touched till shee that was master ouer her husband had sung a Christmas Carrol; whereupon they fell all to such a singing, that there was neuer heard such a catterwalling piece of musike. Whereat the knight laughed so hartily, that it did him halfe as much good as a corner of his Christmas pye.

(1) See *Additional Notes.*

## A jest of a felon at Oxford.

THE Assises being at Oxford, among the rest
there was a Felon that had the benefit of the
Clergy, to haue his booke;[1] but he could read neuer
a word. Which a scholer perceiuing, stood behind.
and prompt him with his uerse that he was to reade ;
and comming to the latter end, he held his thumbe
upon the booke, that the scholler could not see :
wherefore he bade him softly : take away thy
thumbe. He thinking that the same was so in the
booke, sayd aloud: Take away thy thumbe. Which
the judge perceiuing, bade take him away ; and so
he was condemned. And being upon the ladder,
ready to dye, and the rope about his necke, he
sayd : Haue at yon Dasie that growes yonder ; and
so leaped off the gallows.

## Of a Gentleman of Norfolke and his Host.

A GENTLEMAN of Norfolke as hee was riding
towards London in the winter time, and sitting
by the fireside with his Host untill supper could be
made ready, there happened a Rabbit to be at the fire
a rosting, which the gentlemā perceiued to be very
leane, as he thought. Quoth he unto his Host: We
haue Rabbits in our country, that one will drip a

---

(1) **An allusion to the** *neck-verse.*

pottle, and baste it selfe. The In-keeper wondred with himselfe, and did thinke it to be a lye, but would not say so, for maners sake, and because he was his guest; but thinking to requite him. Now truly, quoth he, it is very strãge, but I can tell you of as strange a thing as that ; which the Gentleman [was] very desirous to heare. Quoth he, I had as fine a Grayhound as any was in England ; and if I had happened to goe abroad to my grounds, the Grayhound would alway go with me. And sometime there would start out a Hare before me, which my Grayhound would quickly catch. It fortuned that my dog died, and for very loue that I bare to him, I made me a bottle of his skin to carry drinke withall. So, one time in hay harvest, my folks being making of hay in my grounds, and the weather hote, I filled my bottle with beere, to carry to them, lest they should lack drinke. And as I was going along, there start a hare out of a bush before me; and as it was my custome, I cried: Now, now, now. My bottle, leaping from my girdle, ran and catcht the Hare. What, quoth the Gentleman, methinks that should be a lie. Truly, sir, said the in-keeper, so did I thinke yours was. The Gentleman perceiuing that he was requited for his kindnesse, held himselfe contented.

## A tale of a Printer and a Gentlewoman.

AS a merry conceited Printer was going thorow
S. Martins in London, with a friend of his,
being merrily disposed : quoth hee : I will lay a quart
of wine with you, that I will goe and kisse yonder
Gentlewoman who is comming on the other side of
the way. Wilt thou ? quoth the other, and I wil
lay it with thee. The wager being layd, presently
this Printer crosses the way, and met this Gentlewoman, and with cap and bended knee salutes
her, and taking her by the hand kissed her. The
Gentlewoman [was] somewhat abashed at this
sudden salutation, and could not call to mind where
she had seene or known him. Truly, sir, sayd she
(and made a low curtsie), you must pardon me, for as
yet I do not know you. Truly, nor I you, mistris ;
but I hope there is no hurt done. So saluting
her, [he] went his way, leauing the Gentlewoman
much ashamed, and [causing] much laughing to the
beholders.

## A tale of a Gentleman and his man.

A GENTLEMAN upon a time hauing a man
that could write and read well, rebuked him
one day for idlenes, saying : If I had nothing to
doe I would, for the better comfort of my wit, set

downe all the fooles I know. The fellow, making little answere, tooke his pen and inke, and as his master had wished him, fell to setting downe a Catalogue of all the fooles that he was well acquainted with : among whom, and first of all, he set downe his master, who, reading his name, would needs know the nature of his folly. Marry (quoth he), in lending your Couzin twenty pound this other day : for I thinke he will neuer pay you. Yes, but (quoth his master), what if he do pay me? Then (quoth his man) I will put out your name, and put downe his for a foole.

## 𝕬 𝖉𝖊𝖈𝖊𝖕𝖙 𝖔𝖋 𝖙𝖍𝖊 𝖍𝖔𝖕𝖊 𝖔𝖋 𝖙𝖍𝖊 𝖈𝖔𝖚𝖊𝖙𝖔𝖚𝖘 𝖜𝖎𝖙𝖍 𝖆 𝕿𝖚𝖗𝖓𝖊𝖕.

THE King of Fraunce, Charles the fift, being presented by a poore Gardiner with a Turnep of a huge greatnesse, gaue him for his reward fiue hundred crownes, giuing him charge to lay it up and keepe it safely for him, till hee did call for it. Which bounty being noted of all his Court, and chiefly obserued by one couetous rich officer of his house, caused him, in hope of some greater recompence for a greater present, to present his Majesty with a faire and goodly horse, which the king thankfully receiuing, noting his miserable nature,

and that his gift rather did proceede from hope of
gayne then good will, called for the Turnep, wherewith he rewarded the miserable Asse ; at which he
no lesse fretted, then all that saw it hartily laughed.
And so I wish all such churles to be serued.

## A pretty tale of a Foxe and an Asse.

IN the time out of mind, when men wrote they
cared not what, I find a discourse of a Lyon
which, being King of beasts, upon some, I know
not what cause, called a Parliament, whereto a great
number of his subjects being come as neere to his
presence as they durst, hee caused a proclamation
to be pronounced to the whole assembly, that what
beast soeuer bare a horne in his head should not,
after that day, presume to set foote within that chiefe
wood of his, without his especiall license, and
whosoeuer did violate his commaund should be
held as a traytor, and suffer death without further
Judgement. It fell out within few dayes after, that
a Foxe, hauing one night met with a brood of young
Geese, besides Rabbets and Chickens, and hauing
drawne them to a bush, under which he had layd
them, farre from the high way, chaunced in the
morning to espye a poore Asse comming towards
him, to whom, after a few salutations and questions

touching his passage that way, he tolde the sum-
marie of the aforesayd proclamation ; who answered
him, that it nothing touched him, for that he had no
hornes. Oh, but (quoth the Foxe) take heede, thou
hast long eares and if the Lyon will say that they
be hornes, then they are as ill as hornes ; but if
thou wilt helpe me to carry a little poultry that I
haue taken heere for the Court, I will warrant thee
to goe and come safe. The poore Asse, whose
backe was made for the purpose to beare the Foxe's
burden, followed his counsell, and tooke up the
poultry, which the Foxe made shift to lay upon his
backe ; wherewith hee was no sooner come to the
woodside, but a Woolfe, espying of him, ran towards him, of whom not a little afrayd, he flung
downe his burden, with this out-cry : Let neuer
Asse follow a Foxe, lest he meet with a Woolfe at
his iourneyes end.

## 𝕳𝔬𝔴 𝔞 𝔴𝔬𝔪𝔞𝔫 𝔰𝔢𝔯𝔲𝔢𝔡 𝔞 𝕲𝔩𝔲𝔱𝔱𝔬𝔫, 𝔟𝔲𝔱 𝔶𝔢𝔱 𝔥𝔢 𝔴𝔞𝔰 𝔱𝔬𝔬 𝔤𝔬𝔬𝔡 𝔣𝔬𝔯 𝔥𝔢𝔯.

NOT unlike to Mother Bunch our Hostesse, an
olde woman in Sussex, that brewed good Ale,
there dwelt, that had euery weeke a lusty eater, and
as tall a drinker, [who] used to her house ; but when
he had serued himselfe, he would not pay any thing

at all. The Woman, grieuing to be thus used still, knew not what remedy to haue, for with his swaggering hee domineerd, because hee had bene a souldier. One Tuesday morning he comes thither, saying: Hostesse, what shall we haue to breakefast? I haue nothing of your price (quoth she) at this time. Whereupon he began to sweare so pityfully, that he so feared the woman that she set a dish of sweet butter before him, that shee had kept for others that were to come thither, whereof he began to eate so greedily, that she feared he would eate up all. And thereupon she stept to the dore, as though one had knockt, and came in agayne, and sayd to him: Sir, there is one at the dore would speake with you. Whereupon hee went to the doore. In the meane space she thrust his knife in the fire, and heat it almost red hote. In comes hee againe, saying, there was nobody there. Then belike he is gone, quoth she. Hee, taking his knife againe, would haue cut the butter, but it fell still from the knife; whereat he wondring sayd: Hostesse, I maruaile what ailes my knife? Truely, sir, your knife blushes to see his master so unreasonable. In faith, sayd he, if this knife blush, his fellow here yet looketh pale; and so drawes out his other knife, and eates up the rest of the butter cleane.

## 𝕿𝖍𝖊 𝖆𝖓𝖘𝖜𝖊𝖗𝖊 𝖔𝖋 𝖆 𝕲𝖊𝖓𝖙𝖑𝖊𝖒𝖆𝖓𝖘 𝖒𝖆𝖓 𝖙𝖔 𝖍𝖎𝖘 𝕸𝖆𝖘𝖙𝖊𝖗.

A WORSHIPFULL Gentleman in London, hauing on a time inuited diuers of his friends to supper to his house, and being at supper, the second course comming in, the first was one of the Gentlemans owne men, bringing a Capon, and, by chance, stumbling at the portall doore, the Capon flew out of the platter, and ran along the boords to the upper end of the table, where the Master of the house sate, who, making a iest of it, sayd : By my faith, it is well ; the Capon is come first, my man will come anon too, I hope. By and by, came his man, and takes up the Capon, and layes it in the platter, and sets it on the boord. I thanke you, sir, quoth his Master, I could have done so my selfe. I, quoth his man, tis a small matter, sir, for one to doe a thing, when he sees it done before his face.

## 𝕮𝖊𝖗𝖙𝖆𝖎𝖓𝖊 𝖘𝖚𝖑𝖑𝖊𝖓 𝖘𝖕𝖊𝖊𝖈𝖍𝖊𝖘 𝖔𝖋 𝕯𝖎𝖔𝖌𝖊𝖓𝖊𝖘 𝖙𝖔 𝕬𝖑𝖊𝖝𝖆𝖓𝖉𝖊𝖗.

D IOGENES walking on a time in a Churchyard neere unto a high way that lay in a valley, espied Alexander with a great traine a farre off upon a hille comming downe towards that towne, where

M 2

the Church stoode. Whereupon, minding to put
Alexander out of such proud humours, as he doubted
of him at that time to be possessed with, ran in
all haste unto the Sexten of the Church, for the key
of the doore within which lay the dead mens
skulles and bones which had beene digged up;
where, taking out as many as he could well carrie
in his armes, hee laid them one by one in the way
where Alexander was to passe; who, being come
some what neere unto him, and seeing his paines in
laying of the bones, asked what he meant by it.
Why (quoth Diogenes), I have heard that here
have beene as well the bones of Princes, as poore
people, buried here in this Churchyard, and now I
have beene laying them together, to see if I could
finde any difference whereby I might finde which
were the Princes and which the beggers; but,
truely, they are so like one an other, that I find no
difference at all. Well (quoth Alexander), this is
one of thy dogged humors; but how darest thou
thus trouble me in my time of pleasure, knowing
that I can take thy life from thee, if I list? Why
(quoth Diogenes), doe thou know, that I will die in
spight of thy teeth, and, therefore, care not for thy
threats, knowing death to bee the worst that can
come of them, and my offence no greater then this
in deseruing of them. Which answere Alexander

well noting, knowing his nature, left him to his sullen humors.

## ®f a ðrunken fellow that fell in the fire.

THERE was a notable drunkard of Rochester, whom his wife perswaded, as much as in her lay, to leaue that sinne ; but the more shee spake the worse hee was ; and, because she controuled him, he would al to beat her.  So she let him alone ; and, because his use was still to stay out till almost midnight, she would goe to bed, and bid her maid tarry up for him, and make a good fire ; and so shee did.  One night, when he came home, the maide let him in, and he stoode by the fire, and warmed himselfe ; but his head beeing too heauie for his bodie, downe he fell in the fire all along. The maid ran, crying, Oh, mistresse, mistresse, my Master is fallen into the fire.  No force, mayd (quoth she), let him take his pleasure in his owne house a Gods name, where he will himselfe.

## A pretty tale of a ƒoxe anð a Goose.

IN the time when birds and beastes could speake, and the windes would carry many tales thorow the wood, as it is written by some idle head, there came a Foxe out of a wood, unto a countrey house,

there neere to adioyning, where, finding a broode
Goose, within a kind of open penne, saluted her
in this maner : How doe you, sister? I heard
you were not well of late, which made me come
to visit you, as one who would be glad to doe you
any good that laye in his poore power. The Goose,
sitting ouer her young brood crowding, made him
this answere : Truly, I am not wel; yet I thinke I
and mine should doe much better, if you would
not so often come to visite us; yet for that I
have a payne in my backe, I pray you come in
and feele how it is swelled, that you may the
better teach me what to apply unto it. The Foxe,
very glad of this unlooked for kindnesse, hoping
to haue that he came for, put his head no sooner
within the dore, but a dog, lying closly hidden,
caught him by the nose, and, biting off a piece of
his chappe, with a sudden snatch let him go.
The poore Foxe, making no little haste home to his
borough, no sooner came among his fellow Foxes,
but with great sighes told them, that he was bitten
with a Goose ; which the bitch-foxe hearing, with
an open mouth ran at him, and beat him out of
the hold, with this shamefull reproche : Go, coward,
bite her agayne ; thou shalt neuer come within my
borough ; to be bitten of a Goose, and bring a way
neuer a feather.

## 𝕬 𝖜𝖎𝖙𝖙𝖞 𝖆𝖓𝖘𝖜𝖊𝖗𝖊 𝖔𝖋 𝖆 𝕸𝖆𝖌𝖎𝖘𝖙𝖗𝖆𝖙𝖊 𝖙𝖔 𝖆 𝖒𝖆𝖑𝖎𝖈𝖎𝖔𝖚𝖘 𝖆𝖈𝖈𝖚𝖘𝖊𝖗 𝖔𝖋 𝖆𝖓 𝖔𝖋𝖋𝖊𝖓𝖉𝖊𝖗.

A MALICIOUS fellow, willing to bring a neighbour of his unto all the disgrace he could deuise, and shrewdly suspecting him to haue more then a moneths mind to a fine mistres neere unto him, oftentimes watching his going in and comming out of her house : one day, among other, in the euening, noting his long stay, suspected that there was somewhat to doe more then all the Parish was acquainted with, and therefore seeing the maide gone foorth upon some errand, beeing very earely in the morning, suddenly stept in with a companion of his, and tooke them together at their exercise ; which, being glad of, and that he had witnesse to make his matter good, runnes to the Magistrate of the Citie, who had to deale with such persons and such cases, and told him as much as he had seene, with : oh, Sir, I assure you he is a perillous man for a woman ; and, to tell you the troth, we tooke him in bed with her : what say you to such a fellow ? The Magistrate, some what allyed unto the young man, and wishing rather a secret amendment then an open reprehension, gaue him this answere : Truely, for the matter, it is not well ; but for being taken in bed with her, in truth I can thinke no otherwise, but hee was a sluggard : I know not what to say to him. The accuser, seeing the people smile, and himselfe mocked with this speech, did no further aggrauate the matter, but, with a flea in his eare, went away with his malicious humor.

## Of King Henrie and the Countrey-man.

KING HENRY, ryding a hunting, in the countie of Kent, he came by chance to a great gate, that he must needs passe through, and in the way there stoode a Ploughman, to whom the King sayd, I prethee, good fellow, open the gate. The fellow, perceiuing it was the king, stoode like an Image, and said : No, and it shall please your Grace (quoth hee), I am not worthy to bee in that office ; but I will fetch Master Cooper, that dwelleth but two miles hence, and he shall open you the gate. And so ran away, as fast as euer he could.

## Of the olde man of Monmouth, that gaue his sonne all his goods in his life time.

IN Monmouth dwelt an ancient man, of fayre possessions and great lands, hauing but one sonne to enioy all his substance. His sonne being married, he gaue him all that he had, and so would liue free from all worldly matters, in his olde age, with his sonne in his owne house. After the deed of gift was made, awhile the olde man sate at the upper end of the table; afterwards, they set him lower, about the middle of the table ; next, at the tables end ; and then, among the seruants ; and, last of all, they made him a couch behind the doore and couered him with olde sack-cloth, where, with grief and sorrow, the olde man dyed. When the olde man was buried, the young mans eldest childe sayd unto him : I pray you, father, giue me this olde sackcloth. What wouldst thou doe with it? sayd his father. Forsooth, sayd the boy, it shall serue to couer you, as it did my olde graundfather.

## 𝕳𝖔𝖜 a woman to hide a small fault shewed a greater.

A WOMAN at Romford had for some cause shauen her head, and newly as shee had put off her kercheife off her head, one of her neighbours called for her hastily into the streete. When her neighbour saw her so, she blamed her for comming abroad bare-headed. Shee, remembring her selfe,

whipt up her clothes from behinde her, ouer her
head. And so, to hyde her head, shee showed her
bare tayle.

## How a madde man in Glocestershire answered a Gentleman.

IN Glocestershire dwelt one that cured frantike
mē in this maner : when their fit was on them,
he would put them in a gutter of water, some to
the knees, some to the middle, and some to the
necke, as the disease was on them. So one that
was well amended, standing at the gate by chaunce,
a Gentleman came riding by, with his Haukes and
his Hounds. The fellow called him to him, and
sayd : Gentleman, whither goe you? On hunting,
quoth the Gentleman. What doe you with all those
Kytes and Dogges? They be Haukes and Houndes,
quoth the Gentleman. Wherefore keepe you them?
quoth the other. Why, quoth hee, for my pleasure,
What doe they cost you a yeere to keepe them?
Fourty pounds, quoth the Gentleman. And what
doe they profit you? quoth hee. Some ten pounds
(quoth the Gentleman). Get thee quickly hence,
quoth the fellow ; for if my master finde thee heere
he will put thee in to the gutter up to the throat.

# Of an Hermet by Paris, that lay with all the chiefest Gentlewomen in the Countrey.[1]

THIS notable knaue, that, under colour of holy-nesse, enticed all the chiefest Matrones of the Countrey to folly, at last, his doings were detected and knowne, and he was brought before the Duke of Anioy, which, to heare the number of them for his disport, called his Secretary to write them downe. The Secretary bade him recount them. The Hermet named to him the number of xxvii of the Dukes seruants wiues, and others, and then stoode still and sayd nothing. Is there no more? quoth the Duke. No, and it shall like your Grace, quoth the Hermet. Tell troth, quoth the Secretarie, for if thou doest not, thou shalt be sharply punished. Then sayd the Hermet, sighing: To make up the xxviii, write thine owne wife in the number. Whereupon the Secretarie, for uery griefe, let fall his pen. And the Duke, laughing heartily, sayd : I am glad that he that with so great pleasure hath heard the faultes of other mens wiues, should now come into the same number himselfe.

(1) This tale is found in the *Heptameron* of the Queen of Navarre, first printed in 1549, but the Author or Editor of *Pasquils Jests* probably took it from *Mery Tales and Quicke Answeres*, where it is No. 40, and is entitled : "Of the hermite of *Padowe*."

## Ƭꜧe miserable niggardize of a Justice.

TO conclude with this miserable Justice, who
came to London, to the Terme ; and, lying in
Fleet-street, a companie of excellent Musicians, in
a morning, played very earely at his chamber. But
he, being loth to bestow his money so uainely,
bade his man tell them, hee could not as then
heare their Musike, for he lamented for the death
of his mother. Wherefore, they went their way,
for their hope was deceiued. A Gentleman, a
friend of his, in London, hearing the same, came
to comfort him, and asked him when his mother
dyed. Fayth (quoth hee) some xvi yeeres agoe.
When his friend understood his deceit, he laughed
heartily.

## Ƭꜧe end of tꜧe Ƭales.

## 𝔥ere beginne the 𝔊ulles.[1]

———❦———

## ℭhe first 𝔊ull, upon the wager of the 𝔥orse and the ℭowe for good trauell.

THERE was sometime, not many yeeres since, a merry conceited man, of what profession I doe not well remember, who, hauing occasion to take poste from some hauen towne neere the Sea, came to the Maior of the Towne to complaine of the Constable of the Towne, for his little honestie in prouiding him such ill horses, knowing the nature of his busines, and the haste it required. The Maior, looking upon them as one that had not often made any posting iourneyes, tolde him, that though they were not so good as he had seene, yet they would serue the turne well ynough, and that as then he thought the Towne would yeelde him no better. Whereupon the poster told him, that if hee were no better furnished, that in his

(1) A *Gull* signifies here apparently a person who is soft and easily deceived; but at the time when *Pasquils Jests* made their appearance, the word certainly had a more extended meaning. See *Epigrams*, by [Sir] J[ohn] D[avies], circa 1596, in Marlowe's Works, ed. Dyce, iii. 226. Epigram ii. is *On a Gull*, and professes to be an accurate definition of what that term imported.

Countrey, a man would teache a young Cowe, to
carry him further in a day then the best horse in
that Towne ; and, for a neede, hee coulde doe as
much there, and thereupon hee would lay twenty
poundes. The Maior, discontented with his speech,
tolde him he would lay the wager, tooke money in
earnest, the wordes were set down, witnes set to
their hands, that, in xxiiij houres, he would so dyet
a young Cow, y$^t$ she should carry him further in a
day then the best horse in the Shire. The Cow
was brought into a stable, hey and water set to
her, and in the morning, when he should ride, a
horse brought thither to the place, which, presently, he would haue bound to the Cowe ; which,
being too heauie for the cowe to carry, they all
found the deceite, and the poore Maior beeing
made a good Gull, was forced to confesse his folly,
and to giue the Poster a good piece of money to
be rid of his wager.

### The second Gull, upon the wager of leaping.

A CERTAINE yong, well limmed, broad shoul-
dred and milposte-legged yong man, who (it
should seeme) with following of hounds, was used
to leaping of ditches ; and so, with use, grew to be

held the captaine leaper of that side of the Countrey. One day, among other, wherein games came
about the Countrey, best, second, and third, a great
assembly of the youth of diuers Parishes, striuing
before their best beloues, who had the lightest
paire of heeles, put in their peeces of money, each
one for the best, or the rest, as it fell out. This
gallant yonker, aduancing himselfe, beeing untrust
for the purpose, offers any man a foote before him,
for the price of a quarter of the best malt in the
countrey. But while no man would meddle with
him, one mad-headed fellow standing by him,
suddenly stept to him, and told him that, if
hee might chuse his ground upon the ground
before him, that he would aduenture upon the
aduantage of a foote before him, at the uprising
or standing; he would leape with him for fortie
shillings. The wager was layd, the money put
into a boxe, and the witnesses came to see the
leaping; when he that took the foote before him,
tooke his ground just before a great Elme tree
that grew on the greene hard by; where, beeing
able to leape no further then the tree, the other,
finding himselfe deceiued, was contented to lose
part of his money, to learne him better wit; and
so, like a good Gull, went his way.

## 𝕿𝖍𝖊 𝖙𝖍𝖎𝖗𝖉 𝕲ull, upon a 𝖜ager of going as fast as a horse, and go all one 𝖜ap.

A DAPPER yong fellow, upon a time, having bought him a pretty ambling gelding, was for certaine daies almost neuer off from his backe ; and riding him no long iourney, but, as it were, betwixt London and Mile-end, in the view of many people, willing to make shewe of his horse or horseman-ship, sitting as upright as a picture of Rye dowe : a subtill companion of his acquaintance, meaning to make a Gull of his mastership, told him it was a pretty Nagge, but hee was but slow pased, and that hee would lay fiue pounds that he would go as farre in a daye on foote, as hee should ryde his horse, and goe both one way. The fine and all so fine, beeing much moued to heare his horse so disgraced, accepted his offer, layd the wager, and they put the money into a mans hands of good worth, that stoode by. Which done, the merry fellow, standing in the high way, went backwards. Which the horseman assaying to do, not used to those kind of tricks, his horse, rising aloft, fell backwards with him, with danger of his life; when, rising up, and seeing the other still going backe-wards, called to him, and, with confession of losse, taking backe what hee would giue him, remayned a good Gull for his labour.

## 𝕿𝖍𝖊 𝖋𝖔𝖚𝖗𝖙𝖍 𝕲𝖚𝖑𝖑, 𝖚𝖕𝖔𝖓 𝖆 𝖜𝖆𝖌𝖊𝖗 𝖙𝖔 𝖍𝖆𝖓𝖌 𝖍𝖎𝖒𝖘𝖊𝖑𝖋𝖊.

VPON a time, I haue forgotten when, in a place out of minde, met a company of good fellowes, which, beeing likely to bee some Inne, while the people were all set at dinner, came in an old rich Farmer of the Country, who, beeing well lyned in his purse, and therefore might haue the merrier heart, was so full of talke at dinner, that scarce any men else was heard at the table. Which a Scholler sitting among them wel obseruing, and withall seeing him wel tickled in the head with the good drinke, upon the sudden fell into this speech with him. Honest man, I pray you pardon me, if I say anything that may offend you; I am sory to see the euill that is towards you: you haue bene uery merry, but I feare you will neuer be so againe in this company; for I see in your eyes a spirit of madnesse, which will very speedily bring you to your unhappy ende. For, indeede, within this houre you will hang your selfe in the stable, upon one of the great beames; and that I will lay

3.  ·  N

a good wager, either with you, or anie of this companie. The olde man, much moued at this speech, and yet noting his grauitie, tolde him, that he was sory to see a Scholler haue so much learning and so little wit; but, my friend (qd. hee), if you haue any money in your purse, you shall be rid of it, when you will, upon that wager. Wherupon the Scholler gaue him ten shillings, and told him, that if he did not hang himselfe within an houre after, and first come into the house, and aske forgiuenesse of all the house, hee should giue him but ten pound for it. The Farmer tooke the money, called in for wine and sugar, and made merry withal. At the houres ende, he came to take his leaue of the Scholler and his company, who told him that he must pay ten pounds, for that he had not hanged himselfe. At which words he, finding the deceite, confessed his ignorance, payed for the good cheere, and, trebling the Schollers money, like a true Gull got him home againe.

## The fift Gull, that lost the wager upon the great Hogge.

IN the midst of the Terme, at a certain Alehouse or Inne, where couetous wretches set their half-

starued horses and themselues feede upon browne
bread and redde herrings, using after supper to sit
sixteene at a faggot and a pot of beere, and inquiring of mine host, What newes in the Town?
A cunning companion, that could feede upon the
braines of a Conney, gat him a lodging in the house;
and, getting a company of olde written papers bound
up in skrowles, like lawe cases, would play the
penny-father among them, till he had made his
market with some of them; so, holding an euen hand
among them, talking of many idle things, at last brake
out into a great admiration of the strange wonders
of the world, and of all not the least, of a huge
great Hogge that hee had seene in the Countie of
Lincolne, neere unto the Fennes, where were three
Sowes that were so high, that the tallest man in the
company standing upright, let him reach as high
as he could, he should not touch the backe of it,
and these three Sowes with their pigs were a pore
mans, that would sell them for xii pounds, and if
he had had money, hee would haue bought them,
and haue gotten a hundred pounds by the bargaine. Foure or fiue of those greedy Asses, giuing
no little eare to his talke, entreated him that hee
would bring them thither, and they would beare
his charges. But he, onely leaning to one of them,
whose purse he knew to be full of mony, secretly

in a morning stole away with him, and rode
downe with him into the Countrey; where keeping
of a certaine blinde house of lodging, kept the
poore man at his house fiue or sixe dayes, to see
these great Sowes, and in the end brought him
unto a pretty Sowe, by whom he caused him to
stand upright and reach up his hand as high as he
could, when he asked him if he did now touch her
backe. Who answered, No; for hee was too high
aboue it. Well (quoth he), this is the Sowe that
you shall haue for foure poundes of your money,
that I haue receiued of you; which he had deliuered him the night before. The poore man,
finding his greediness kindely met withall, and that
he must take the Sowe, or lose al, was content
with losse of halfe his money, to returne againe,
as good a Gull as he went out.

## The sixt Gull, upon a lifting Dogge.

AN idle-headed fellow, new come out of the
Countrey, and determining, after a little money-
spending, to returne home with a budget full of
newes, met by chance with an odde wagge, cousin
Germaine to a Page; who, finding his humor, and
meaning to fit him in his kinde, fell into this honest
kinde of parlee with him: Oh, old huddle and twang,

what newes in the Countrey, that you are come to
towne? hast thou beene at a play yet? Yea (quoth
the good clowne), that I haue, two or three. But,
Sirra, what newes where you keepe? I am sure
you heare all the world. No great newes (quoth
the wag), but onely of the huge great lifting Dogge,
that came lately out of Barbary, they take but
two-pence a peece of euery one that seeth him :
he is at the signe of the Carnation Hedgehog, in
Westminster, neere to y^e Gatehouse ; go thither
when thou wilt in my name, and thou shalt see
him for a penny. The poore Asse, little mis-
trusting the boyes waggery, went in all haste,
seeking for such a signe as was not to be found.
But, being demaunded wherefore he sought, one of
the Pages, coparteners in his tricks, told him, if he
would giue him but a quart of wine, he would
bring him to the Dog. The fellow, weary with
seeking for the Carnation Hedgehogge, was contented, for the abridging of his further travaile, to
giue him both wine and sugar, with such appurte-
nances as cost his purse aboue an ordinary. Which
done, and the shot payed, out this youngster leads
this little wit, from one lane to another, till, hauing
traced most streets to be thought upon, at last he
brought him out at the townes end, to a poore womās
house, that kept a little Iseland curre, whom,

shewing unto this good Goose : Looke you (quoth
he), he lifts up his tayle so high, that you may
kisse his **** if you list.   And with those words,
laughing, ran a way, crying, Oh Gull, Gull, get thee
home into the countrey, and carry newes of the
lifting Dogge.


## 𝕿𝖍𝖊 𝖘𝖊𝖚𝖊𝖓𝖙𝖍 𝕲𝖚𝖑𝖑, 𝖋𝖔𝖗 𝖙𝖍𝖊 𝕻𝖎𝖌𝖌𝖊𝖘 𝖙𝖍𝖆𝖙 𝖜𝖊𝖗𝖊 𝕳𝖊𝖓𝖓𝖊𝖘.

TRAUAILING upon the way to London, out of
what country I know not, a certayne pretty
quick-witted fellow ouertooke a company of horse-
men, who to passe away $y^e$ time, fell to talke of
such things as came in their heads : some of Horses,
some Hawkes, some Hounds, some Hares, and some
Connies ; but towardes their iourneyes end, they
fell to talking of wonders, each one recounting
what he had seene : some the long ditch at
New-market, other the stones by Salisbury, and
some the top of Powles, and other of the Lyons
in the tower; but, among all this, the youth in
a basket that ouertooke the company, began to
tell of a most miraculous thing that he had seene,
and that but two nights before : that, in a towne
some fourty myles behinde him, at the signe of the
Whip and the Egge shell, he did see twelue pigges

in a yard, going by two Sowes, and in the morning
they were all Hennes. Many seemed to wonder
at it, and the more at his sober protesting of his
truth in his tale. Whereupon, one simple man of
the company, desirous to carry newes home of
such things as he had seene abroad, desired this
fellow, at his comming backe againe, to beare him
company to that Towne, and into his way back
againe, and he would beare part of his charges
for his kindnes. This being betwixt themselues
agreed upon, their businesse being dispatched
together, they rid home together, where, being
well dried after a wet iourney, going to supper,
they had one of the Pigges well rosted in his
house, whose name was Henne: and in the
morning, asking for these Henne Pigges, he shewed
him all the rest. Wherewith, finding himselfe
sweetly deseyued, ashamed to tell the world how
he was abused, like a good poore Gull, gat him
out of the Countrey.

### The eyght Gull, upon the Gardens.

I T fell upon a time, much about Sturbridge faire,
that many mad people, minding to throwe away
a little money, for lacke of company in the City,
would needs go make merry in the Country ; among

whom was one iolly lusty wench, that had made
her selfe fatte with good ale and laughing. This
piece of houshold stuffe, being hostesse of I know
not what Inne, say her husband what he list,
would make one among her friends; and being
some three or fourescore miles out of London,
in a Countrey market Towne, where were some
such girles as thought their pennies good silver,
and their ware worth money: after they had
beene merry some few dayes, and almost emptied
a poore Tauerne of al his runlets, inquiring, as
the fashiō is, after newes, this good mistris, falling
to her turne to talke of wonders, told them that
one of the greatest wonders that euer shee saw,
or heard of, was of late in the Citie, done by a
stranger, touching gardens and the preseruation of
flowers, for she had seene it with her eies : that he
had taught diuers how to take in their gardens
euery night at their windowes, and let them out
againe euery morning. Which thing the neighbours that came with her seemed to soothe up,
that they had heard of the like, but they had
neuer seene it. But she with solemne othes still
affirmed that she had seene it, and could bring
them to it. While they all gaue eare unto it, one
chiefe woman of the company, who had her purse
well lyned, and cared not for to spend a little

money for the satisfying of her humor, upon a
beliefe of her solemne protestations, told her that
if she might be assured to come to the sight of
that she spake of, shee would take some of her
neighbours with her, and shee would beare her
companie back to London. To be short, the
matter was agreed upon, the wonder was beleeued,
the day appointed for their iourney, and together
they came to London, where they lay all at her
house, had good cheere, and payed well for it.
But after they had gone abroad with the Hostesse
to see sightes, Cheapeside, the Exchange, Westminster, and London bridge, had beene upon the
toppe of Powles, beene at the Beare-garden, seene
a play, and had made a Tauerne banquet, looking
into their purses for to discharge their expences,
were willing to see this strange sight of these
gardens, which shee had dayly promised to bring
them to, but stil making excuse, that they were
in the Countrey, and not yet come to London
againe, that had such gardens to be seene ; in the
ende, [she] brought them to a little lane, whereout at
a garret window, shee shewed them a poore widdow
setting out certaine boords, and upon them certaine
earthen pottes, in which were diuers kindes of
flowers and herbes, as Gilly-flowers, Carnations,
and such like. The woman, seeing her selfe with

her company mocked with this iest, made little
shew of anger, but seemed to laugh it out, and
with this tricke of mistris Hostesse to gather some
mony with her wit, tooke a Gull with her into
the Countrey, to feede a foole when she found
him.

## The ninth Gull, that wisht for the Wood.

AMONG madde Countrey wenches, that, when
they sit a milking, will be talking of their
sweete hearts, it was my happe, not long since, lying
close under a bush, to heare a merry tale of a bird
little wiser then a Woodcocke. There was a yong
fellow that was well furnished for implements of
houshold, mary his wealth was not great, and his
wit but little, and his spirit of a weake constitution.
For as it fell out, a rich widdowe, that was past a
girle, and therefore knew what to do with a good
thing when she had it, hearing diuers reports of
such persons as she was wished to make much
of, among al she heard of one yong man, a neighbours sonne of hers, to bee a sufficient man to
doe her much good seruice, either within the
house or without, either for plowing, or threshing,
or sowing, or such countrie worke as best fitted

her occupation. This yong man she sent for, and as farre as modesty might, shee made shew of her affection, which the Goose not perceiuing, she caried him . . . .[1] into her chamber, where she told him she must haue his helpe to remoue a chest. The fellow understanding nothing more then was tolde him, went up with the widdow, and all alone from one chamber to another, the doores shutting after them, where shee, often smiling at his either shamefastnes or foolishnesse, in the ende carryed him to a chamber where stoode a chest that hee could not remoue ; when, saying he would fetch companie to helpe him, she answered, No, now she was otherwise minded. And so leading downe againe the good Asse, she neuer sent more for him. A friend of his, meeting of him comming forth, hoping of his good hap, knowing his beeing aboue with her alone, asked him how he had sped. Whose answere was, Oh, I wisht I had had her in the wood, and then I would haue tolde her my minde. Now what a notable Gull was this, I leaue to all good humord wenches to consider.

---

(1) Two or three words, not material to the sense, are illegible here from the copy of the old ed. I have used having been clumsily repaired at this passage.

## The tenth Gull, that shooke his gloues.

THIS tale was no sooner ended, but another
wench began to quite her in this sort : Nay,
then, I will tell thee of as good an Asse as that
was for his life. In our Towne, not long ago, one
of the chief of our Parish, who was twise Church-
warden, and in election to be Bailife, a good fat gross
Churle, hauing a good house of his owne, and well
to take to, married a widow that dwelled three miles
off, who, hauing good cattell and corne, and some
household of her owne, by the motion of good
friends, made a match together. But this Churle,
being trouble with some sixteene diseases, lay
himselfe in one bed, and his wife in an other by
him, who, hauing a kinde of more then good liking
to a yong man in the house, some kinsman of his,
with sheepes-eyes, and smiles, and such odde kind
of wicked kindnes, she made him understand her
minde ; and beeing agreed one night to come into
her chamber when hee was asleepe, shee told him,
for feare of the worst, that he should take a paire
of her gloues, and flappe them to and fro in his
hand, which would make a noyse like unto a great
Spaniell that used often to shake his eares ; which
lesson he forgot not. Night was come, the candles

out, they in bedde, and he came creeping like a dogge. But the doore creaking, the old man halfe awake, or not fast asleepe, asked who was there ; when the fellow shaking of his gloues together, made him thinke it was the dogge, when saying, Oh, Troll, he lay still as though he slept. But the fellow missing his way in the darke, running his head against his masters bedpost, upon a sudden the old man start up his head with, How now, who is there ? The poore man amazed, forgetting to flappe his gloue, answered, Forsooth, it is the dog. Whereat his mistris laughing, bad hang him up. Whereat the fellow, as it were, following in, and seeking to driue him foorth, cryed out, Come out. But in the morning, as I heard, the Gull was put in a coope, where I heard no more of him.

### The eleuenth Gull, upon the Cole-wort.

IT is a tricke among many Travailers, if they light into companie that they thinke haue not passed the Seas, to tel wonders that wise men ought not to beleeve upon the first hearing. Among which kind of people, it fell out one day at an Ordinarie, that a certaine idle cōpanion, that loued to heare himself speake, and would talke more then either

he understood or euer heard of, hearing diuers at
the table talking of the diuersitie of soyles, and
the natures of fruits, began himselfe with a fine
and all so fine kinde of lisping utterance, to tell
that he had seene many countries, and noted the
diuersities of their natures ; but of all, one especially hee noted for the fertilities of the soyle,
where, among many kindes of rootes, Gowrdes,
Melons, and such other kind of fruits, there grewe
in one waste peece of ground, neere unto a garden,
a Colewort of that hugenesse for height and bredth,
that foure score Tinkers upon a sunny day sate at
worke together under the shadow of it.  Nowe while
euery body wondered at his tale, and some, that
he was not ashamed to lye so broad that no body
could lie by him, one well conceited spirit of the
company, upon the sudden, thinking to quite him
in his kind, brake out into this speech : Why it
is not so strange as that which I heard was in
the same place, that all those tinkers did worke
together upon one kettle.  For what use? (quoth
the Travailer).  Mary, Sir (quoth the other), to
seethe your Colewort in.  At which speech finding
his lye hit him, with as much speede as he could,
like a lying Gull, gat him away from the company.

## 𝕿𝖍𝖊 𝖙𝖜𝖊𝖑𝖋𝖙𝖍 𝕲𝖚𝖑𝖑, 𝖚𝖕𝖔𝖓 𝖙𝖍𝖊 𝖈𝖗𝖞 𝖔𝖋 𝕳𝖔𝖚𝖓𝖉𝖘.

I READ among the discourses of country actions, that a Gentleman of the Countrie, that loued home-sportes, as Hawking, Hunting, Ducking, Fowling, and Fishing, and such like, but of all, especially a good cry of Hounds, of which he kept the best in al the Country, upon a morning riding forth, neere a wood side, start a hare, who led the Hounds a chase thorow the wood, where the winding of the hornes, the hollowing of the hunts-men, and the mouthes of the dogs made such a countrey pleasant sweet noyse, that the Master of the sport, sitting still upon his horse, as one half ravisht with his pleasure, esteeming no musicke comparable to such a cry, sodainely brake out into this speech among them that were neere him : Oh what a heauenly noise is this ! List, list, for Gods sake ; is not this a heauenly noyse ? Whereat one Gull of the company, who, as it should seeme, neuer heard any dog but a Mastiffe, holding up his eare as it were towardes the Skie, to heare some noyse from the heauens, brake out into these words : Oh Lord, where is this heauenly noyse ? Why, harke (quoth the Gen-tleman), list awhile, dost thou not heare ? No

(quoth the Gull); the curres keepe such a bawling, I can heare nothing for them.　Whereat
the Gentleman laughing, and yet inwardly chafing
at the fooles wit, rode away from him, and left him
to learne more understanding.

#### ffinis.

# THE
# CONCEITS OF OLD HOBSON.

3.                                    B

*The Pleasant Conceites of Old Hobson the Merry Lon-
doner. Full of Humourous Discourses and Witty
Merriments. Whereat the Quickest Wittes may
laugh, the wiser sort take pleasure. Printed at
London for John Wright, and are to be sold at
his Shoppe neere Christ-Church gate.* 1607. 4°.

THE tract is in this edition dedicated to Sir W. Stone,
in the following terms :—

TO THE RIGHT WORSHIPPFULL,

## SIR WILLIAM STONE, KNIGHT,

MERCER TO THE QUEENES MOST
EXCELLENT MAIESTY.

YOUR friendly disposition (Right worshippfull), giving
grace to well meaning minds, hath imboldned me
amoungst others to testifie that good will in outward
shew, which my heart of long time hath secretly
bore to your worship, and now taking oportunity, I
present to your favorable censure this small booke,
contayning many quick flashes of the witty iests of old
Hobson the merry Londoner, lately a cittyzen of good
estimation, and I thinke not alltogether forgotten of
your worship. Receave this little treatise (I beseeche
you) with favour answerable to my good will ; and, as
your leasure shall serve, bestow now and then a little
reading therefore which, if it please you to doe, I doubt

not but you will like well of the labour, and besides
the honest recreation which it affordeth, apply what
your worship maketh choyce of unto your private
pleasure ; and thus wishing your prosperity, acceptance
of this my guift, and a good opinion of the giver, I
conclude, hoping that my honest wish

shall not be voyd of a

happy successe.

Your Worships most humble to command.

RICHARD IOHNSON.

*Pleasant Conceits of Old Hobson, the Merry Londoner,
full of Humorous Discourses and witty merryments,
whereat the quickest wits may laugh, and the wiser
sort take pleasure. London. Printed by W. Gilbertson,* 1640, 12*mo.*

Of this edition, which I have unfortunately not been able to examine,
only one copy is known, and that wants the last leaf. From a notice
attached to the copy in question in the catalogue of a collection of Shakespearian literature, sold in 1857, it appears that the ed. of 1640 presents
considerable variations, and has additional matter, probably pilfered, like
the contents of ed. 1607, from some other book of the same kind, and
transplanted by the compiler of the later impression to his own pages
without the slightest ceremony or judgment, as is the case with the
tract, as edited by Johnson himself.

The curious little tract here reprinted professes to
narrate pleasant episodes in the life of William Hobson,
who followed the business of a haberdasher of small
wares in the Poultry during the reigns of Edward VI,
Mary, and Elizabeth, and who, in later life, acquired some

wealth, and occupied a distinguished position in the City. Hobson, who seems to have been a bluff and plain-spoken, but charitable and generous,[1] man, and to have enjoyed besides a certain reputation as a humourist, was born quite at the beginning of the reign of Henry VIII ; he died at an advanced age in 1581, and was buried in St. Mildred's Church in the Poultry. William Hobson is, of course, a distinct person from Hobson the Cambridge carrier, with whom he was confounded by Malone. In 1617, appeared a pamphlet by Gervase Markham entitled *Hobson's Horseload of Letters;* this publication refers not to the haberdasher, but to his provincial namesake.

There can be no doubt that recollections of Hobson's eccentric sayings and doings long survived him, and that, among the Londoners, and the apprentices especially, his name continued, for some time after his death, to be highly popular.  So much indeed does this seem

(1) "*Dr. Nowell.*  I know him well ;
A good, sufficient man ; and since he purchas'd
His freedom in the city, Heaven hath bless'd
His travail with increase.
   *Lady Ramsey.*  I have known old Hobson
Sit with his neighbour Gunter, a good man,
In Christ's Church, morn by morn, to watch poor couples
That come there to be married, and to be
Their common fathers, and give them in the church,
And some few angels for a dower to boot.
Besides, they two are call'd the common gossips,
To witness at the font for poor men's children.
None they refuse that on their help do call :
And, to speak truth, they're bountiful to all."
—Heywood's *If You Know Not Me, You Know No Bodie.* 1606.

to have been the case, that in the second part of his play
*If You Know Not Me, You Know No Bodie*, printed in
1606, 4°, Thomas Heywood made the honest haberdasher one of the dramatis personæ, and gave a good
deal of prominence to him.[1] It is not improbable, that
Heywood's drama suggested to the editor of the *Pleasant Conceits* the idea of his publication.

The " Pleasant Conceits of Old Hobson " were collected by Richard Johnson, a popular writer of the day.
As a picture of the manners of the time, they have their
value and interest, and the occasional descriptions
of Hobson's personal appearance and oddities are,
doubtless, tolerably reliable.   For some of the touches
Johnson was indebted to his more distinguished contemporary who, it may be observed, has almost carica-
tured Hobson's propensity to drag in, at every other
sentence, his favourite " Bones a God " or "Bones a me."

It may be worth noticing that, in Heywood's play,
there is a passage (Shakesp. Soc. ed. p. 136), which
seems to assign to Hobson the dictum, which forms
the otherwise rather obscure title of that production.
In Act I. Sc. I., the ensuing dialogue takes place
between Hobson and Her Majesty :—

" *Hob.* God bless thy grace, Queen Bess !
*Queen.* Friend, what are you ?
*Hob.* Knowest thou not me, Queen ? then, thou knowest nobody.
Bones a me, Queen, I am Hobson, old Hobson ;
By the stocks ! I am sure you know me."

(1) Two Historical Plays on the Life and Reign of Queen Elizabeth.
By Thomas Heywood.  Edited by J. P. Collier, Esq. (Shakespeare Soc.
1851, p. 74, *et alibi.*)

A similar expression is put by the dramatist into the mouth of *Hobs*, the Tanner of Tamworth, in the *First Part of Edward IV*, 1600 (Shakesp. Soc. ed. p. 43).

As to many of the jests, it should be known that they have not the slenderest claim to originality ; they were, as in so many other cases, merely "ancient tales new told," stories transplanted by Johnson, who adapted them without difficulty or scruple to his own purposes from the *C. Mery Talys* and similar collections.

In preparing the present piece for the press, the Editor has amended the pointing, which in the original is very faulty and capricious, but has retained the orthography without the slightest alteration.

# THE PLEASANT LIFE OF OLD HOBSON THE MERRY LONDONER, FULL OF HUMOROUS DISCOURSES, AND WITTY MERRIMENTS, WHEREAT THE QUICKEST WITS MAY LAUGH, AND THE WISER SORT TAKE PLEASURE.

### *Master*[1] *Hobsons description.*

IN the beginning of Queene Elizabeths most happy raigne, our late deceased Soveraigne, under whose peacefull goverment long florished this our country of England, there lived in the citty of London a merry cittizen, named old Hobson, a haberdasher of smale wares,[2] dwelling at the lower end of Cheapside, in the Poultry : as well knowne through this part of England, as a sargeant knows the counter-gate. He was a homely plaine man, most commonly wearing a buttond cap close to his eares, a short gowne girt hard about his midle, and a paire of slippers upon his feete of an ancient fashion ; as for his wealth, it was answerable to

(1) Orig. reads *Masters.*

(2) See Thynne's *Debate Between Pride and Lowlines,* a Poem (circa 1565), p. 34 of reprint, and *Autobiography of Dr. Simon Forman,* ed. Halliwell, p. 6.

the better sort of our cittizens, but of so mery a disposition that his equal therein is hardly to be found. Hereat let the pleasant disposed people laugh, and the more graver in carriage take no exceptions : for here are merriments without hurt, and humourous iests savoring upon wisdome : read willingly, but scoffe not spitefully : for old Hobson spent his dayes merrily.

### 2. *Of Master Hobsons Proverbs.*

Not many yeares since there was Sir Iohn Baynes, (by the common voyce of the citty) chosen Shriefe of London, which man in former times had beene Master Hobson's prentice ; and ridinge alonge the streete with other aldermen about the citty businesse, [he] was saluted by Master Hobson in this maner : Bones a God man! what a cock-horse knave! and thy master a-foote ; heres the world turnd upside downe. Sir Iohn Baines, hearing this his masters merry salutation, passed along with a pleasant smyle, makinge no answere at all. Upon slight regard, Master Hobson tooke occasion to say as followeth : here's pride rydes on horse-backe, whilste humilitye goes a foote. In speakinge these words, came foure other alldermen rydinge after Master Shreife, whose names were these :

Allderman Ramsey, Allderman Bond, Allderman Beecher, and Allderman Cooper, at whose passage by he made this pleasant rime :—

| | |
|---|---|
| 1. Ramsay the rich | 3. Beecher the gentleman |
| 2. Bond the stout | 4. and Cooper the loute. |

This pleasant rime, so sodaynely spoken by Master Hobson, is to this day accounted for his proverbe in London.

### 3. *Of Master Hobson and Iohn Tawnycote.*[1]

MASTER HOBSON, being a haberdasher of small wares (as I sayd before), and his shoppe on a time full of customers, his negligent prentises carelessly

---

(1) See Heywood's *If You Know Not Me, You Know No Bodie,* 1606, Act I. Sc. 1.

"*Hob.* What, are your books made even with your accounts?

*1st Pren.* I have compar'd our wares with our receipt,
And find, sir, ten pounds difference.

*Hob.* Bones a me, knave,
Ten pounds in a morning? here's the fruit
Of Dagger-pies and ale-house guzzlings.
Make even your reckonings, or, bones a me, knaves,
You shall all smart for't.

*2nd Pren.* Hark you, fellow Goodman :
Who took the ten pounds of the country chapman,
That told my master the new fashions?

*1st Pren.* Fore God, not I.

*3rd Pren.* Not I.

*Hob.* Bones a me, knaves,
I have paid soundly for my country news.
What was his name?

*1st Pren.* Afore God, I know not.

creditted a Kentish pedler with ten pounds of
commodities, neither knowing his name nor his
dwelling place, which oversight, when maister
Hobson understood, and noting the simplicity of
his servantes and their forgetfulnes, demanded
what apparrell the pedler had on? Mary, sir
(quoth one of the prentises), he had on a tauny
cote. Then (quoth Maister Hobson), put downe
Iohn Taunycote, and so was the pedler, by the
name of Iohn Taunycote, entred to the booke.
About a month after, the same pedler came againe
to London to buy ware, and comming to Maister
Hobson in a russet cote, willed him to turne over
his booke for ten poundes that one Iohn Rowlands
owed him. Ten pounds (quoth Maister Hobson),
that Iohn Rowlands oweth me! I remember no
such man. Bones of God, knave, thou owest mee
none! But I doe, saith the pedler: whereupon
the booke was serched, but no Iohn Rowlands
was to be found. I thinke thou art mad, quoth
Hobson, for thou owest me nothing. But I doe,
quoth the pedler, and will pay it. Being in this

> *2nd Pren.* I never saw him in the shop till now.
> *Hob.* Now, bones a me, what careless knaves keep I!
> Give me the book. What habit did he wear?
> *1st Pren.* As I remember me, a tawney coat.
> *Hob.* Art sure? then, set him down John Tawney-coat.
> *1st Pren.* Ten pound in trust unto John Tawney-coat.
> *Hob.* Bones a me, man, these knaves will beggar me."

strife a long time, one of his servants said, that hee had found in the booke such a debte by one Iohn Tawny-cote. That is myselfe, replyed the Pedler; I was then Iohn Tawny-cote, though I am now Iohn Russet-cote; so paid hee the ten pounds by the same name to Maister Hobson, and received twenty more upon his owne word and name of Iohn Rowland,[1] the which twenty pound hee shortly after paid for suertyshippe; and so by this his over-kind heart, paying other mens debtes, hee grew so poore, and into such necessity, that he was forced to maintaine his living by hedging and ditching, and other such like country labours.

(1) In Heywood's Play, Act I. Sc. 1. the name is sometimes *Rowland*, and sometimes Rowland *alias Goodfellow*.

"*2nd Apprentice.* Master, I have found out one John Tawney-coat, Had ten pounds' worth of ware a month ago.

*Taw.* Why, that's I, that's I! I was John Tawney-coat then, Though I am John Grey-coat now.

*Hob.* John Tawney-coat! Welcome, John Tawney-coat.

*Taw.* 'Foot! do you think I'll be outfac'd of my honesty?

*Hob.* A stool for John Tawney-coat.—Sit, good John Tawney-coat; Honest John Tawney-coat, welcome John Tawney-coat.

*Taw.* Nay, I'll assure you, we were honest, all the generation of us. There 'tis, to a doit, I warrant it: you need not tell it after me. 'Foot! do you think I'll be outfac'd of mine honesty?

*Hob.* Thou art honest John, honest John Tawney-coat. Having so honestly paid for this, Sort up his pack straight worth twenty pound. I'll trust thee, honest John; Hobson will trust thee; And any time the ware that thou dost lack, Money, or money not, I'll stuff thy pack.

*Taw.* I thank you, Master Hobson; and this is the fruit of honesty."

Within a while after this, Maister Hobson, comming into Kent to seeke up some desperate debts,
came to Dartford, where finding this poore man
ditching for a groat a day, in pitty of him said :
how now, John Tawny cote, bones a God, man,[1]
thou canst never pay me with this poore labour;
come home, knave, come home, I will trust thee
with twenty pound more ; follow thy old trade of
pedling again, and one day thou maiest pay me all.
Thus the pedler had a new credit of Maister Hobson, by which good meanes he grew rich, that in
time he bought his freedome of London, and
therein grew so welthy a Cittisen, that he became
one of the maisters of the Hospital,[2] and when he
died, he proved a good benefactor to the same
house.

(1) The forms of oaths are generally so capricious and variable, that it
would be idle and useless to seek the precise origin of some of those found
in the jest-books and anecdote-literature of early times.  The oath which
occurs above of course requires no explanation.   It is sometimes worded
differently, as "God-a-Bones !" &c.   But our own ancestors ought not
to be regarded as peculiarly fantastic in their profanity.  It was the same
with their neighbours ; and even now the Frenchman swears by cabbages
and pigs !

(2) "*Lady Ramsey*.  Amongst these, I hold Hobson well deserves
To be rank'd equal with the bountiful'st.
He hath rais'd many falling, but especially
One Master Goodfellow, once call'd Tawney-coat,
But now an able citizen, late chosen
A master of the Hospital."
          —*If You Know Not Me, &c.* Part 2, 1606.

### 4. *How Maister Hobson made a light Banquet for his company.*

UPON a time, Maister Hobson invited very solemnly the whol livery of his company to a light banquet, and for the same provided the greatest taverne in all London in a redines. The appoynted houre being come, the cittizens repaired thether richly atired, the better to grace Maister Hobsons banquet; but expecting great cheare and good intertainement, they were all utterly disapoynted : for what found they there, thinke you ? Nothing, on my word, but each one a cup of wine and a manchet of bread on his trencher, and some five hundred candles lighted about the roome, which in my mind was a very light banquet, both for the belly and for the eye. By this merry jest, hee gained such love of his companie, that hee borrowed gratis out of the hall a hundred and fiftie pound for two yeares.

### 5. *How Maister Hobson chauk'd his Prentisses the way to the Church.*[1]

EVERMORE when Maister Hobson had any buisines abroad, his prentises wold ether bee at the taverne,

(1) This is taken from *Scogin's Jests*, where Scogin chalks his *wife* the way to church. Hence comes, perhaps, the phrase "walk your chalks," to which, however, a somewhat different origin has been assigned.

filling there heads with wine, or at the Dagger in
Cheapeside, cramming their bellies with minced
pyes.    But above al other times, it was their
common costome (as London prentises use) to
follow their maisters upon Sundays to the Church
dore, and then to leave them, and hie unto the
taverne; which Maister Hobson on a time perceving one of his men so to doe, demanded at his
comming home, whot the preachers text was.    Sir
(quoth the fellow), I was not at the beginning.
What was in the midle? (quoth Maister Hobson).
Sir (quoth the fellow), then was I asleepe.    (Said
Maister Hobson againe) what was then the conclusion?    Then replyed his servant: I was come,
Sir, away before the end; by which meanes he
knew well he was not there, but rather in some
tipling house, offending Gods maiesty and the
lawes of the land.    Therefore the next Sunday
morning after, Maister Hobson called all his servants together, and in the sight of many of his
neighbors and their prentises, tooke a peece of
chauke, and chaukd them all the way along to
the Church derectly, which proved a great shame
to his owne servants, but a good example to all
others of like condition: after this was there never
the like misdemenour used among them.

## 6. *How Maister Hobson hung out a Lanterne and Candle light.*

In the beginning of Queene Elizabeaths raigne, when the order of hanging out lanterne and candle light first of all was brought up, the bedell of the warde, where Maister Hobson dwelt, in a darke evening crie[d]¹ up and downe : hang out your lantornes, hang out your lantornes, using no other words: whereupon Maister Hobson tooke an empty lantorne, and, according to the beadles call, hung it out. This flout by the Lord Maior was taken in ill part, and for the same offence [Hobson] was sent to the Counter : but [he] being released the next night following, the beadle, thinking to amend his call, cried with a loud voice : hang out your lantorne and candle. Maister Hobson hereupon hung out a lantorne and candle unlighted, as the beadle againe commanded, whereupon he was sent again to the Counter ; but the next night the beadle, being better advised, cryed : hang out your antorne and candle light, hang out your lantorne and candlelight ; which Maister Hobson at last did to his great commendations, which cry of lanthorne and candlelight² is in right manner used to this day.

(1) Orig. reads *crieng.*

(2) *Lanthorne and Candlelight* is the title of a pamphlet published by

## 7. *How Maister Hobson bayted the Divell with a Dog.*[1]

NOT farre from Maister Hobsons house, there dwelled one of the cunning men, otherwise called fortune tellers, such cossoning companions, as at this day (by their crafts) make simple women beleeve, how they can tell what husbands they shall have, how many children, how many sweet-harts, and such like : if goods bee stole, who hath them, with promise to helpe them to their losses againe : with many other like deceiptfull elusions. To this wise man (as some termes him) goes Maister Hobson, not to reap any benefit by his

Thomas Decker in 1608-9; but I suspect that the expression was already proverbial and familiar when Decker availed himself of it as the title of a piece intended to be popular.

(1) In the *Knave of Clubs*, 1600, by S. Rowlands, this trick is played by a "cousening knave" on a butcher :—

> " At length, out of an old blind hole,
> Behind a painted cloth,
> A devill comes with roaring voyce,
> Seeming exceeding wroth,
> With squibs and crackers round about
> Wilde fier he did send,
> Which swaggering Ball the butcher's dog
> So highly did offend,
> That he upon the devill flies,
> And shakes his bones so sore,
> Even like an oxe most terrible,
> He made Hobgoblin roare."
> —*Knave of Clubs*, 1600 (Percy Soc. ed. p. 17).

crafty cunning, but to make a jest and tryall of his experience. So, causing one of his servants to lead a masty[1] dog after him, staying at the cuning mans doore with the dog in his hand, up goes Maister Hobson to the wise man, requesting his skil : for he had lost ten pound lately taken from him by theeves, but when and how he knew not well. The cunning man, knowing Maister Hobson to be one of his neighbors, and a man of a good reputa- tion, fell (as he made showe) to coniuring and casting of figures, and after a few words of incanta- tion, as his common use was, he tooke a very large faire looking glasse,[2] and bad Maister Hobson to looke in the same, but not to cast his eyes back- ward in any case ; the which hee did, and therein saw the picture of a huge and large oxe with two broad hornes on his head, the which was no other- wise but as hee had often deceitfully shewd to others : a cossoning fellow, like the cunning man himselfe, clothed in an oxe hide, which fellow he maintained as his servant to blinde the peoples eyes withall, and to make them beleeve hee could shew them the Divill at his pleasure in a glasse. This vision Maister Hobson perceving, and gessing

(1) **Mastiff.**
(2) *i. e.* a beryl or mirror. See Aubrey's *Miscellanies*, ed. 1857, p. 154.

3                                             C

at the knavery thereof, gave a whistle for his dog, which then stayed below at the doore in his mans keeping; which whistle was[1] no sooner hard, but the dog ran up stayers to his maister as he had beene mad, and presently fastned upon the poore fellow in the oxe hide, and so tore him as it was pittifull to see. The cunning man cried : for the passion of God : take off your dog! No (quoth Maister Hobson), let the Divill and the dogge fight ; venture thou thy devill, and I will venture my dog. To conclude, the oxe hide was torne from the fellows backe, and so their knaveryes were discovered, and their cunning shifts layd open to the world.

8. *How Maister Hobson alowed his wife two men to waight on her to the Market.*

As Mai. Hobson increased in riches, so increased his wife in pride, in such sort that she would seldom goe out of doores without her man before her.[2] Upon a time, having buissnes to Cheapside market amoungst many other of her neighbors, the more to shew her haughty stomack, [she] desired

(1) Orig. reads *being*.
(2) A curious picture of the merchant's wife of the Elizabethan era is given by Nash in his *Pierce Penniles*, 1592 (Shakesp. Soc. ed. p. 21).

of her husband that she might have her man to attend her, who, seeing her disposition, willingly consented thereunto, and thereupon called two of his lustiest men, put them in armor with two browne-bills on their necks, placing one of them before her, the other after, and so proferred to send her forth to market. She, in a nicenes,[1] tooke such displeasure hereatt, that for a mounth after she lay sicke in her bed, and would eate nothing but caudles[2] made of muskadine.

## 9. *Of an Epitaph that Maister Hobson made for a dead man.*

THERE was a very rich cittyzen (dwelling not far from London bridge) who[3] in his life time was never knowne to doe any deed worthy of memorie ; who, dying, left Maister Hobson his onely executor to dispose of his goods, as also to lay upon his grave a faire marble stone ; and as upon marble stones there bee commonly ingraven certaine verses in the maner of an epitaph of the mans conversation there-

(1) Fit of foolishness. The adj. *nice* is employed by Chaucer in the sense of foolish. See Naves in voce *Nice* (edit. 1859).

(2) *i.e.* cordials. *Caudle* is the form of the word generally found in early English works. See, for instance, *Comedie of Patient Grissil*, 1603 (Sh. Soc. ed. p. 88), and *Wife Lapped in Morels Skin*, circa 1550 (Sh. Soc. ed. p. 71).

(3) Orig. reads *whom.*

under buried, so Maister Hobson considered what epitaph he would set upon his friends grave, [and] knowing the few good deeds he did in his life time, caused these two verses following to be ingraven upon the marble stone.

EPITAPH.

He was begotten, borne, and cryed,
He lived long time, fell sicke, and died.

### 10. *How Maister Hobson proved himselfe a Poet.*

MAISTER HOBSON, having ocasion to ride into the wild[1] of Kent, where in that age scollers were very scarce, during the time of his taring there, there hapned to be buried one Iohn Medcaufe, a very sufficient farmer, upon whose grave was written these verses following, in faire Romaine letters.

I desire yee in the Lords behalfe,
To pray for the soule of poore Iohn Caufe.

Maister Hobson, noting the simplicity of the verses, writ underneath as followeth :—

O thou, Death, more suttell then a foxe,
Thou mightst a let this caufe lived[2] to be an oxe,
To have eat grasse, hay and corne,
And like his sire to have wore a horne.

---

(1) Weald.
(2) Probably the word should be *live;* but Hobson's poetical efforts, as reported by Johnson, are so deplorably sorry, that it seems scarcely worth while to take much trouble in ascertaining the true reading. In MS. Ashmole, No. 38, this story is attributed to Tarlton the Jester. See vol. ii. p. 253.

11. *How Maister Hobson found his Factor in France with a French Curtizan.*

MAISTER HOBSON, having in France a factor which dealt for him in marchandise, and lacking divers sorts of wares to furnish his chapmen for Bristowe faire, sent to his aforesaid factor (being a mery conceited youth) for certaine matches of such commodities as were then most in request. He, mistaking his maisters meaning, sent him al the matches used for gun-pouder that could be bought in France, to the valew of two thousand poundes worth. Maister Hobson, receaving them, and seing himselfe matcht with a commodyty of matches, thought all was not well in France, and that his man necklected his busines there. To know the truth thereof, the next morning very early, not re-vealing it to his wife, in a night gowne, a buttoned cap, and in a payre of slippers,[1] [he] tooke shipping

(1) "*Hob.* Mother a me, leave off these parables,
And tell me plainly, is he not a wencher?
*Tim.* By yea and by nay, sir, without parable, I am no tell-tale. I have seen him in company with Madonna such a one, or such a one : it becomes not flesh and blood to reveal. Your worship knows he is in France, the sea betwixt him and you, and what a young youth in that case is prone unto—your gravity is wise. I'll not say so much as I saw him drinking with a French lady or lass in a tavern, because your gravity is wise ; but if I had, it had been less than, perhaps, you imagine on such a wild youth as he, no question, does deserve.
*Hob.* Mother a me, 'tis so. In a French tavern,

at Billinsgate, and so passed over into France, when, after some inquiry made of his mans life and conversation, he found him in a lewd house, reveling with a most gallant French curtezan, whome Maister Hobson after a smile or two saluted in this manner: what now, knave? what, a wenching, knave? at rack and manger, knave?[1] Bones of me, cannot a snatch and away serve your turne, knave? Is this

Kissing the lady, and the sea betwixt us.
I am for you, Master John ; thus in my gown and slippers,
And nightcap and gown, I'll step over to France."
    —*If You Know Not Me, You Know No Bodie*, 1606, Act I. Sc. 1.
(1) " *John.* Zounds! my master.
*Hob. Sancte amen!* Man John, a wenchart knave, rack and manger knave? Bones a me, cannot a snatch and away serve your turn, but you must lie at rack and manger? Is this the ware you deal with, servant John?
*John.* Chapman's ware, sir.
*Hob.* Sirrah, sirrah, the dealing with such ware belongs not to our trade. Bones a me, knave, a 'prentice must not occupy for himself, but for his master, to any purpose.
*John.* And he cannot occupy for his master without the consent of his mistress.
*Hob.* Come, y'are a knave,
*John.* Of your own bringing up, sir.
*Hob.* Besides, thou canst not keep open shop here, because thou art a foreigner, by the laws of the realm.
*John.* Not within the liberty ; but I hope the suburbs tolerate any man or woman to occupy for themselves: they may do't in the city, too, an they be naturalized once.
*Hob.* Ay, but sirrah, I'll have none of my English 'prentices Frenchified. Bones a me, knave, I'll have thee deal with no such broken commodities.
*John.* Your worship must have such as the country yields, or none at all. But, I pray ye, sir, what's our trade?
*Hob.* What say'st thou, knave?
*John.* That your worship is a haberdasher of all wares.

the French wares you deale withall, knave ? His
man, seeing himselfe so taken napping, for a time
stood amazed, not knowing what to say, but re-
covering his sences, he gave his maister this pleasant
answere : though, sir, this ware is a broken commodity, yet may wee deale with them, being dealers
with all wares, or rather haberdashers of small wares,
which is seldome lik'd of French gentlewomen.
Maister Hobson at this pleasant answere could not
choose but pardon him, and so came they both over
into England, where now this rack and a manger is
growne to a proverbe.[1]

12. *How Maister Hobson got a Pattent for the Sale
of his Matches.*

THE commodity of matches which his factor sent
him from France, being slow of saile, considering

*Hob.* Bones a me ! a haberdasher of small wares.
*John.* And that the worst trade in all Christendom, and especially for
French women."—*If You Know Not Me,* &c. 1606, Act I. Scene 1.

(1) This proverb is, *To lie at rack and manger, i.c.* To live plentifully.
　　　　" Yet must ye be at further danger,
　　　　If ye doo intend to use them oft ;
　　　　Keepe them both at rack and maunger.
　　　　Aray them wel, and lay them soft."
　　　　　　*The Schole-house of Women,* 1542.
　　" I have found out a cunning way with ease
　　To make her *cast her coat,* when ere I please ;
　　And if at *Rack and Manger* she may be,
　　Her *Colts tooth* she will keep most wantonlee."
　　　　　　*Wild's Poems,* 1670, p. 59.

the little use for them being a time of pease,[1] like
a witty cittizen Maister Hobson hies himselfe to
court to the Queene Elizabeth, for then she raigned,
and having a pattent ready made for the sale of the
aforesaid matches. Where, so soone as hee came
into the Queenes presence, hee kneeled downe,
and desired her grace to give an asignement to his
pattent, declaring what it was, and the great losse
he was like to sustaine by that commodity. The
Queene, perceaving for what intent he came, and
considering the great benefit that would come by

(1) "*Boy*. Here's a letter sent you from John Gresham.
*Hob*. Oh, an answer of a letter that I sent,
To send me matches against Bristow fair,
If then any were come.
*Boy*. I cannot tell, sir, well what to call it ; but, instead of matches of
ware, when you read your letter, I believe you will find your factor hath
match'd you.
*Hob*. What's here ? what's here ?        [*Read the letter*.
'As near as I could guess at your meaning, I have laboured to furnish
you, and have sent you two thousand pounds' worth of match.'
How ? bones, knave ! two thousand pounds' worth of match ?
*Boy*. Faith, master, never chafe at it ; for if you cannot put it away for
match, it may be the hangman will buy some of it for halters.
*Hob*. Bones a me, I sent for matches of ware, fellows of ware.
*Boy*. And match being a kind of ware, I think your factor hath match'd
you.
*Hob*. The blazing star did not appear for nothing.
I sent to be sorted with matches of ware,
And he hath sent me naught but a commodity of match,
And in a time when there's no vent for it.
What do you think on't, gentlemen ?
I little thought Jack would have serv'd me so."
                                        *Heywood*, Act I. Sc. 1.

such a grant, and meaning to give it to some gentleman nere unto hir, as a recompence for his service,
said unto Maister Hobson : my friend (sayd the
Queene), bee content : for thou shalt not have thy
pattent sealed, nor will I give thee thy request.
Maister Hobson, hearing the Queenes denial, said :
I most hartely thanke your maiesty, both I and all
mine are bound to thanke and pray for your high-
nes ; and so making lowe obeysance, went his way.
At these his words the Queene much marvailed,
and when he had gone a litle from her, she caused
him to be sent for backe againe, whome, when he
was returned, the Queene asked, if he did well
understand what answer her grace did give him.
Yes truely, saide Maister Hobson. Whàt said I ?
(quoth the Queene) Marry, your grace bad me be
content, for I should not have my desire, nor my
pattent sealed. Why did youe then (qd. the Queene)
give me such great thanks ? Because (said Maister
Hobson) your grace gave mee so soone an answere
withoute either longer sute or losse of time, the
which would have beene to my very much harme
and great hinderance : for I have at home a mighty
charge of househould, to which I am bound in
duety to looke diligently, and to maintaine care-
fully. The Queene, marking well the wisdom and
discreet answer of Maister Hobson, and now con-

ceaving a new favour towards him, sayd : now shall
you give me twice thanks, for you shall have your
pattent sealed, and your desiers performed that
you sue for.  So casting her eyes upon the Lord
Chauncelour, [she] commaunded the same by him to
be done, which was accomplished with all speede ;
whereby in short time, hee had quickè saile of his
commodity of matches to his hearts content, and
his welthes great encrease.[1]

13. *Master Hobsons Iest of Ringing of Bells upon
Queene's Day.*

UPON Saint[2] Hewes day, being the seventeenth of
November, upon which day the tryumph was holden
for Queene Elizabeths hapy goverment, as bonfiers,
ringing of bells and such like ; but in the parish
where Maister Hobson dwelled, he being Church-
warden, was no ringing at all, by reason the steeple
was a-mending and the bells downe ; and being
asked by a servant of the Queenes house, why they
ringed not, he answered, because they had no bels
in their steeple.  Then qd. the Queens man : may
you very wel sel away your steeple.  Why so, qd.

---

(1) Unluckily for Hobson's credit, this story is taken from the *Mery
Tales and Quick Answers,* ed. 1567, No. 139.

(2) Orig. reads *Satint.*

Maister Hobson? Because, quoth the other, it standet emty and vacant. To whom Maister Hobson replyed againe : we may better sell awaye our pulpet : for these twelve mounths was there never a sermon in the same, and it rather stands empty and vacant. After this the parson of the church preached every Sonday following.[1]

14. *Of a Begers Answear to Maister Hobson.*

A POORE begger man, that was foule, blacke and loathsome to behould, came on a time to Maister Hobson, as he walked in Moore feelds, and asked something of him for an almes : to whom Maister Hobson said : I prethee, good fellow, get thee from me, for thou lookst as thou camst lately out of hell. The poore begger man, perceving hee would give him nothing, answered ; forsooth, Sir, you say true, for I came lately out of Hell indeed. Why didst not thou tarry there still, quoth Maister Hobson. Nay Sir, quoth the begger, there is no roome for such begerr men as I am : for all is kept for such gentlemen cittizens as you be. This wity answere caused Maister Hobson to give the poore man a teaster.[2]

(1) This tale had already appeared in *Mery Tales*, &c. ed. Berthele (circa 1530), where it is the 12th tale.

(2) Sixpence. In *Mery Tales*, &c. (ed. Berthelet) this identical anecdote is related as an adventure between Skelton the poet and a beggar :

## 15. *How long Maister Hobsons Daughter mourned her Husbands Death.*

MAISTER HOBSON had a daughter which was a very faire and young woman, the which for her husband that laye a dying, made great sorrow and lamentation, and would not bee comforted by any perswasions, wherefore her father came to her and sayd : daughter, leave of your mourning, for if God take away your husband, I will speedily provide you another of as great a welth and credit as he is now of, and farre more young and lusty. But yet, for all this, would shee not leave mourning, and grew greatly displeased that her father made any motion of another husband, protesting that she would never marry more. But now marke the variable minds of women ! Her husband was no sooner dead and buried, the charges of his buriall paid for, and shee with her friends set at supper to comfort her, betweene sobbing and weeping, she whispered her father in the eare and said : father, where is the same man, that ye said should bee my husband ? Thus may you see (quoth Maister Hobson)[1] the nature of women kind, and how long

it is the 13th Tale. It does not, however, occur in the *Mery Tales of Skelton*, 1567.

(1) This is almost a literal copy of the 10th Tale of *Mery Tales*, &c. (edit. Berthelet). So much for Master Hobson's wit !

they mourne for their husbandes, after they bee
dead. These words made the yong woman never
after to aske her father for a husband.

### 16. *How Maister Hobson caused his Man to set up a Signe.*

MAISTER HOBSON having one of his Prentices new
come out of his time, he,[1] being made a free man of
London, desired to set up for himself. So taking a
house not far from saint Laurence Lane, furnished
it with store of ware and set the signe of the May-
denhead. Hard by, was a very rich man of the same
trade, [who] had the same signe, and [who] reported
in every place where he came, that the yong man
had set up the same signe that he had, onely to get
away his customers, and dayly vexed the yong man
there withall who, being greved in · mind, made it
knowne to Maister Hobson, his late maister who,
comming to the rich man, said : I marvell, Sir
(quoth Maister Hobson), why you wrong my man
so much as to say he seketh to get away your customers. Mary, so he doth (quoth the other): for
he hath set up a signe called the Maidenhead, as
mine is. That is not so (replied Maister Hobson):
for his is the widdoes head, and no mayden-head ;
therfore you do him great wrong. The rich man,

(1) Orig. reads *and*.

hereupon, seeing himself requited with mocks, rested satisfied, and never after that envied Maister Hobsons man, but let him live quietly.[1]

### 17. *Of Maister Hobsons Iest of a Louse and a Flea.*[2]

UPON a time, Maister Hobson going to my Lord Maiors to dinner amongst the livery of his company, and being waited on by one of his prentices, the said prentise spied a louse creeping upon the side of his gowne, and tooke it off. Maister Hobson, espying him to doe some thing in secret, asked him what it was. The fellow, being ashamed, was loath to tell him ; but, being importuned by his maister, said it was a louse. Oh ! (qd. Maister Hobson) this is good lucke : for it sheweth me to be a man, for this kind of vermine chiefly breedeth on mankind ; and thereupon gave five shillings to his man for his labour. Another of his prentises, being a pickthanke knave, and having h[e]ard that his fellow had five shillings given him for taking a louse from of his maister, [went to his maister] having his gowne likewise on, and made as though he tooke a flea from the same, and convayed it

(1) This pointless story seems quite original.

(2) This is merely a new application of No. 24 of *Mery Tales and Quick Answers* (ed. Berthelet). In the older book it is related of Louis XI. of France and one of his servants. See also Taylor's Works, 1630, i. 105.

privilyaway. But when maister Hobson constrayned him to tell what it was, with much dissembling shamefastnes he said it was a flea. Maister Hobson, perceving his disimulation, said to him : what ! dost thou make mee a dogge : for fleas be most commonly bread upon dogs ? And so, [for] the five shillinges he lookd for he had given fiveteene stripes : for, quoth Maister Hobson, there is great difference betweene one that doth a thing with a good mind, and him that doth a thing by disimulation.

18. *How one of Maister Hobsons men quited him with a merry Iest.*

MAISTER HOBSON had a servant that hee had long before made a freeman, and was still at Maister Hobsons commandment, and did him much good service ; wherefore, upon a time, hee came unto his maister and said : sir, I have done your service long time iust and truly, wherefore I pray you bestowe some thing upon mee to begin the world withall. Fellow, quoth Maister Hobson, thou sayst true, and hereon have I thought many times to doe a good turne ; now will I tell thee, what thou shalt doe. I must shortly ride to Bristowe faire, and if thou wilt beare my charges thether, I will give thee such a thing as shall be worth to thee a hundred pounds. I am content (quoth the fellowe). So all the way as hee road his man bore his charges, and paid for all things dewly, till they came to their last lodging, and there after supper he came to his maister and said : sir, I have borne your charges as you commanded me ; now I pray you let me know what the thing is, that will be worth to me a hundred poundes. Did I promise thee such a thing? (quoth his maister.) You did (quoth the fellow). Shew it me in wrighting (quoth his maister). I have none (qd. the fellow). Then thou art like to have nothing (quoth his maister) ; and learne this of me : when so ever thou makest a bargaine with any man, looke that thou take a wrighting for thy security, and be wel advised how thou givest thy bond to any man ; this thing hath [1] benefitted me in my time a hundred pounds, and so may it likewise do thee. Thus when the poore fellow saw there was no remedy, he held himselfe content, and all that night pondred in his mind how to grow [to a] quittance with his maister. So, on the morrow, when his maister had dispatched his buissines in the towne, and was set forward back again towards London, he taried a litle behind to recon with the hostes where he lay, and of her he bor-

---

(1) Orig. reads *had*.

rowed as much mony on his maisters cloke as came to all the charges that they spent by the way. Maister Hobson had not riden past two miles but that it begon to raine, wherupon he called for his cloke of another servant that rod by, who said that it was behind with his fellow who had it with him. So they tooke shellter under a tree, till he overtooke them. When he was come, maister Hobson most angerly sayd : thou knave, why comst not thou away with my cloke ? Sir, and it please you (quoth the poore fellow), I have layd it to pawne for your charges all the way. Why, knave, quoth maister Hobson, didest not thou promisse to bear my charges to Bristowe ? Did I, quoth the fellow ? Yes (quoth Maister Hobson), that thou didest. Shew me a wrighting then therefore (said the fellow). Whereunto Maister Hobson (seeing himselfe so cunningly overreached) answered but litle.[1]

### 19. *Of Maister Hobsons riding to Sturbrige Faire.*[2]

MAISTER HOBSON on a time, in company of one of his neighbors, roade from London towards Sturbrige faire. So the first night of there iorny they lodged

---

(1) This is a reproduction with very slight variation of No. 54 of *Mery Tales and Quick Answers* (1530), where it is related of Mr. Justice Vavasour and his man Turpin.

(2) *i.e.* Stourbridge Fair.

" *Tawnycoat.* God bless you, Master Hobson.

at Ware in an Inne where great store of company was, and in the morning, when every man made him ready to ride, and some were on horsbacke setting forward, the cittizen his neighbour found him sitting at the Inne gate, booted and spurd, in ·a browne studdy, to whome hee saide : for shame, Maister Hobson, why sitte you heare? Why doe you not make yourselfe redy to horsebacke, that we may set forward with company? Maister Hobson replyed in this manner : I tarry (quoth he) for a good cause. For what cause? quoth his neighbour. Marry, quoth Master Hobson, here be so many horses, that I cannot tell which is mine owne, and I know well, when every man is ridden and gone, the horse that remaneth behind must needs be mine.[1]

*Hob.* Bones a me, knave, thou'rt welcome.  What's the news
        At bawdy Barnwell, and at Stourbridge Fair?"
Heywood's *If You Know Not Me, You Know No Bodie*, 1606, Act, I. Sc. 1.
        " Women-dancers, Puppet-players,
        At Bartholomew and Sturbridge fairs."
                        Dixon's *Canidia*, 1683, Part V. p. 87.
        " A fire licking a child's Hair
        Was to be seen at *Sturbridge Fair*,
        With a lambent flame all over a Sweating Mare."
                                Ibid. p. 148.
    See Taylor's Works, 1630, ii. 8.  Auctions of books used in former times to be occasionally held at this fair.
    See also Gutch's *Collectanea Curiosa*, ii. 11, *et seqq.*
    (1) No. 72 of the *Mery Tales and Quick Answers* (1530) is entitled, " Of the Two Yong men that rode to Walsingham," and is identically the same as the above.

20. *How Maister Hobson found a Farmers purse.*[1]

THERE was a certaine farmer that lost forty pounds betwixt Cambridg and London, and being so great a summe, he made proclamation in all market townes thereabouts, that whosoever had found forty and five pounds, should have the five pounds for his labour for finding it, and therefore he put in the five pound more than was lost. It was Maister Hobsons fortune to find the same some of forty pounds, and brought the same to the Baylife of Ware, and required the five pounds for his paines, as it was proclaymed. When the country farmer understood this, and that he must needs pay five pounds for the finding, he sayd that there was in the purse five and forty pounds, and so would hee have his own mony and five pounds over. So long they strove that the matter was brought before a justice of peace, which was then one Maister Fleetwood, who after was Recorder of London. But when Maister Fleetewood understood by the bayleife that the proclamation was made for a purse of five and forty pound, he demanded where it was. Here, quoth the baylie, and gave it him. Is it just forty pound, said Maister Fleetewood?

(1) This is an almost exact copy of No. 16 of *Mery Tales*, &c. (1530), where it is related of Mr. Justice Vavasour and his man Turpin.

Yes truly (quoth the bayleife). Here, Maister Hobson, sayd Ma. Fleetwood, take you this mony: for it is your owne, and if you chance to find a purse of five and forty pound, bring it to this honest farmer. That is mine, quoth the farmer: for I lost iust forty pound. You speake to late (quoth Maister Fleetewood). Thus the farmer lost the mony, and maister Hobson had it according to iustice.

### 21. *How Maister Hobson was a iudge betwixt two women.*[1]

THERE dwelled not farre from Maister Hobson two very ancient women; the youngest of them both was above three-score yeares of age; and uppon a time sitting at the taverne together, they grew at varience which of them should be the youngest (as women indeede desier to bee accoumpted younger then they be); in such manner that they layd a good supper, of the valew of twenty shillings, for the truth thereof, and Maister Hobson they agreed upon to bee their judge of the difference. So after Maister Hobson had knowledge thereof, the one came to him, and as a present, gave him a

(1) See Wright's *Latin Stories*, p. 73 (Percy Society); *Mery Tales and Quick Answers* (1530), No. 22; and *Jack of Dover*, 1604, (vol. ii. p. 334). In the last, this tale is told, with very slight variations, of "The Foole of Lancaster."

very faire pidgion pye, worth some five shillings, desiering him to pass the vardet of her side. Within a while after, the other came, and gave Maister Hobson a very faire grayhound, which kind of dogges he much delighted in, praying him likewise to be favourable on her side ; wherefore hee gave iudgment that the woman that gave him the grayhound was the yonger, and so she woun the supper of twenty shillings, which she [that had given him the pidgion-pye] perceiving, came to him and sayd : sir, I gave you a pidgion pie, and you promised the verdit should goe on my side. To whom Maister Hobson said : of a truth, good woman, there came a grayhound into my house, and eate up the pidgion pye, and so by that meanes I quite forgot thee.

## 22. *Of the pride of Maister Hobsons wife.*

MAISTER Hobsons wife carrying something[1] a stately mind, and delighting in brave apparell, upon a time walking abroad with other women her neighbours, they espied a payre of silke stockins upon her legges, and desiring the like, never let their husbands to live in quiet after, til they had silke stockins of the same fashion. So within a

(1) *i.e.* somewhat.

weeke or two following, their husbandes came
complayning to Maister Hobson, and said : sir
(quoth one of them), the ŝufferance of your wives
pride hath spoyled all ours : for since she hath
worne silke stockings, our wives have growne so
importunate, that they must needs have the like,
and you are the cheifest cause in suffering her to
weare the same.  Oh ! my good neighbours (qd.
M. Hobson), I have great cause in doing so, and it
bringes me much quietnes.   As how ? (qd. one of
them).   Mary, thus (neighboures): for, seeing I
cannot please her above the knee, I most needs
please her belowe the knee, and the only thing to
please a woman is to let her have her will.[1]

### 23. *Of Maister Hobsons rewarding a poet for a bookes dedication.*

UPON a new yeares day, Maister Hobson sitting at
dinner in a poets company, or one, as you may
tearme him, a writer of histories, there came a
poore man and presented him a cople of orringes,
which hee kindly tooke as a new yeares guift, and
gave the poore man for the same an angell of gould,
and thereupon gave it[2] his wife to lay it up among
other jewells, considering that it had likewise cost

(1) This story is taken from *Jack of Dover, His Quest of Inquiry*, 1604
(vol. ii. p. 316).   It is there told of the " Foole of Bedford."
(2) *i.e.* the gift.

him an angel; the which she[1] did. The Poet,
siting by and marking the bounty of Ma. Hobson
for so small a matter, he went home and devised a
booke contayning forty sheets of paper, which was
halfe a yeare in writing, and came and gave it to
Maister Hobson in dedication, and thought in his
mind that he, in recompencing the poore man so
much for an orringe, would yeeld far more recompence for his booke, being so long in studying.
Maister Hobson tooke the poets booke thankfully,
and perseving he did it onely for his bounty shewed
for the orring given him, willed his wife to fetch
the said oringe, which he gave to the poet, being
then almost rotten, saying : here is a jewell which
cost me a thousand times the worth in gould ;
therefore I think thou art well satisfied for thy
bookes dedication. The poet, seing this, went his
way, all ashamed.[2]

(1) Orig. reads *he.*

(2) In *Mery Tales and Quick Answers* (1530), No. 23, this story is
told of Louis XI. of France and a husbandman of Burgundy. See also
Lovelace's Poems, ed. Hazlitt, p. 229; and Day's *Parliament of Bees*,
1641, 4°, *Dedication.* In the *Pleasant Comedie of Patient Grissil*, 1603 ;
Act III. Sc. 1, the marquis says :—

    "I robb'd my wardrobe of all precious robes,
    That she might shine in beauty like the sun ;
    And in exchange I hang this russet gown
    And this poor pitcher, for a monument
    Amongst my costliest jems."—

This tale reads not unlike a prank of George Peele the dramatist and
poet.

### 24. *How Maister Hobson gave one of his servants the halfe of a blind mans benefit.*

MAISTER Hobson beeing still very good to poore and most bountyfull to aged people, there came to him usually twice or thrice a weeke a silly poore ould blinde man to sing under his window, for the which he continually gave him twelve pence a time. Maister Hobson had[1] one of his servants so chorlish and withall so covitous, that he would suffer the blind man to come no more, unles he shard halfe his benefit : the which the blind singing man was forst to give, rather then to loose all. After twice or thrice parting shares, Maister Hobson had thereof intelligence, who, consulting with the blind man, served his servant in this maner ; [since] still he looked for halfe whatsoever he got. So this at last was Maister Hobsons guift, who gave com-mandement that the blind man should have for his singing three-score jeerkes with a good wippe, and to be equally parted as the other guifts were ; the which were presently given. The blinde mans were but easie, but Maister Hobsons mans' were very sound ones, so that every jerke drewe bloud. After this he never sought to deminish his masters bounty.[2]

(1) Orig. reads *having.*
(2) See Wright's *Latin Stories* (Percy Soc.), p. 122, and *Mery Tales and Quick Answers* (1530).

### 25. *How Maister Hobson found out the pye stealer.*[1]

In Christmas holy-dayes, when Ma. Hobsons wife had many pyes in the oven, one of his servants had stole one of them out, and at the taverne had merrilie eaten it. It fortund that same day some of his friends dined with him, and one of the best pyes were missing, the stealer whereof at after dinner he found out in this maner. He caled all his servants in friendly sort together into the hall, and caused each of them to drinke one to another both wine, ale and beare, till they were al drunke; then caused hee a table to be furnished with very good cheare, whereat hee likewise pleased them. Being set all together, he said : why sit you not downe, fellowes ? We be set all redy, quoth they. Nay, quoth Maister Hobson, he that stole the pye is not set yet. Yes, that I doe (quoth he that stole it); by which meanes he knew what was become of the pye : for the poore fellow being drunke could not keepe his owne secretts.[2]

---

(1) See Doran's *History of Court Fools*, pp. 1, 2.

(2) This is only *Mery Tales and Quick Answers*, No. 85, newly applied. See also the *Philosopher's Banquet*, 1614, p. 240.

### 26. *Of Maister Hobson and a doctor of physicke.*[1]

UPON a time, when Maister Hobson lay sicke and
in very great payne, there came unto him a Doctor
of Physicke, that tould him he could not escape,
but must needs die of that sicknes.   Maister Hobson, a while after, not by the Doctors helpe but by
the will of God, recovered, and was whole of his
disease : yet he was very lowe, and bare brought ;
and as he walked forth on a day, he met the said
Doctor which, doubting whether it ware the sicke
man or no, sayd : are not you, Sir, the man called
Maister Hobson ?  Yes, trewly (quoth he).   Are
you alive or dead, sayd the Doctor.   I am dead,
quoth Maister Hobson.   What doe you here then,
sayde the Doctor ?  I am here, quoth Maister
Hobson, because I have experience in manye earthly
things, and God hath sent me to the world againe
with a commandement to take up all phisitions
that I can get, and send them thether to him ;
which saying made Maister Doctor as pale as ashes
for feare.   Maister Hobson, seing this, sayd unto
him : feare not, Maister Doctor, though I said al,
phisitions : for you are none, and there is no man

(1) No. 48 of *Mery Tales and Quick Answers* (1530) is precisely
similar in its details.

that hath witte will take you for one : therfore you
are not in my charge ; farewell.

### 27. *How Maister Hobson answered a popish fryer.*

IN the rainge of Queen Mary, when this land was
blinded with superstition, there was a Popish frier
that made an oration in the Charter-house yard,
where many formes were placed full of people to
hear the same oration, amoungst which number sat
Maister Hobson, which fryer, much extolling him
that was then Pope of Rome, comparing him to
Saint Peter, for in degree he names him above all
the holy Fathers in time past, as Doctors, Marters,
Prophets, yea and above more then prophets, Iohn
Baptist.   Then, in what high place, sayd the frier,
shall we place this good man ?   What place, I say,
is fit for him, or where shall he sit ?   Maister Hobson, hearing him speake so prophanly, and sitting
amoungst the audience, start [1] up and sayd : if thou
canst find no other, then set him here in my place :
for I am weary ;—and so went his way.[2]

(1) *i.e.* stert, the old præterit of *start.*
(2) This is No. 119 of *Mery Tales and Quick Answers,* ed. 1567.  It is
there told of a friar who preached on Saint Francis.  It is not found in
edit. Berthelet.

### 28. *How Maister Hobson answered Musitions.*

UPON a time, Maister Hobson lying in Saint
Albones, there came certaine musitions to play at
his chamber dorre to the intent, as they filled his
ears with their musicke, he should fil their purses
with mony : where upon he had one of the servants
of the inne (that waited upon him) to goe and tell
them, that hee could not then indure to heare their
musicke, for he mourned for the death of his
mother. So the musitians, disapoynted of their
purpose, went sadly all away. The fellow, that
heard him speake of mourning, asked him how
long agoe it is since he buried his mother. Truely
(quoth Maister Hobson), it is now very neare forty
yeares agoe. The fellow, understanding his subtilty,
and how wittily he sent away the musitians, laughed
very hartely.[1]

### 29. *Of Master Hobson teaching his man to use money.*[2]

MAISTER HOBSON had a servant so covetous, and
withall so simple witted, that all the money he

(1) In *Mery Tales*, &c. (edits. Berthelet and Wykes), No. 77, this
anecdote is related "of the covetous ambassador who would hear no
music."

(2) No. 79 of the *Mery Tales*, &c. (1530), relates "how Dionysius of
Syracuse served a covetous man." The story is the same.

could gather together he hid in the ground, of the
which Maister Hobson having some inteligence
fell a coniuring for it in this maner. With a good
wand he so belabored my yong man, that he presently revealed where it lay, the which summe of
money Maister Hobson tooke quite away, all saving
a smale summe, the which the poore fellow put to
so good a use, in buying and selling, that in short
time he greatly increased it. When Maister Hobson understood what he had done, and what good
use he put his money too, [he] sayd : sirra, [since]
you can tell how to use money, and learne to make
profit thereof, I will restore to thee all againe ; and
so he did, which made the fellow ever after a good
husband.[1]

### 30. *Of Maister Hobsons sore eyes and his answer to Phisitions.*[2]

UPON a time, when Master Hobson had sore eyes,
there came a certaine phisition to him, thinking to
have some recompence for his councell, warning

---

(1) Of course *husband* is used here in its less usual sense of *economist.*
In Heywood's play, Hobson is made to say :—
  " Men of our trade must wear good husbands' eyes ;
  'Mongst many chapmen, there are few that buys."
  (Act I. Sc. 1.)
(2) This tale is partly copied from *Mery Tales and Quick Answers*
(1530), No. 88.

him that he should in any case forbeare drinking,
or ells by the same loose his eyes, to whom Master
Hobson sayde : it is much more pleasure for me
to loose my eyes with drinking, then to keepe them
for worms to eate them out. Another time a
phisition came to Maister Hobson and said : sir,
you looke well, and greeve at nothing and have a
healthfull countenance. True (quoth Maister Hobson): for I have not to doe with any phisitions, nor
with phisicke ; to whom he replied : sir, said he,
you have no cause to blame the physition, for his
phisicke never did you hurt. Thou saist true,
quoth Maister Hobson : for, if I had proved phisicke,
I had not beene now heare alive. Another phisition
came to him on a time and said : sir, you be a very
ould man. Very trew, quoth Maister Hobson : for
thou wert never my phisition. Such maner of
checkes and floutes would he stil give to them that
spoke to him of physicke : for in all his life hee
never tooke any.

### 31. *Of Maister Hobsons iest of the signe of Saint Christopher.*

MAISTER Hobson and another of his neighbours,
on a time walking to Southwarke Faire, by chance
drunke in a house, which had the signe of Sa.

Christopher, of the which signe the good man of
the house gave this commendation. Saint Christopher (quoth he), when hee lived upon the earth,
bore the greatest burden that ever was, which was
this : he bore Christ over a river. Nay, there was
one (quoth Maister Hobson), that bore a greater
burden. Who was that (quoth the inkeeper). Mary,
quoth Maister Hobson, the asse that bore both him
and his mother. So was the Inne-keeper called
asse by craft. After this talking merely[1] together,
the aforsaid Inne-keeper, being a litle whitled with
drinke, and his head so giddy that he fell into the
fire, people standing by ran sodainely, and tooke
him up. Oh ! let him alone (quoth Maist. Hobson),
a man may doe what he will in his owne house,
and lie wheresoever he listeth. The man, having
little hurt, with this sight grew immediately sober,
and after foxed[2] Maister Hobson and his neighbour so mightely that, comming over London bridge,
being very late, [they] ranne against one of the
cheane posts, at which Maister Hobson, thinking
it to bee some man that had iustled him, drew out
his dodgion dagger, and thrust it up into the very
hillts into the hollow post; where-upon verely hee

---

(1) *i.e.* merrily.
(2) *i.e.* made them drunk. See Nares (edit. 1859) in voce *fox*, and the
examples quoted of the use of the word in this sense.

had thought he had kil'd some man. So runing away, [he] was taken by the watch, and so all the jest was discovered.[1]

### 32. *Of Maister Hobsons answere to a messenger of the Lord Maiors.*

UPON a time, Ma. Hobson had arested one of my L. Maiors kinsmen for a certaine det owing him ; and [he] being in the counter, my Lord Maior sent one of his officers for to intreat Maister Hobson to be favorable to his kinsman, telling a long tale, and to little purpose, whome Maister Hobson answered in this manner : my friend (quoth he), what thou saydst in the beginning I doe not like of, and what was in the middle I doe not well remember, and for thy conclution, I understand it not ; and this was all the favour Maister Hobson shewed to my Lord Maiors kinsman.

### 33. *How Maister Hobson bid an alderman to diner.*

THIS Maister Hobson on a time had a servant that was over full of words, and toe much talkative. Being offended therewith, [hee] gave him still[2] in

---

(1) This is, singularly enough, two or three of the *Mery Tales and Quick Answers* rolled into one. See Tales No. 2 and No. 8 of that collection.      (2) Continually.

charge to say nothing, and to answer to that hee was demaunded, and no more. So upon a day Maister Hobson made a great diner, and sent his said servant some two dayes before to invite an Alderman of London there-unto. So upon the day when diner time came, all the guestes stayd for the said Alldermans comming till two of the clocke, and so at last Maister Hobson sayd unto his servant : didst thou bid Maister Alderman to diner ? Yes, truly (said he). Why cometh he not then ? (quoth Maister Hobson). Mary (quoth the fellow), hee said hee could not. Why touldst thou not me so ? quoth Maister Hobson. Because, quoth the fellow, you did not aske me. Here-upon (though long first), they went all to diner,[1] and being mery together drinking of wine, there came in a certaine ruffen, and stole one of the fairest sillver cupps away, the which, the fellow seing, said never a word, but let him goe. Which when Maister Hobson missed, he demanded of his servant where it was. Sir (quoth the fellow), a theefe came in, and stole it away. Why didst not thou stay him ? (qd. Maister Hobson). Mary, sir (quoth he), because he asked no question of me. After

(1) Thus far the *Mery Tales*, &c. No. 35. The remainder is peculiar to the present collection, and possibly may be entitled to the merit of originality. In *Mery Tales* the story is told "of the wise man Piso, and his Servant."

3                                                                  *E*

this, Maister Hobson, noting the simplenes of his servant, let him have his toung at free liberty.

### 34. *How Maister Hobson grew out of love with an image.*

IN the raing of Queene Mary, when great superstition was used in England, as creeping to the crosse, worshipping of images and such like, it was Maister Hobsons chaunce amongst other people to be in the Church, and kneeling to an image to pray, as it was then used, the same image by some mishapp fell downe upon Maister Hobson, and broke his head, upon which occation he came not thether in halfe an yeare after; but at length by the procurement of his neighbours he came to the Church againe, and because he saw his neighbours kneele before the same image, he kneeled downe likewise, and said thus: wel, I may cap and kneele to thee, but thou shalt never have my heart againe so long as I live: meaning, for the broken head it had given him.[1]

(1) A reproduction of No. 75 of *Mery Tales*, &c. (1530). See also Taylor's *Wit and Mirth*, No. 13.

### 35. *How Maister Hobson said he was not at home.*

ON a time Master Hobson upon some ocation came to Master Fleetewoods house to speake with him, being then[1] new chosen the recorder of London, and asked one of his men if he were within, and he said he was not at home. But Maister Hobson, perceving that his maister bad him say so, and that he was within (not being willing at that time to be spoken withall), for that time desembling the matter, he went his way. Within a few dayes after, it was Maister Fleetwoods chaunse to come to Maister Hobson's, and knocking at the dore, asked if he were within. Maister Hobson, hearing and knowing how he was denyed Maister Fleetwoods speach before time, spake[2] himselfe aloud, and said hee was not at home. Then sayd Maister Fleetwood : what, Master Hobson, thinke you that I knowe not your voyce ? Whereunto Maister Hobson answered and said : now, Maister Fleetewood, am I quit with

(1) As Mr. Halliwe points out, Fleetwood's recordership commenced in 1569, and therefore it might be presumed, that this story was assignable to that period. See, however, *Mery Tales and Quick Answers* (1530), No. 112, where the same anecdote is related of Scipio Nasica and Ennius the poet. (2) Old edition has *speake.*

you : for when I came to speake with you, I be-
leeved your man that said you were not at home,
and now you will not beleeve mine owne selfe; and
this was the mery conference betwixt these two
merry gentlemen.

𝔉inis.

# CERTAYNE CONCEYTS & JEASTS.

*Heereafter follow Certaine Conceyts and Jeasts, as well to laugh downe our harder vndigested Morsells, as breake vp with myrth our Booke and Banquet, collected out of Scotus Poggius and others.*

THE title here copied occurs at p. 239 of a scarce volume entitled *The Philosophers Banquet;* London, Printed by T. C. for Leonard Becket, 1614, 8°. The Second Édition. The First Edition appeared in 1609, 8°, with a much less ample title, and a third was published in 1633. These "Conceyts and Jeasts" form the concluding portion of the work, and although they possess no striking merit, the Editor thought it desirable to render them accessible, and at the same time make the present collection more complete.

HEEREAFTER FOLLOW certaine
Conceyts & Ieasts ; as well to laugh
downe our harder vndigested Morsells, as breake vp with myrth
our Booke and Banquet.
*Collected out of* Scotvs
Poggivs, *and*
*others.*

1. A CERTAYNE Poore-man met king Phillip, &
besought him for something, because he was his
kinsman. The king demanded frō whence descended. Who answered: from Adam. Then the
K. commaunded an Almes to be giuen. Hee replyed, an Almes was not the gift of a king; to
whome the king answered : if I should so reward
all my kindred in that kinde, I should leaue but
little for myselfe.[1]

2. A certaine Iewe vpon their Saturday or
Saboth was fallen into a Ditch. A Christian, passing by and seeing him there, came vnto him to
haue pulled him out ; but the Iewe answered,
their Sabaoth was not to be violated.

(1) This is No. 86 of *Mery Tales and Quicke Answeres.*

Vppon the morrow the Christian passing by againe, the Iewe cryed vnto him, that hee would now helpe him out ; vnto whome hee answered : this is nowe my Sabaoth, and must not be broken ; and so left him.

3. A certaine Thiefe had stollen the Goose of a poore woman ; and when vpon the Sabaoth the priest, admonishing his parishioners thereof, commaunded them all to sit downe, they[1] answered : we all sit downe.

No (quoth he), you sit not all downe : for hee that stoale the Goose sitteth not. Who answered rashly ; but I doe. To whom the priest answered : thou shalt presently restore her againe, or I will excommunicate thee.[2]

4. A certaine Player, being vpon the Sea in a Tempest, beganne very greedily to eate salte Meates, saying, that he feared hee should haue too much drinke to digest them.

5. An other man beeing vppon the Sea (in a great Tempest, and daunger of Ship-wracke), was commaunded to cast something foorth that might best be spared, to lighten the burthen of the

---

(1) Old edition has *who.*
(2) See No. 85 of *Mery Tales and Quicke Answeres.*

Shippe. Who answered, hee would caste out his wife.[1]

6. A certaine Player beeing sicke, and lying vppon his Death-bedde, the Priest came vnto him, and exhorted him to make his Will, which he said he would most willingly and quickly doe : for (quoth hee) I haue nothing but two Geldings to dispose, and I bequeath and giue them to the Knightes and Barons of the Land.

And when the Priest asked him, why hee gaue them not rather to the poore, he answered : I doe as you teach vs, to be imitators of God ; and hee hath giuen all to the Rich, and nothing to [the] poore, and therefore I will follow him, in doing the like.

7. A certaine Ladie commended a knight exceedingly for his excellent actiuitie and behauiour, in Torney and Tilte, and at the ende of his course (being very desirous to see and salute him), he proued to be her Husband ; and then shee cared not, nor liked him so well.

8. It is saide that there are foure kinde[s] of Fooles : amongst all other as chiefe, the first, that threatens so long, that no man feares him : the

(1) See *Tarlton's Jests*, vol. ii. p. 234

second, that sweares so much, that no man belieues him : the third, that giues so much that he keeps nothing for himselfe : the fourth, that when hee hath no other to serue, refuseth to serue himselfe.

9. There was a certaine Foole, that alwayes, when the Sun shone, would weepe, and when the Raine rained, would laugh ; and his reason was, because after Sunne-shine followed Raine, but after Raine, Sunne-shine ; which alludeth to the Prouerbe : *Tempestas sequitur Serenum.*

10. A certaine Rusticall clowne came to an Arch-Deakon, and tolde him he had marryed a Woman which was poore, but heertofore had bene rich; and, asking his aduise, if he might not put her away and marry a Richer, [he] was answered, he might not ; vnto whom this clowne replied : why, Syr, you haue put away your poore benefice, and taken a Richer.

11. A certayne meane Priest had a Concubine, and the Arch-Deacon, vnderstanding thereof, commaunded that hee should eyther forsake his Concubine, or the Church; and he forsooke the Church and kept his concubine ;[1] and afterwards his Concubine forsooke him, because he could not keepe her.

1) See the *Jests of Scogin*, vol. ii. p. 80.

12. A poore olde woman being sicke and weake, bequeathed after her death to the Priest her Henne, because shee had nothing more. Now the priest came and tooke her away, shee yet liuing. (Quoth shee) nowe I perceyue, that our priest is worse than the Diuell, because I haue oftentimes bid the Diuell take her, and the Foxe take her : yet still I had her, but the Priest not.

13. A certaine olde woman, being almost blinde, agreed with a Physition to helpe her, which comming vnto her, and finding much Houshold-stuffe that shee had, euery time that he drest her, he tooke something away, vntill at last he left nothing but the empty house. Now the woman at last recouering her sight, finding her house empty, and her goods conuayde away, would not giue the Physition his hyre, who therefore brought her before the Iudge, to whome shee pleaded, that she was not perfectly cured, but that she saw lesse then before ; because before she saw many things in her house, where now she could see nothing at all.[1]

14. Aristotle demaunded of one, why hee, being a man of so large a stature and bodie, would be marryed to a woman so small and vnanswereable

---

(1) See *Mery Tales and Quicke Answeres*, No. 89.

therevnto as hee was. To which he replyed : Since that I was to make choyce out of thinges that were euill, I thought it most wisedome to choose the least.[1]

15. A certaine boysterous Rusticke, yet prompt and conceyted, trauelling on the way with a long pike-Staffe on his necke, was suddenly and furiously assaulted by a great Mastiue-Dogge, which came vpon him with open mouth and violence, as if hee would at once deuoure him.

Who presently, to withstand the daunger by Rescue of himselfe, runnes the pike and sharpe ende of his staffe into his throate, wherevppon hee presently dyed. Which the Owner thereof seeing, comes eagerly vnto him, and betweene threatning and chyding asked him, why hee strooke him not rather with the blunte ende of his staffe. Why, Syr (quoth hee), because your dogge ranne not at me with his tayle.

16. A certaine poore man came into a Barbers shoppe, and desired to be shauen for Gods-sake, because he had no money ; which the Barber performed, but with so great inclemencie, that at euery stroke hee fetched Teares from his eyes, making him to crye out pittifullie.

(1) See *A C Mery Talys*, No. 61.

In the meane time, a Dogge comes crying into the shoppe, beaten out of the kitchin ; which this poore man seeing, noting another to partake of his miserie, said vnto him : art thou likewise shauen for Gods-sake ?

17. A certaine vain-glorious Souldyer bragged, in all places where he came, of 9 kings that he had of his kindred ; & going about to name them, could reckō but 6. A player standing by told him he knew the rest : [for they were] the 3 Kings of *Collen.*[1]

18. A certaine Souldyer, ordaining a Feast, caused a Priest to wash first ; to whó[m] the priest said : we wash first, but sit downe last. The Morall of that, saide the Souldier, is, you should be first cleane, and last drunke.

19. One, buying a Horse, would know of the seller, if he were worth his money. Who answered he was. He then demanded of him, why he solde him. He answered : because I am poore, and he eateth ouermuch. Hath he not (quoth hee) no euill condition ? He answered : not, but that he will not climbe Trees.

Now this chapman, hauing bought him, and

(1) . *e* of Cologne

brought him home, hee bitte all that came neere him. (Quoth hee) the fellowe told me true : for he saide, he would eate ouer-much ; and afterwards comming to a wooddē bridge, he would by no meanes goe ouer, which he likewise noting, sayd : truly, he doth not climbe Trees.[1]

20. A certaine Priest, hauing shewed the hay-nousnesse of Vsurie, his Sermon being ended, [and] comming to Absolution, he commanded that euery one should stand vp in theyr turnes, to receyue theyr Blessings, as they were called. First (sayd he) let Smithes arise ; which [they] hauing done, and receyued theyr Blessings, sate downe agayne. Then hee saide to the Drapers : arise ; and so to the rest. Afterwardes (he sayde), let Vsurers arise to their benediction. And when none stood vp (although there were many there), these men (qd. the Priest) how will they appeare in the day of Iudgmen†, to receyue their euerlasting Malediction, which dare not appeare before men, to receyue theyr benediction ?

21. A certaine vsurer of Mentz, drawing neare vnto his Death, bound his Friendes by oath, that in his graue they should put a purse full of Money,

----

(1) This is one of the Jests of Howleglas or Owleglas. See edition ackenzie, No. 93.

vnder his head; which [was] done accordingly. His sepulcher [being] afterwards opened, that it might bee taken out, there was seene a Diuell powring melting golde downe his throat with a ladle.

22. A certaine Thiefe meeting a Priest in a wood, sayde : I would be confest, because to-day passing here-through, I met an other priest, from whome I haue taken his horse; for which I ask thee to enioyne me penance. Giue mee (saith the Priest) fiue shillings for the celebrating of your Masse. The Thiefe bethinking himselfe, gaue vnto him ten. Beholde (quoth he), heere is fiue shill : for that horse which I tooke from him, and fiue shil : likewise for this horse, which I will take from thee ; and so, since you make so faire a Market, absolue me for both together.

23. A certaine player, seeing Thieues in his house in the night, thus laughingly sayde : I knowe not what you will finde here in the dark, when I can find nothing my selfe in the light.

24. One asked a prostitute Ladie of Florence, how her children so likely resembled her husband Agrippa, shee so vsually commercing with others. Who answered : I suffer no other to bourde my Shippe, before her Carriage be full. *Guicch:*

25. A certaine man followed his wife to Confession, who, when the priest had inioyned her pennance, tooke her behind the Altar to inflict it, which her husband seeing, said : good sir, she is very tender, let me receyue it for her; when the wife, beeing prostrate there, saide : I will suffer for my selfe; Strike harde: for I am a grieuous sinner.

26. Boetius in his booke, *De Disciplinâ Scholast:* relateth of a certaine youth which, not brideled in his younger yeares by his parents, nor corrected for his petty introductions to Thieuerie: at last, through greater liberty and offence was convicted and condemned to dye.  Being brought to the Gallowes, (espying his Father) he desired to kisse him before his death, which admitted to doe, he bitte off his nose, because he corrected him not in his childehood.

27. A certaine old woman, as mistrustfull as couetous, hidde vnder her seate in the church 20. pounds ; which the clarke, thereof vnderstanding, had stollen away, which this woman comming afterwards, and finding not there, suspecting immediately which way it should be gone, as also contriuing how it might be recouered, she commanded her Guyde, that was to leade her amongst the Officers of the Church, to take speciall notice if any one laughed, or changed his countenance

more then other, when they sawe her approache, to
him to conduct her ; which was done accordingly,
and falling out to the Clarke, to him shee₁ was
brought. To whō she thus said : good sir, I am a
weake and blinde woman, expecting euery day to
dye, and for the good opinion I haue of you, who
I intend shall celebrate my Obsequie, I imparte
this Secrecie vnto you, that, vnder my seate in the
Church, I haue (as in a sure place,) put 20. pound,
which euery day I intend to increase, and at my
death to leaue it to you. Thus hauing said, with
thanks from him she departed ; and hee likewise,
for his better Vsurie and increase, to reprieue the
money to her former keeper : which being done,
shee returns the next morning and fetches it clean
away, and so deceiued the deceiuer.

28. A certaine Bishop, hauing preached of the
humilitie of Christ, and his lowlinesse in ryding
on an Asse : his Sermon being ended, and he
mounted vppon his palfrey, a certaine old woman
came vnto him, and tooke him by the brydle,
saying : I pray you sir, is this the Asse that Christ
rode vpon ?

29. On a time, certaine lame men assembled
to a Church, there to be cured by a holy Priest,
and would not be expulsed : which seeing, the

3·            *F*

priest sayde vnto them : giue me all your staues,
and it shall be done.    Who asked, to what ende.
Why (quoth hee), they shall make a Fire, in the
which the most lamest of all shall be burned, and
with the ashes of him shall all the rest be cured ;
which hearing, forgetting their lamenes, they ran
all away.

30.  Q. Eliz: on a time in her progresse, comming
to Couentrie, the Mayor and Aldermē meeting her
at the townes-end, as it fortuned, in a water, the
Maiors horse euer proffered to drinke, which he,
by keeping vp his raines, suffered not.    The Qu:
perceiuing asked him why hee let not his horse
drinke.    Who answered, it was not fitting for his
horse to drinke before her Maiesties ; whereat she,
smiling, gaue the raines to her steed ; but he refused.
Why by this (quoth she), M. Mayor, wee see the Prouerbe verified : *A man may bring his horse to the
water, but he will choose whether he will drinke.*

31.  One asked a Paynter why, seeing that he
could drawe such excellent proportions, hee begote
such deformed children.    Hee answered : I drawe
at the one in the Day, but I worke at the other in
the Night.

32.  A certaine Husband-man, with great coste,

had kept his Sonne to the schoole, that he might
be instructed with knowledge and learning; who,
after the expence of much time and Money, returned home to his Father, full fraught with
learning (as he supposed) when suddenly, to
manifest himselfe vpon the first occasion, seeing
at supper 3. Egges to be set vpon the table : who
ist (quoth he) in all this parish, besides my selfe,
that can approoue with plaine arguments in 3.
egges 5. to be contained ? To whom his Father
sayd : thou proposest an impossible thing : yet
let me see how thou vndertakest to prooue it.
Then his sonne began like a sophyster to argue.
Hath not he that hath 3. egges, 2. egges, & so
hauing 2. & 3. hath 5. True (saith his father),
iudging his vaine Arte worth a vaine reward :
therfore take thou the 2. eggs that thy art hath
brought foorth : for I will take these 3. that the
henne hath layde.

33. A certaine conceyted Traueller being at a
Banquet, where chanced a flye to fall into his
cuppe, which hee (being to drinke) tooke out for
himselfe, and afterwards put in againe for his
fellow : being demanded his reason, answered,
that for his owne part he affected them not, but
it might be some other did.

There is extant to this Ieast, an Epigram of Syr Thomas Moores, which I haue here inserted, as followeth :—

*Muscas è Cratere tulit Conuiua, priusquā*
*Ipse bibit: reddit rursus vt ipse bibit;*
*Addidit et causam; muscas ego nòn amo, dixit;*
*Sed tamen e vobis nescio an quis amat.*

Which I English thus :—

*Out of his Glasse, one tooke a Flye,*
*In earnest or in ieast*
*I cannot tell; but hauing drunke,*
*Return'd it to the rest.*

*And for hee would offencelesse seeme,*
*Hee shewed his reason too :*
*Although I loue them not my selfe,*
*It may bee some heere doo.*

34. The friends of a certaine widdow being a queene,[1] gaue her counsell to imitate the example of the Turtle : hauing lost her mate, to mourne and sorrowe for a time, before she imbraced any other husband ; to whom she answered : why doe you propose the example of the Turtle to me ? if I were pleased to imitate birdes, I would rather take vnto me the example of the sparrow.

(1) *i. e.* a quean.

35. Likewise a certaine merry wench, being taught by a Poetaster that sometimes at his leasure would recite metamorphoses, as how the kings fisher was changed into a bird,[1] the sisters of Meleager into Meliagri birdes :[2] the Daughters of Pyerias into Pies, Progne into a Swallow ; and others of that kind ; when vnimagined the wench demaunded of him that, if she were to choose a metamorphosis out of two, the goose or the henne, whether [3] he thought she would incorporate. Who answered, the Goose, because she should still keepe her head aloft. Nay (qd. she), rather the Hen, because she knowes her daily venery, whereas the Goose but onely the spring.

36. Iohannes Andreas, a noble lawyer, in the proheme of his 6. booke of Decretalls, reporteth of one Iames de Castello, a Bononian, sent Embassador to Pope Boniface 8. B. of Rome, being a man of eminent knowledge and learning, but of exceeding little stature, insomuch that,

(1) The author appears to have had a rather dim notion on the subject of mythological lore. He here alludes to the legend of Ceyx and Alcyone, who were changed by Jupiter, as a punishment for their pride, into birds—he, into a sea-gull (not a *king-fisher*), and she, into a halcyon (ἀλκυών), also a species of gull.

(2) *Meleagridæ*, a sort of fowl, belonging to the same class as the turkey.

(3) *i. e.* which of the two.

deliuering his Embassage, the Pope, imagining
that hee kneeled on his knees, made vnto him
long action with his Hand, that he should rise
vppe ; vntill one of his Cardinalles gaue him to
vnderstand, that hee was a certaine Zacheus.

37. A certaine couetous suspicious Vsurer,
hauing Receyued a summe of Money, committed
it to the custodye of his mans-hose ; who notwithstanding iealous of loosing that he neuer looked
off (as if he feared the Diuell would carry it away),
still questioned his Man, as hee followed his heeles,
with—Roger, hast thou the same still ?  Yea (saith
hee).  I pray thee put thy hands in thy pocket and
feele ; which Roger so did, and had it.  Shortly
after, it happened (as a plague for his iealousie,)
certaine Thieues set vppon them, and robbed
them of it, bound them hand and foote, and so
departed their way.  Where hauing layne some
little time, this olde Myser, somewhat rowsing
vppe himselfe with his former comfort, saith to
his man : Roger, thou hast not the same still : and
he answered No.  He willed him to put his hands
in his pocket and feele ; but *Rogers* hands were
bound, and he could not.

# TAYLOR'S WIT AND MIRTH.

Wit and Mirth. Chargeably Collected Ovt of Taverns, Ordinaries, Innes, Bowling-Greenes and Allyes, Ale-houses,[1] Tobacco-shops, Highwayes, and Water-passages. Made vp, and fashioned into Clinches, Bulls, Quirkes, Yerkes, Quips, and Jerkes. *Apothegmatically bundled vp and garbled at* the request of old John Garretts[2] Ghost.

---

Dedicated
To the truely Loyall harted, learned, well accomplished Gentleman, Master Archibold Rankin.

*Sir,—Being enioyned by the Ghost or* Genious *of old* John Garret *(a man well known and beloved) to collect, gleane, or gather, a bundle or trusse of mirth, and for his sake to bestrow the stage of the melancholly world with it; and withall to present it to some one generous spirit, who was old* Johns *friend; I thought vpon many to whom I might haue made my Dedication, who were both Royall, Honourable, Worshipfull, and all well-affected towards him. As to mention one for all, that* Jewell *of the world, and richest Jem of her sex, that Magazine of the two inestimable Jewels,* Patience *and* Fortitude ; *to that illustrious, peerelesse Princesse I*

---

(1) Taverns and pot-houses supplied Taylor, no doubt, with a large proportion of his matter for the *Wit and Mirth.* See *The Young Gallants Whirligig*, 1629, by F. Lenton (Halliwell's repr. p. 126), and Heywood's *Fair Mayd of the Exchange*, 1607 (Shakesp. Soc. ed. p. 50).

(2) See *Wits Recreations*, 1640 (repr. 1817, p. 226); and *Marriage of Wit and Wisdom*, &c. (Shakesp. Soc. ed. p. 86).

*might have recommended it, to whose seruice, and for whose happinesse, his life and best endeauours, with his prayers and implorations at his death, were vnfainedly consecrated. But my manners conceiuing the subject of this Booke, of altogether to triuiall a nature, to be sheltred vnder the shadow of the wings of transcendent and admired majestie; I stept so many steps downe the staires with my inuention, where by good fortune I met with you, whom I knew did loue that old honest mirrour of mirth, deceased; and whom the world better knows, are a true deuoted friend to honest harmelesse mirth, and laudable recreation.*

*I therefore entreat you, that (when your more serious affaires will permit) you would bestow the looking vpon these my poore and beggarly wardrobe of witty Jests, whom I dare not call* Apothegmes.

*And because I had many of them by relation and heare-say, I am in doubt that some of them may be in print in some other Authors, which I doe assure you is more than I doe know; which if it be so, I pray you but to conniue or tollerate, and let the Authors make twice as bold with me at any time.*

*Thus wishing euery one to mend one whereby the rent and torn garments of Thred-bare Time may be well and merrily patched and repaired, crauing your pardon, with my best wishes, I remain,*

Yours euer in the best of my best studies hereof,

JOHN TAYLOR.

The preceding inscription to Archibald Rankin with the Poem called "John Garret's Ghost," is taken from Taylor's Works, 1630, folio, which has also been adopted as the text of the *Wit and Mirth.* Five years later, appeared an edition of the latter, with some omissions, under the following title :—"Wit and Mirth, being 113 pleasant Tales and witty Jests," Lond. 1635, 8vo. In the folio there are 138 articles, exclusively of other incidental matter.[1]

Taylor's *Wit and Mirth* deserves, on the whole, to be considered one of the best collections of this kind ever published. Many of the anecdotes are peculiarly racy and droll, without being offensive, and the greater part relate to persons who lived in or about the period of the compiler. On the other hand, a few of the stories partake of the grossness incidental to this class of literature, and two or three were deemed by the Editor so totally unsuited for publication at the present day, that he has taken the liberty of expunging them. In all other respects, the text is exactly the same as it stands in the folio of 1630. With the exception of the *Life of Old Parr,* 1635, and the *Relation of a Journey into Wales, &c.* 1652, 4°, none of Taylor's pieces has hitherto been reprinted. Some years ago, a TAYLOR CLUB was projected for this purpose ; but, probably from want of encouragement, the scheme

---

(1) Other editions formerly existed, and, indeed, may still exist. In "An Advertisement of Books, Printed for, and sold by F. Coles, T. Vere, and J. Wright," on the last page of the *History of Montelion, Knight of the Oracle,* 1673, 4°, occurs "Witt and Mirth, by J. Taylor, in 8°."

was unfortunately abandoned. The 8vo. of 1635 I have not seen.

Taylor the Water-Poet was one of the favourite authors of Robert Southey, who has given an account of his life and writings in his *Uneducated Poets*, and has quoted him largely in his *Common-Place Book*.

John Garret, at the request of whose ghost the Water-Poet professes to have formed the present collection, was a jester of the period, mentioned by Bishop Corbet and others. Heylin, author of the Cosmography, speaks of "Archy's bobs, and Garrets sawcy jests." In his dedication of the *Wit and Mirth*, Taylor alludes to Garret as "that old honest mirrour of mirth deceased."

Taylor, to forestal possible cavils at his plagiarisms from others, or adoption of good sayings already published and well-known, expressly says in the dedication : "Because I had many of them [the jests] by relation and heare-say, I am in doubt that some of them may be in print in some other Authors, which I doe assure you is more then I doe know."

## John Garrets Ghost.

THE doores and windowes of the Heauens were barr'd,
And Nights blacke Curtaine, like a Ebon Robe,
From Earth did all Celestiall light discard,
And in sad darknesse clad the ample Globe;
Dead midnight came, the Cats' gan catterwaule,
The time when Ghosts and Goblings walke about :
Bats flye, Owles shrick, and dismall Dogs do bawle,
Whiles conscience cleare securely sleeps it out.
At such a time I sleeping in my bed,
A vision strange appear'd vnto my sight ;
Amazement all my senses ouer spread,
And fill'd me full with terrour and afright.
A merry graue aspect me thought he had,
And one he seem'd that I had often seene :
Yet was he in such vncouth shape yclad,
That what he was, I could not wistly weene.
His cloake was Sack, but not the Sacke of Spaine,
Canara, Mallago, or sprightfull Shery,
But made of Sack-cloth, such as beares the graine,
Good salt, and coles, which makes the Porters weary ;
Lac'd round about with platted wheaten straw,
For which he nothing to the Silke-man owed :
A wearing neuer mentione'd in the Law,
And yet, far off, like good gold lace it show'd.
Lin'd was his mantle with good Essex plush,
Pyde Calues skins, or Veale sattin, which you will :
It neuer was worne threedbare with a brush,
It (naturally) sau'd the labour still.
A hat like *Grantham* steeple : for the crowne
Or Piramide was large in Altitude :
With frugall brim, whereby he still was knowne
From other men amongst a multitude.

A Princes shooe he for a jewell wore,
Two ribbonds, and a feather in his beauer,
Which shape me thought I oft had seene before ;
Yet out of knowledge where, as't had bin neuer.
He in his hand a flaming torch did hold,
And as he neerer did approach to me,
My hayre 'gan stand on end ; feare struck me cold ;
Feare not, I am *John Garrets* Ghost, quoth he ;
I come to rowze thy dull and lazy Muse
From idlenesse, from Lethe's hatefull lake :
And therefore stand vpon no vaine excuse,
But rise, and to thy tooles thy selfe betake.
Remember me, although my carkasse rot,
Write of me, to me, call me Foole or Jester ;
But yet I pray the (Taylor) ranke me not
Amongst those knaues that doe the world bepester ;
Thou wrot'st of great *O-Toole* and *Coriat,*
Of braue *Sir Thomas Parsons,* Knight o' the Sun ;
And *Archy* hath thy verse to glory at,
And yet for me thou nought hast euer done.
Write that in *Ireland* I, in *Mars* his trayne,
Long time did vnder noble *Norris* serue ;
Where (as I could) I stood 'gainst Pope and Spaine,
Whilst some were slaine, and some w<sup>th</sup> want did starue ;
Where shot, and wounds, and knocks I gaue and tooke,
Vntill at last, halfe maimed as I was,
A man decrepit, I those warres forsooke,
And (with my Passe) did to my country passe ;
Where getting health I then shooke hands with death.
And to the Court I often made resort,
When *Englands* mighty Queene *Elizabeth*
Allow'd me entertainment for disport ;
Then by the foretop did I take old time :
Then were not halfe so many fooles as now ;
Then was my haruest, and my onely prime,

My purse receiuing what my wit did plow.
Then in such compasse I my jests would hold,
That though I gaue a man a gird or twaine,
All his reuenge would be to giue me gold,
With commendations of my nimble braine.
Thus liu'd I, till that gracious Queene deceast,
Who was succeeded by a famous King,
In whose blest Sons reigne (I with yeeres opprest)
Me to my graue sicknesse and death did bring.
And now (kind Jacke) thou seest my ayrie forme
Hath shaken off her jayle of flesh and bone ;
Whilest they remaine the feast of many a worme
My better part doth visit thee alone.
And as betweene vs still, our good requests,
Thou neuer me, I neuer thee, deny'd :
So for my sake collect some merry jests,
Whereby sad time may be with mirth supply'd.
And when 'tis written, find some good man forth,
One (as thou think'st) was, when I liu'd, my friend ;
And though thy lines may be but little worth,
Yet vnto him my duty recommend,
So farewell, *Jacke*, dame *Luna* 'gins to rise ;
The twinkling stars begin to borrow light ;
Remember this my suit, I thee aduise,
And so once more, good honest Jacke good night.
With that, more swifter then a shaft from bow,
He cut and curried through the empty ayre,
Whilest I, amaz'd with feare, as could as snow,
Straight felt my spirits quickly to repayre.
And though I found it but a dreame indeed :
Yet for his sake of whom I dreamed then,
I left my bed, and cloath'd my selfe with speed,
And presently betooke me to my pen.
Cleere was the morne, and Phœbus lent me light,
And (as it followeth) I began to write.

## (1.)

MYSELFE caried an old fellow by water, that had
wealth enough to be Deputy of the Ward, and wit
sufficient for a Scauenger; the water being somewhat rough, hee was much afraid, and (in stead of
saying his prayers,) he threatned me, that if I did
drowne him, hee would spend a hundred pound,
but hee would see me hanged for it; I desired him
to be quiet and feare nothing, and so in little space
I landed him at the Beares Colledge on the Bank-
side, alias Paris Garden. Well (said he), I am glad
I am off the water : for, if the boat had miscaried, I
could have swum no more than a Goose.

## (2.)

AN old Painter (at the repairing of a Church) was
writing sentences of Scripture vpon the wals; by
chance, a friend of mine came into the Church, and
reading them, perceived much false English. Old

man, said my friend, why doe you not write true English? Alas, Sir (quoth the Painter), they are poore simple people in this Parish, and they wil not goe to the cost of it.[1]

### (3.)

Two men being sate at a Table, one against the other : the one of them, hauing a cup in his hand, dranke to the other, saying : here, Opposite, I will drinke to you. Opposite! said the other (being angry), what is that? I would not have thee put any of thy nicknames upon me : for thou shalt well know that I am no more opposite then thy selfe, or the skin betweene thy browes.

### (4.)

A WEALTHY Monsieur in France (hauing profound reuenues and a shallow braine) was told by his man that he did continually gape in his sleepe ; at which he was angry with his man, saying, hee would not beleeue it. His man verified it to be true ; his master said that hee would neuer beleeue any that told him so, except (quoth hee) I chance to see it with mine owne eyes ; and therefore I will have a great Looking glasse hanged at my beds feet for the purpose, to try whether thou art a lying knaue or not.

(1) See *Additional Notes.*

## (5.)

THE said Monsieur commanded his man to buy him a great Hat with a button in the brim to button it vp behind ; his man bought him one, and brought him. He put it on his head with the button before, which when he looked in the glasse and saw, he was very angry, saying: thou crosse vntoward knaue, did I not bid thee buy a hat with the button to hold it vp behind, and thou hast brought me one that turnes vp before ? I command thee once more goe thy wayes, and buy mee such a one as I would have, whatsoever it cost me.

## (6.)

*This anecdote has been suppressed for an obvious reason.*

## (7.)

AN exceeding tall Gentlewoman was riding behinde a very short little man, so that the mans head reached no higher then her breast ; which the aforesaid Monsieur perceiuing said : Madam, you will ride a great deale better, if you put your legge ouer that same pummell of your saddle.

Another time he chanced to meet a Lady of his acquaintance, and asked her how shee did, and how her good husband fared ; at which word she wept,

3.              G

saying, that her Husband was in heauen. In heauen,
quoth he ; it is the first time that I heard of it, and
I am sorry for it with all my heart.

### (8.)

ONCE the said Monsieur saw a fellow that had a
Jack-Daw to sell. Sirra, quoth he, what wilt thou
take for thy Daw? Monsieur (said the fellow), the
price of my Daw is two French Crownes. Wherefore, said the other, dost thou aske so much for
him? The fellow replied, that the Daw could speak
French, Italian, Spanish, Dutch and Latine: all
which tongues hee will speake after he is a little
acquainted in your Lordships house. Well, quoth
he, bring thy Daw in, and there is thy money. In
conclusion, Jack-Daw (after a moneth or fiue weekes
time), neuer spake otherwise than his fathers speech,
*Kaw, Kaw:* whereat the Monsieur said, that the
Knaue had cozened him of his money; but it is
no great matur; there is no loste in it: for, quoth
he, though my Daw doe not speake, yet I am in
good hope that he thinks the more.

### (9.)

ANOTHER time hee commanded his man to buy
some sweet thing to burn in his Chamber: for (quoth

he) my Chamber stinkes most odoriferously. His man brought Frankincense in a paper ; and as hee was going for fire, his master tasted of it, and finding it sticke in his teeth, and relish very bitter, he called his man cozening knaue, that would bring him such bitter trash for his money ; and straightwayes commanded him to buy a pound of the best Sugar, and burne it straight to sweeten and perfume his Chamber.

## (10.)

THIS Gallant in his youth was much addicted to dicing, and many times when he had lost all his money, then hee would pawne his cloake, and so goe home without either cloake or coyne, which grieued the Lady his mother very much ; for remedy whereof she caused all his doublets (of what stuffe soeuer) to be made with canuasse painted backs, whereon was fashioned two fooles, which caused the Gentleman euer after to keepe his cloake on his back, for feare two of the three should be discouered.

## (11.)

Will Backstead the Plaier[1] cast his Chamber-lye

(1) Respecting William Backstead, or *Barkstead,* see Collier's *Memoirs of the Principal Actors in Shakespeare's Plays,* 1846, p. xxx. and *note.*

out of his window in the night, which chanced to
light vpon the heads of the watch passing by ; who
angerly said : who is that offers vs this abuse ? Why,
quoth Will, who is there ? Who is here? said one of
the pickled watchmen ; we are the Watch. The
Watch! quoth William; why, my friends, you know;
*Harme watch, harme catch.*

### (12.)

A CARDINALL of Rome had a goodly faire house
new built, but the broken brickes, tiles, sand, lime,
stones, and such rubbish as are commonly the rem-
nants of such buildings, lay confusedly in heapes,
and scattered here and there. The Cardinall demanded of his Suruayor, wherefore the rubbish was
not conueyed away. The Suruayor said, that he
purposed to hyre an hundred carts for the purpose.
The Cardinall replyed, that the charge of carts might
be saued, for a pit might bee digged in the ground
and bury it. My lord, said the Suruayor, I pray
you what shall wee doe with the earth which we
digge out of the said pit? Why, you horseson
Coxcombe, said the Cardinall, canst thou not dig
the pit deepe enough, and bury all together.

Barkstead published in 1607, 8°, *Myrrha, the Mother of Adonis, or Lust's
Prodigies,* a Poem, and in 1611, 8°, *Hirem, or the Fair Greek,* a Poem.

(13.)

A POORE Country man,[1] praying deuoutly super-
stitious before an old Image of S. Loy,[2] the Image
suddenly fell downe vpon the poore man, and
bruised his bones sorely, that hee could not stirre
abroad in a moneth after; in which space the
cheating Priests had set vp a new Image. The
Country man came to the Church againe, and
kneeled a farre off to the new Image, saying :
*Although thou smilest and lookest faire vpon me : yet
thy father plaid me such a knauish pranke lately,
that ile beware how I come too neere thee, lest thou
shouldest haue any of thy Fathers unhappy qualities.*

(14.)

A LADY, hauing beene ten yeeres in suite of Law,
had a triall at last, where the Judgement went on
her side ; whereupon she would presently express
her joy by inuiting some of her neerest tenants and
neighbours to supper ; amongst whom was a plaine
downe-right country Yeoman, to whom the Lady

(1) See No. 75 of *Mery Tales and Quicke Answers*, ed. Berthelet
(1530). The story is found in other jest-books before Taylor's time. See
the *Pleasant Conceits of Old Hobson*, 1607. Old Edition has *may*.

(2) S. Loy was the patron of smiths :—

" Am I past shame, thou peeld apish boy ?
Thou malapert knave, controlest thou me ?
Thou shalt fare the worsse, I swere by Saint Loy."
*The Book in Meeter of Robin Conscience.*

said : Tenant, I thinke I have tickled my Adversary now, though it were long first; I trow hee will make no hags of his medling with mee. The honest Yeoman replyed: Truly, Madam, I did euer think what it would come to at last : for I knew, when he first medled with your Lady-ship, that hee had a wrong Sow by the eare.[1]

### (15.)

ONE asked a fellow, what Westminster-Hall was like. Marry, quoth the other, it is like a Butlers Box at Christmas amongst gamesters : for whoso-euer loseth, the Box will bee sure to bee a winner.

### (16.)

A PROPER Gentlewoman went to speak with a rich Mizer that had more gowt than good manners. At her taking leaue, hee requested her to taste a cup of Canara. Shee (contrary to his expectation) tooke him at his word, and thanked him. He commanded Jeffrey Starueling his man to wash a glasse, and fill it to the Gentlewoman. Honest Jeffrey fil'd a great glasse about the bigness of two Taylors thimbles, and gave it to his master, who kist it to save cost, and gaue it to the Gentlewoman,

---

(1) This anecdote is found in some modern collections (see the *Complete London Jester*, ed. 1771), and the same remark applies, of course, to many others which occur in the *Wit and Mirth.*

saying that it was good Canara of six yeeres old at
the least; to whom shee answered (seeing the
quantitie so small): sir, as you requested me, I have
tasted your wine; but I wonder that it should be so
little, being of such a great age.[1]

### (17.)

A SOULDIER vpon his march found a horse-shooe,
and stucke it at his girdle, where, passing through a
wood, some of the enemy lay in ambush, and one
of them discharged his musket, and the shot by
fortune light against the fellowes horse-shooe. A
ha! qd. he, I perceiue that little armour will serue
a mans turne, if it be put on in the right place.

### (18.)

ONE being in a Chamber with his friend, looking
out at a window, hee saw one riding on a horse in
the street. Said hee: doe you see that horse? Yea,
qd. the other. Then said hee: you may sweare you

---

(1) This witticism is much older than Taylor's age. I have not met
with it in any other English jest-books which have happened to fall
in my way; but it is the same story, in a somewhat altered shape,
which occurs in the 'Εταίραι of Lucian. Lucian, however, gives a
better finish and point to the matter: for he makes his heroine, whose
lover has brought her a very small cask of wine, which he warmly com-
mends as very choice and very old, answer drily that she thinks "it is
very little of its age."

haue seene the best horse in England.   How doe
you know that? said the other.   I know it well, said
hee, for it is my horse, and I am sure that hee is
the best, and yet I dare sweare that I have one in
my stable worth ten of him.


(19.)

AN unhappy boy, that kept his fathe[r]'s sheepe in
the country, did vse to carry a paire of Cards in
his pocket, and meeting with boyes as good as
himself, would fall to Cards at the Cambrian game
of whip-her-ginny, or English one and thirty; at
which sport hee would some days lose a sheepe or
two; for which, if his father corrected him, hee
(in reuenge) would driue the sheepe home at night
ouer a narrow bridge, where some of them falling
besides the bridge were drowned in the swift brooke.
The old man, being wearied with his vngracious
dealing, complained to a Justice, thinking to affright
him from doing any more the like.   In briefe,
before the Justice the youth was brought, where
(vsing small reuerence, and lesse manners) the
Justice said to him : Sirrah, you are a notable villaine;
you play at Cards, and lose your fathers sheepe at
one and thirty.   The Boy replied, that it was a lye.
A lye, quoth the Justice, you saucy knaue, dost thou

giue me the lye ? No, qd. the boy, I gaue not you the lye, but you told me the lye : for I neuer lost sheepe at one and thirty : for, when my game was one and thirty I always wonne. Indeed, said the justice, thou saist true; but I have another accusation against thee, which is, that you driue your fathers sheepe ouer a narrow bridge, where some of them are oftentimes drowned. That's a lye too, quoth the boy : for those that go ouer the bridge are well enough ; it is onely those that fall beside, which are drowned. Whereto the Justice said to the boys father: old man, thou hast brought in two false accusations against thy sonne : for he neuer lost sheepe at one and thirty : nor were there euer any drowned, that went ouer the bridge.

### (20.)
### *A Quiblet.*

A CAPTAINE, passing through a roome where a woman was driuing a buck of clothes, but he thinking she had been brewing, saw a dish, and dipped some small quantity of the lye,[1] which he, supposing to be mault-wort, dranke vp, and presētly began to swear, spit, spatter and spaule.

(1) A composition used in washing, which may be found described in the Dictionaries. The older form of the word was *ley*. Thus, in the *Mery Tales of Skelton*, 1567, we find *hote ley* for *hot lye*.

The woman asked him what he ayled. He told her, and called her some scurvy names, saying, he had swallowed Lye. Nay, then I cannot blame you to be angry : for you being a souldier and a Captaine, it must needs trouble your stomacke to swallow the Lye.

### (21.)

A COUNTRY fellow (that had not walked much in streets that were paued) came to London, where a dog came suddenly out of a house, and furiously ran at him. The fellow stooped to take vp a stone to cast at the Dog, and finding them all fast rammed or paued in the ground, quoth hee : what strange country am I in, where the people tye vp the stones, and let the dogs loose.

### (22.)

AN honest Mayor of a Towne, being all Mercy and no Justice, louing ease and quietness, and vnwilling to commit any offence or offender : one said of him that hee was like the herbe *John* in a pottage pot : for that herbe did not giue any taste at all either good or bad, but an excellent colour ; so the Mayor did neither good nor harme, but (as an image of a Mayor's authority) filled up the roome.

(23.)

A JUSTICE of the Peace, being angry with a pilfer-
ing Knaue, said : Sirrah, if thou dost not mend thy
manners, thou wilt be shortly hanged, or else I
will be hanged for thee. The bold knaue replyed :
I thanke your worship for that kind offer, and I
beseech your worship not to be out of the way,
when I shall haue occasion to vse you.

(24.)

CERTAINE Justices of the Peace,[1] being informed
of the odious abuses daily committed by drunkennesse in their Jurisdictions, did, according to their
places and duties, meet at a market towne, and
sate two dayes, hearing informations, and working
reformations. At last, they concluded that the Ale
and Beere were too strong, and therefore commanded that from thence forth smaller drinke
should bee brewed, whereby these vnruly people
might sometimes goe to bed sober. But one mad
tospot fellow being much grieued at this order,
hauing made himselfe halfe pot-shaken, without

---

(1) Of the extent to which habits of intoxication were carried in
England in Taylor's time by both sexes, a pretty good notion is derived
from the pamphlets of the period. See Ward's *Woe to Drunkards*,
1622, 8vo.

feare or wit came to the Justices, and asked them, if they had sate two dayes about the brewing of small drinke; to whom one of the Justices replyed: yes. Why, then, quoth the drunkard, I pray you sit three daies more to know who shall drinke it : for I will none of it.

### (25.)

THERE was a Scottish Gentleman that had sore eyes, who was counselled by his Physitians to forbeare drinking of wine ; but hee said hee neither could nor would forbeare it, maintaining it for the lesser euill, to shut vp the windowes of his body, then to suffer the house to fall downe, through want of reparations.[1]

### (26.)

VPON the death of Queene Elizabeth, there was a Mayor of a Country Towne sitting in consultation with his Brethren, to whom he grauely said : My Brethren and Neighbours, I doe heare that the Queene is dead, wherefore I thought it exceeding fit wee should despaire to this place that, being, dessembled together, we might consult of our estates :

---

1) This jest appears to be imitated from the *Merie Tales & Quicke Answeres*, No. 88. See that Tale, and the note attached to it, and also he *Pleasant Conceits of Old Hobson*, 1607 (*suprà*, p. 45).

for I doubt mee wee shall haue another Queene or a King, and I stand in great feare that the people will be vnrude, so that wee shall bee in danger of strange Resurrection.

## (27.)

ANOTHER Mayor that was on hunting, (by chance) one asked him how hee liked the Cry. A p** take the Dogs! saith hee, they make such a bawling, that I cannot heare the Cry.

## (28.)

AN old Justice was fast asleepe on the Bench, when poore Malefactor was judged to bee hanged ; at which word the Justice suddenly awaked and said to the Thiefe : *my friend, I pray let this bee a warning to you; looke you doe so no more, for wee doe not show euery man the like fauour.*

## (29.)

AN old Recorder of a Citty in this Land was busie with a Country Mayor. In the meane space, they were interrupted by a fellow that was brought before him for killing of a man. My Lord asked the fellowes name, who answered, his name was

*Gilman.* Said my Lord : take away *G,* and thy name is *Ilman;* put *K* to it, thy name is *Kilman,* and put to [it] *Sp* and thy name is *Spilman. Thou art halfe hang'd already* (as the prouerbe sayes) : for thou hast an ill name, let a man vary it how hee can.

The Mayor all this while stood by musing at my Lords canuassing the mans name, and afterward being at home among his owne good people, he had an offender brought before him for getting a wench with child. Master Mayor asked him his name. The fellow said : if it please your worship my name is *Johnson.* Then Master Mayor (striuing to imitate my Lord) said : take away *G* and thy name is *Ilman,* put *K* to it, it is *Kilman,* put *Sp* to it, and thy name is *Spilman ;* thou art a knaue ; thou hast an ill name, and thou shalt bee hanged, &c.

(30.)

*A Quiblet.*

MASTER Field the Player,[1] riding vp Fleet street a great pace, a Gentleman called him, and asked him, what Play was played that day. Hee (being

---

(1) Nathaniel Field, the author and actor. A copious account of him will be found in Collier's *Memoirs of Shakespearian Actors,* 1846.

angry to be stayd vpon so friuoulous a demand)
answered, that he might see what Play was to be
playd vpon euery Poste. I cry you mercy (said the
Gentleman), I tooke you for a Poste, you road so
faste.

### (31.)

ONE, being long vexed with the spirit of jealousie,
came suddenly into his house, and found a man
(whom he suspected) somewhat too busie with his
wife ; to whom hee said : now, good fellow, I
thanke thee : for thou hast cured me of a strange
hellish torment; my suspition is cleared; and
apparent knowledge hath giuen mee such ease of
heart, that I will be jealous no more.

### (32.)

A SKILFULL Painter was requested to paint out a
faire Courtezan (in plaine English, a W****). I pray
you spare that cost, said the Painter : for, if shee
be a right w****, she daily paints herselfe.

### (33.)

SEIGNEUR *Valdrino* (pay-master to the Campe of
Alphonsus, King of Aragon), a man exquisite in
Courtship and compliment : as two or three were

at strife laying wagers what Countryman he was,
a blunt bold Captaine asked what was the matter.
Why Captaine, said one, we are laying a wager
what Countriman my Lord Treasurer Valdrino is.
Oh, said the Captaine, I can tell you that ; I am
sure he was borne in the land of Promise : for I
haue serued the King in his wars these seuen
yeeres without pay, and euer when I petition to
my Lord, he payes me with no coyne but promises,
which makes me halfe assured that hee is that
Countryman.

### (34.)

A NOBLEMAN of France (as hee was riding) met
with a yeoman of the Country, to whom he said :
my friend, I should know thee, I doe remember I
haue often seene thee. My good Lord, said the
Countriman, I am one of your Honers poore
tenants, and my name is T. I. I remember thee
better now (said my Lord); there were two brothers
of you, but one is dead ; I pray which of you doth
remaine aliue ?

### (35.)

THE aforesaid Noble man hauing had a Harper
that was blinde, playing to him after supper some-

what late, at last hee arose, and commanded one
of his seruants to light the Harper downe the
staires, to whom the Serving-man sayd : my Lord,
the Harper is blind. Thou ignorant knaue, quoth
my Lord, he hath the more need of light.

### (36.)

A YOUNG fellow wisht himselfe the richest Cuckold in England, to whom his mother said very
angerly : you foolish couetous boy, why dost thou
desire such a wish ; hath not thine owne Father
enough in store for thee ?

### (37.)

A W**** *Rampant* made her husband a Cuckold
*Dormant*, with a front *Cressant*, surprized by the
watch *Guardant*, brought to the Justice *Passant*,
with her play-fellow *Pendant*, after a coursie
*Couchant.* The Justice told her that her offence
was haynous in breaking the bonds of matrimony
in that adulterate manner, and that she should
consider that her husband was her *Head.* Good
sir, quoth shee, I did euer acknowledge him so,
and I hope it is no such great fault in me, for I
was but trimming, dressing, or ad-horning my
*Head.*

3. H

### (38.)

A MAN being very sickly, one said to his wife : I maruell your husband doth not weare a night-cap. Truly (quoth shee), within this six monthes that my husband hath bin sicke, although his legges be shrunke, yet hee hath outgrowne all his night-caps.

### (39.)

A BOY, whose mother was noted to be one not ouer laden with honesty, went to seeke his Godfather, and enquiring for him, quoth one to him : who is thy Godfather ? The boy repli'd : his name is good-man Digland the Gardiner. Oh, said the man, if he be thy Godfather, he is at the next alehouse; but I feare thou takest Gods name in vaine.[1]

### (40.)

A SCHOLLER, riding from Cambridge towards London, his horse being tyred (a lazie disease often befalling such hacknies), met a Poste on the way, who, notwithstanding he did what he could to make

(1) It is scarcely necessary to mention that this anecdote is elsewhere applied to no less persons than Shakespeare and Sir William Davenant, the latter speaking of the great dramatist as his godfather, and being reproved as above.   But the term *godfather* was not always used in so strict a sense formerly as now.   See Rich's *Farewell to Militarie Profession*, 1581 (Shakesp. Soc. repr. p. 28).

his horse giue him place, by spurre, switch and bridle: yet the Poste was faine to giue him the way; to whom (in anger) he said: thou paltry fellow, dost thou not see I am a Poste? The Scholler straight replyed: and thou ignorant fellow, dost thou not see that I ride vpon a Poste?

### (41.)

A FELLOW, hauing more drinke than wit, in a winter euening made a foolish vowe, to take the wall of as many as hee met betwixt the Temple-bar and Charing-crosse; and comming neere the Sauoy, where stood a Poste a little distance from the wall, the drunkard tooke it for a man, and would haue the wall, beginning to quarrell and giue the Poste foule words; at which a man came by, and asked the matter, and whom he spake to. He answered, hee would haue the wall of that fellow that stood so stifly there. My friend, said the other, that is a Poste, you must giue him the way. Is it so? said the fellow, a p** vpon him; why did he not blow his horne?

### (42.)

A SAYLOR being on a tyred horse, riding from Douer to London, his company prayed him to ride faster:

to whom he answered : I can come no faster ; doe
you not see that I am be calm'd ?

### (43.)

Two Gentlemen were jesting, and one of them cast
away the others hat ; but the other catcht his hat
off, and put it on his owne head.  Now fie, fie,
quoth the other, thou spoylest my hat.  Wherewith ?
said the other.  Marry (said hee that was bear-
headed), thou spoylest my hat with putting a calues
head into it.

### (44.)

### The Figure Conuersion.

If a Vintner doth draw me good wine vpon money
or credit, then hee is fitter to draw then hang ; but
if he draw me bad wine for good money, then hee
is much fitter to hang then to draw.

### (45.)

A man hauing beene with a Doctor of Physicke to
haue his aduise about some griefe he had, when
he came home, his wife asked him, what newes.
Marry, said he, my Physician doth counsell me to
drinke Asses milke euery morning fasting.  Why,
husband, quoth the Woman, I pray you tell me,
doth Master Doctor give sucke ?

## (46.)

A BRAUE and valiant Captaine, whom I could name, had a scarfe giuen him here in England, and he sayling ouer into the Low-Countryes, an old Romane Catholike Lady of his acquaintance was very importunate to beg his scarfe of him. The Captaine asked her what shee would doe with it, and said it was not fit for her wearing. Shee answered him that, if he would giue it her, that Jesus Christ should weare it in the Church vpon holy daies, meaning the Image. Madam, said the Captaine, if you will bring me word, that euer his father wore such a scarfe, then I will giue you this for him.

## (47.)

BETWEENE the houres of twelve and óne at noone, one asked mee what it was a clock : I answered him, it was little or nothing. Hee demaunded of me what I meant by my answer. I reply'd that, it being not one of the clocke, it was to bee reckned or counted for nought: for that, which is lesser then one, is little or nothing.

## (48.)

A GENTLEWOMAN[1] cheapned a Close-stoole in Pauls Church-yard, and the shop-keeper did aske her too much money for it, as shee thought. Why, mistris, said hee, I pray you consider what a good locke and key it hath. Shee replyed, that shee had small vse for either locke or key: for she purposed to put nothing into it, but what shee cared not who stole out.

## (49.)

A COUNTREY woman at an Assize was to take her oath against a party. The said party entreated the Judge that her oath might not bee taken The Judge demaunded why he excepted against her. My Lord (quoth hee), shee is a Recusant or Romane Catholique, and they hold it no matter of conscience to sweare any thing against vs. Come hither, woman, said the Judge, I doe not thinke thou art a Recusant; I am perswaded, that for fourty shillings thou wilt sweare the Pope is a knaue. Good my Lord, said shee, the Pope is a stranger to mee; but, if I knew him as well as I know your Lordship, I would sweare for halfe the mony.[2]

(1) This silly and coarse story is copied in *Laugh and Be Fat* (1801), 12°, p. 9.

(2) The practice of perjury which, it is well known, formerly prevailed to a much larger extent than at present in our courts of justice, has sup-

## (50.)

A CARDINALL kept a knauish foole for his recreation, to whom hee said : sirrah foole, suppose that
all the world were dead but thou and I, and that
one of vs should be turned to a Horse, and the
other of vs to an Asse ; say, which of these two
wouldest thou choose to bee ? The foole answered :
Sir, you are my master, and for that respect it is fit
that your worship should choose first, and I will
be contented to take that which you leaue. Why
then, said the Cardinall, I would bee a horse. No,
said the foole, let me intreat your worship to bee
an Asse : for I would bee an Asse to chuse of all
things. Why ? quoth the Cardinall. Marry, said the
foole, because that I haue knowne many Asses
come to bee Justices ; but I neuer knew any horse
come to the like preferment.

## (51.)

A GRAUE discreet Gentleman had[1] a comely wife,
whose beauty and free behauiour did draw her
honesty into suspition, by whom hee had a sonne
almost at mans estate, of very dissolute and wanton

plied the compilers of jest-books with a good deal of material for their
purpose. A story is told somewhere of a counsel who on one occasion
received a Roland for his Oliver from a country witness for taunting him
with venality.

(1) Old ed. has *having.*

carriage. I muse, said one, that a man of such
stayd and moderate grauity should haue a sonne
of such a contrary and froward disposition. Sir,
reply'd another, the reason is that his pate is stuffed
with his Mothers wit, that there is no roome for
any of his fathers wisedome; besides, the light-
nesse of her heeles is gotten into her sonnes
braines.

### (52.)

A RICH Grasier dwelling 150 miles from Oxford,
hauing a sonne that had seuen yeeres beene a
student there, at last sent for him home, to whom
hee said : sonne, I doe heare that you are well
practised in the rudiments of learning, but that
withall you are addicted to an idle veine of the
poore and threadbare art of Poetry, which I
charge thee to leaue and auoyd, as thou tenderest
my fauour : for my mind is not to haue thee liue
beggerly, and dye poorely. Yet I will ask thee one
Poeticall question, which is : wherefore thinkest
thou that so beautifull a creature as Venus was so
besotted to match her selfe with so ill fauored a
knaue as Vulcan? In truth, father, quoth the young
man, I can yeeld you no reason for it; but I wonder
at it; and yet I doe admire as much, wherefore my
mother married with you.

## (53.)

A MAN, going with his Wife by a deepe riuer side, began to talke of Cuckolds, and withall he wisht that euery Cuckold were cast into the riuer; to whom his wife replyes : husband, I pray you learne to swimme.

## (54.)

A MAN [was] riding through a village with his dog running by him, which dogs name was called Cuckold, leaping and frisking into euery house hee past by where the doore was open. Whereupon the man, being afraid his dogge would bee lost, cals and whistles : here, here, Cuckold ! to whom an old woman said : whom dost thou miscall ? I would haue thee know that no Cuckold doth dwell in this house. Good woman, said the man, you mistake mee ; I doe call nobody but my dog. Now out vpon thee, thou misbeleeuing knaue, said shee, where learnest thou that manners to call a dog by a christian bodies name ?

## (55.)

[THERE was] a Lusty Miller that, in his younger daies had beene much giuen to the flesh and the deuill ; so that not one pretty maid or female seruant did or could bring grist to his mill to be grownd, but the knaue miller would doe his best to vndermine and blow vp their chastity, and withall hee would bargaine with as many as his temptations ouercame that, at his day of marriage, euery one of them should giue him a cake. In process of time the miller was married, and those aforesaid free-hearted wenches sent each one their cakes, to the number of 99. His wife the Bride, who also went for a maid, did muse and aske what was the meaning of so many cakes. The miller told her the truth of all without any dissembling, to whom his wife answered : if I had beene so wise in bargaining as you have beene in your time, the young men of my acquaintance would haue sent me 100 cheeses to eat with your cakes.[1]

*This bawdy Miller in a trap was catch[t],*
*Not onely married, but most fitly match[t] :*
*In this the prouerb is approued plaine,*
*What bread men breake, is broke to them againe.*

### (56.)

THERE was a faire ship of two hundred tuns lying at the Tower-wharfe at London, where a Country-man passing by most earnestly looked on the said

---

(1) See *Merie Tales and Quicke Answeres*, No. 73.

ship, and demanded how old shee was. One made
answer that she was a yeere old. Good Lord blesse
mee, said the Country-man, is shee so big growne
in one yeere! what a greatnesse will shee bee by
that time shee comes to my age!

> *This mans blind ignorance I may compare*
> *To* Aqua vitæ *giuen* to a Mare :
> *Let each man his owne calling then apply,*
> Ne sutor vltra crepidam, *say* I.

### (57.)

TWELUE Schollers [were] riding together, [and] one
of them said : my masters, let vs ride faster. Why,
quoth another, me thinks wee ride a good pace,
I'l warrant it is foure mile an houre. Alas, said
the first, what is foure mile an hour amongst all vs?

> *Let not man boast of wit or learning deepe:*
> *For ignorance may out of knowlidge creepe.*
> *Amongst* 12 *men* 4 *mile an houre to ride :*
> *He that hath wit, to each his share diuide.*

### (58.)

AN Apprentice in the market did aske the price of
an hundred Oysters. His friend perswaded him not
to buy them, for they were too small. Too small!

replyed the Prentice, there is not much loss in that :
for I shall haue the more to the hundred.

> *If vp the hill a measur'd mile it be,*
> *Then downe the hill's another mile, I see:*
> *A groat to pay, 4 pence will quit the cost;*
> *What's won in t'hundred, in the shire is lost.*

### (59.)

SIXE Gentlemen riding together were in doubt that
they were out of their way ; wherefore they rode a
slight shot to an old shepheard, one of them enquiring of him if that were the way to such a town,
and how far it was thither. Sir, quoth the Shepheard, that is the right way, and you haue sixe
miles thither. Quoth one of the Gentlemen : what
a lying old knaue art thou! it cannot be aboue foure
miles. The Shepheard reply'd : Sir, you offer like a
chapman, and you shall haue it for foure miles ; but
Ile assure you it shall cost euery one of these Gentlemen sixe miles, before they come thither.[1]

(1) This story is found in other jest-books. See Thoms' *Anecdotes and
Traditions*, 1839, p, 32, where it is No. 56 of *The Merry Passages and
Jests*, collected by Sir Nicholas L'Estrange. This particular anecdote
Sir Nicholas notes as having from " Brother Spring," *i.e.* L'Estrange's
brother-in-law, Sir William Spring, created a baronet in 1641. Whence
Taylor derived the story, it is hard to tell : but he seems entitled to be regarded as the earlier authority in this case, since his *Wit and Mirth*
was printed in 1630, when L'Estrange was not more than 27. We need
scarcely observe that the point is not very material.

*Here rashnesse did the Gallants tongue o'rship,*
*To whom the Shepheard gaue a pleasing nip:*
*Thus softest fire doth make the sweetest Mault,*
*And mild reproofes makes rashness see his fault.*

### (60.)

A MAN was very angry with his maid, because his eggs were boyled too hard. Truely, said she, I haue made them boyle a long houre; but the next you haue shall boyle two houres, but they shall be tender enough.

*The boyling of this wenches eggs, I find,*
*Much like vnto a greedy mizers mind:*
*The eggs the more they boyle are harder still,*
*The mizer's full, too full: yet wants his fill.*

### (61.)

Two learned good-fellowes [were] drinking a pipe of Tobacco. It being almost out, that he that drunke last did partly feele the ashes to come hot to his lippes, giuing the pipe to his friend, said: Ashes to Ashes. The other, taking the pipe and being of a quicke apprehension, threw it out to the dunghill, saying, Earth to Earth.

*Thus wit with wit agrees like cake and cheese;*
*Both sides are gainers, neither side doth leese.*

*Conceit begets conceit,—jest jest doth father,*
*And butter falne to ground doth something gather.*


### (62.)

ONE said, a Cittizen was a man all in earnest, and in no part like a jest; because the Citizen was neuer bad, or the jest neuer good, till they were both broke.

*What's one mans yea, may be anothers nay;*
*The Sun doth soften wax, and harden clay:*
*Some Citizens are like to jests; for why,*
*They'll breake in jest, or bankrupt policy.*


### (63.)

A GALLANT with a galloping wit was mounted vpon a running horse toward a town named Tame, within ten miles of Oxford, and riding at full speed, he met an old man, and asked him : sirrah, is this the way to Tame? Yes, sir, hee replyde, your Horse, I'l warrant you, if hee were as wild as the diuell.

*This is a ridle to a foole, me thinks,*
*And seemes to want an* Oedipus *or* Sphinx,
*But, Reader, in my booke I hold it fit* [1]
*To find you lines; your selfe must find you wit.*

(1) *i. e.* sufficient.

## (64.)

A COMPLEMENTAL Courtier that in his French, Italian, and Spanish cringes, congès and courtesies, would bend his body, and bow euery way like a tumbler, a Mercers servant espying his marmositicall Apishnesse, said : Oh, if my master could haue bowed but halfe so much, I am certainly perswaded that hee had neuer broke.

*Too much of one thing oft proues good for nothing,*
*And dainties in satiety breed lothing :*
*Th' ones flattery, mingled with the others pride,*
*Had serued them both, both might liue long vnspide.*

## (65.)

I MY selfe gaue a booke to King James once in the Great Chamber at Whitehall as his Maiesty came from the Chappell. The Duke of Richmond[1] said merrily vnto me : Taylor, where did you learne the manners to giue the King a booke, and not kneele? My Lord, said I, if it please your Grace, I doe giue now ; but when I beg any thing, then I will kneele.

(1) Lodovick, or Lewis, Stuart, Duke of Richmond and Lennox, ob. 1624. Taylor wrote an elegy on him under the title of *True Loving Sorrow*, &c. which is printed in his *Works*, 1630, vol. ii. p. 333. The event was also commemorated in a poem by Abraham Darcie the annalist. See *Autob. of Sir S. D'Ewes*, i. 241, and Burn's *Parish Registers*.

*Be it to all men by these presents knowne,*
*Men need not kneele to giue away their owne.*
*Ile stand vpon my feet, when as I giue,*
*And kneele, when as I beg more meanes to liue;*
*But some by this may vnderstand,*
*That Courtiers oftener kneele than stand.*

(66.)

THE trayned Souldiers of a certaine Shire which I could name, to the number of 6000, as they were mustring and drilling vnder their seuerall Captaines, a yeomans sonne being there as a raw souldier in his corslet, his father standing by, said : I vaith, it does mee much good at heart to zee how trim a vellow my zonne is in his hardnesse.[1] The young fellow, hearing his fathers commendations of him, began very desperately to shake his pike, and looking exceeding grim, said, with a fearfull, horrible, terrible countenance : O vather, chad lather[2] nor a groat that all wee had but one Spaniard here,

*One Spaniard mongst 6000 pitty twere,*
*Better ten thousand Britains bold were there,*
*Led by braue Leaders, that might make Spain quake,*
*Like Vere, or Morgan, Essex, Blunt, or Drake.*

(1) *i.e.* harness.
(2) *i. e.* rather.  Apparently a Shropshire provincialism : for in a copy of the *Tale of the Basyn,* supposed to be in the Salopian dialect, we find *lother* for *the other* or *t'other.*

## (67.)

ONE said, that hee 'could neuer haue his health in *Cambridge*, and that if hee had liued there till this time, hee thought in his conscience that hee had dyed seuen yeeres agoe.

*I will not say the man that spake so, ly'd ;*
*Seuen yeeres agoe, no doubt, hee might haue dy'd :*
*He by his trade perhaps might be a dyer,*
*And daily dy'd to liue, and him no lyer.*

## (68.)

A COUNTRY fellow was much grieued that hee had not gone seuen miles to a market towne to haue seene the Baboones. Why, said his wife, it is too farre to goe and come in a day to see such bables; especially 'tis too great a journey on foot. O, quoth hee, I could haue gone thither with my neighbour Hobson on foot, like a foole as I was, and I might haue rid backe vpon my neighbour Jobsons mare, like an ass as I am.

*Thus in the* preter tense *a* foole *he was,*
*And in the* present tense *he is an* Asse ;
*And in the* future foole *and* asse *shall bee,*
*That goes or rides so far such sights to see.*

## · (69.)

THERE was a lusty young Scholler preferred to a Benefice in the Country, and commonly on

Sundayes and holy-dayes, after euening prayer, hee
would haue a dozen bouts at cudgels with the
sturdiest youths in his parish. The Bishop of the
Diocesse, hearing of it, sent for the parson, telling
him that this beseemed not his profession and
grauity, and if that he did not desist from that
vnmeet kind of exercise, he would vnbenefice him.
Good my Lord (said the Parson), I beseech you
to conceiue rightly of mee, and I doubt not but
my playing at cudgels will be counted tollerable ;
for I doe it of purpose to edifie the ruder sort of
my people. How so ? said the Bishop. Marry, my
Lord (quoth the Parson), whatsoeuer I doe teach
them at morning and euening prayer, I doe beat
soundly into their heads at cudgels afterward, for
their better remembrance.

*I wish that all the Fencers in our Nation*
*Were onely of this* Parsons *congregation :*
*That he his life and doctrine shoulde explaine,*
*By beating them, whilst they beat him againe.*

### (70.)

A JUDGE vpon the Bench did aske an[1] old man· how
old he was. My Lord, said he, I am eight and
fourscore. And why not fourscore and eight ? said
the Judge. The other repli'd : because I was eight,
before I was fourescore.

(1) Old ed. has *as.*

*Eight's before eighty, all men may descry:*
*Yet wee name eighty first contrarily.*
*Pull off my* Boots *and* Spures, *I you beseech,*
*When* Spures *and* Boots *is rather proper speech.*

## (71.)

A FELLOW made his boast, that hee rode 220 miles
with one horse, and neuer drew bit. That may bee
(quoth another); perhaps you rid him with a halter.

*The prouerbe saies : hee that will* swear *will* lie,
*He that will* lie *will* steale *by consequency :*
Swearers *are* lyers, *lyers most are* thieues,
*Or God helpe* Taylors *and true* Vnderthrieues.

## (72.)

ONE saw a decayed Gentleman in a very threedbare cloake, [and] said to him : Sir, you haue a
very watchfull cloake on. Why? said the poore
Gentleman. The other answered: I doe not
thinke it [has] had a good nap this seuen yeeres.
The Gentleman replyed : and truly, sir, mee thinkes
you want a nap as well as my cloake, for you talke
idely for want of sleepe.

*The prodigall at Poverty doth scoffe,*
*Though from his backe the* begger's *not farre off.*
*Here flout with flout and bob with bob is quitted,*
*And proud vain-glorious folly finely fitted.*

## (73.)

A DILIGENT and learned Preacher on a Sunday in the afternoone was preaching, whilest most of the zealous Vestry men (for their meaner edification) were fast asleepe in their pues. In the mean space, a young child cryed somewhat aloud at the lower end of the Church, which the Preacher hearing called to the Nurse, and said : Nurse, I pray thee still thy childe, or else it may chance to awaken some of the best men in our parish.

*Men sleepe at Sermons, sure their braines are adle,*
*Sly Satan lulls them, and doth rocke the cradle :*
*When men thus doe no ill, 'tis vnderstood,*
*The diuell hinders them from doing good.*

## (74.)

A CHORISTER or singing man, at service in a Cathedrall Church, was asleepe, when all his fellowes were singing ; which the Deane espying, sent a boy to him to waken him, and asked him, why hee did not sing. Hee, being suddenly awaked, prayed the boy to thanke master Deane for his kind remembrance, and to tell him that hee was as merry as those that did sing.

*They say he's wise that can himselfe keepe warme,*
*And that the man that sleeps will think no harme ;*
*He sung not, yet was in a merry mood :*
*Like John Indifferent, did not harme nor good.*

### (75.)

A KIND of clownish gentleman had halfe a Brawne
sent him against Christmas ; hee very liberally gaue
the seruing-man halfe a shilling that brought it ;
the seruing-man gaue the Porter that carried it
eight pence before the gentlemans face. Sirrah,
said hee, are you so prodigall to reward the Porter
with eight pence, when I giue you but sixpence ?
thou bearest the mind of a prodigall Gallant, although
by thy foote thou seemest a lubberly clowne.
Good sir, said the fellow, I confesse I haue a very
clownish lubberly paire of feet, but yet I am perswaded that a paire of your worships shooes would
fit them well.

*Here's* Bore *and* Brawne *together are well met,*
*He knew that giuing was no way to get;*
*The world gets somewhat by the prodigall,*
*When as the* mizer *gets the diuell and all.*

### (76.)

A GRIPING Extortioner, that had beene a maker of
beggers for the space of forty yeeres, and by raising

rents, and oppression, had vndone many families, saies on a time in anger to a poore fellow that had stolen a sheepe of his : ah, villaine, darest thou rob mee ; I vow and sweare there is not so d——d a rogue in the world as thou. To whom the fellow answered : I beseech your good worship remember your selfe, and bee good to me for Gods sake and for your owne sake.

*This Rascals eye is with a bleame so blinde,*
*That in the poore mans hee a moat can find;*
*The* Wolfe *himselfe a temperate feeder deems,*
*And euery man too much himself esteemes.*

## (77.)

A SERUING man and his mistris was landing at the Whitefryars stayers ; the stayers being very bad, a waterman offered to helpe the woman, saying : giue me your hand, Gentlewoman ; Ile helpe you. To whom her man replyed : you saucy fellow, place your words right ; my mistres is no Gentlewoman ; shee is a Lady.

*All is not gold (they say) that glitters bright,*
*Snow is not sugar, though it looke as white :*
*And 'tis approued to be true and common,*
*That every Lady's not a Gentlewoman.*

(78.)

A SERUINGMAN going in haste in *London* (minding his businesse more than his way), a Gallant justled him from the wall almost into the kennell. The fellow turned about, and asked the Gentleman why hee did justle him so. The Gentleman said : because hee would not give the wall to a saucy knave. The Seruingman replyed : your worship is not of my mind, for I will.

*Here Pride, that takes Humility in snuffe,*
*Is well encountred with a counter buffe,*
*One would not giue the wall vnto a knaue,*
*The other would, and him the wall he gaue.*

(79.)

A JUSTICE of the Peace was very angry with a country yeoman, because hee came not to him at his first sending for him ; and after he had bountifully bestowed two or three dozen of knaues vpon him, hee said to him : Sirrah, I will make you know, that the proudest saucy knaue that dwels under my command, shall come before mee, when I send for him. I beseech your worship, said the man, to pardon mee, for I was afraid. Afraid of what ? said the Justice. Of your worship, answered the fellow. Of mee, said the Justice ; why wast

thou afraid of mee? Because your worship lookes
so like a Lyon, said the man. A Lyon! quoth the
Justice, when didst thou see a Lyon? May it
please your worship (the fellow replyed), I saw a
Butcher bring one but yesterday to *Colebrooke*
market with a white face, and his foure legs
bound.

> *This fellow was a knaue or foole, or both,*
> *Or else his wit was of but slender growth;*
> *He gaue the white-fac'd* Calfe *the* Lyons *stile,*
> *The Justice was a proper man the while.*

### (80.)

DIUERS Gentlemen being merry together, at last
one of their acquaintance came to them (whose
name was Sampson). Aha, said one of them, now
wee may bee securely merry; no Sergeant or
Bailiffe dare touch vs: for, if a thousand Philistines
come, here is Sampson, who is able to braine them
all. To whom Sampson replyede: Sir, I may boldly
venture against so many as you speake of, prouided that you will lend me one of your jaw bones.

### (81.)

Two Playsterers being at worke for mee at my house
in Southwarke,[1] did many times patch and dawbe

---

1) At one period of his life, the Water-Poet kept an inn there.

out part of their dayes labour with prating; which I, being digging in my garden, did ouer-heare that their chat was of their wiues, and how that if I were able (quoth one), my wife should ride in pompe through London as I saw a Countesse ride yesterday. Why, quoth the other, how did shee ride, I pray? Marry, said hee, in state, in her Horslitter. O base, quoth the other, Horslitter; I protest, as poore a man as I am, I would haue allowed my wife a three-peny trusse of cleane straw.

## (82.)

SIR Edward Dyer [1] came to towne on some businesse, just at the time as the Gate was newly shut, and the Warders going away with the keys. Hee, looking through the gate, called to one of them, saying: Hoe, fellow! I pray thee open the gate and let me in. None of your fellow, Sir, but a poore knaue. Why then, said Sir Edward, I pray thee, poore knaue, let me in. Nay, no knaue neither, quoth the Warder. Why then, said the Knight, hee was a knaue that told me so.

(1) Probably the poet of that name. See Warton's H. E. P. edit. 1824, iv. 99; *Notes and Queries,* 2 S. xi. 163; Aubrey's *Lives,* ii. 338. Davies of Hereford has lines to Dyer in his *Microcosmos,* 1603. Dyer survived till May, 1607. His death probably occurred at his residence in Southwark, where Taylor was once an innkeeper. He was of the same family as Chief Justice Dyer, who died in 1581.

(83)

ONE met his friend in the streete, and told him
he was very sorry to see him looke so ill, asking
him what he ailed.   Hee replyed, that he was now
well amended, but hee had beene lately sicke of
the Poxe.   What Pox, the small pox? said his
friend.   Nay, quoth the other, my minde was not
so base, for I had the bigest pox that I could get
for my money.

(84.)

AN honest Hostesse of mine at Oxford rosted an
old shoulder of a Ram, which in the eating was
as tough as a Buffe Jerkin.   I did aske her what
the reason was that the mutton was so tough.   She
said she knew not, except the Butcher deceiued
her in the age of it, and she would tell him on
both sides of his eares, like a knaue as he was.
Nay, quoth I, I thinke there is another fault in it,
which will excuse the Butcher, for perhaps you
roasted it with old wood.   In troth (quoth the
hostesse) it is like enough, and my husband neuer
doth otherwaies but buy old stumps and knots,
which makes all the meate we either roast or
boyle so exceeding tough that no body can eat it.

(85.)

ONE hearing a clocke strike three when he thought
it was but two, said : This Clocke is like an hypo-
critical Puritane ; for though he will not sweare,
yet hee will lye abbominably.

(86.)

DICKE Tarleton said that hee could compare
Queene Elizabeth to nothing more fitly than to a
Sculler ; for, said he, Neither the Queene nor the
Sculler hath a fellow.[1]

(87.)

Two obstinate rich fellowes in Law (that had each
of them more money than wit), by chance one
of them comming out of Westminster Hall, met
with his adversaries wife, to whom he said : In
troth good woman I doe much pity your case, in
that it is your hard fortune that such a foole as
your husband should have so discreet and modest
[a] wife. The woman replide : In truth Sir, I doe
grieue more that so honest a wife as you have
should have such a wrangling knaue to her husband.

(1) This anecdote is not included in *Tarlton's Jests*, 1611, 4to.

(88.)

A POORE labouring man was married and matched
to a creature that so much vsed to scold waking,
that she had much adoe to refraine it sleeping,
so that the poore man was so battersang'd and
belabour'd with tongue mettle, that he was weary
of his life.  At last, foure or fiue women, that were
his neighbours (pitying his case), came in his
absence to his house, to admonish and counsell
his wife to a quiet behauior towards her husband;
telling her that she was a shame to all good
women, in her bad vsage of so honest a painefull
man.  The woman replyed to her neighbours, that
shee thought her husband did not loue her, which
was partly the cause that she was so froward
towards him.  Why (said an old woman), I will
shew thee how thou shalt proue that he loues thee
dearly; doe thou counterfeit thy selfe dead, and
lye vnder the table, and one of vs will fetch thy
husband, and he shall find vs heavy and grieuing
for thee; by which means thou shalt perceiue by
his lamentation for thee, how much he loues thee.
This counsell was allowed and effected.  When the
poore man came home, he hearing the matter
(being much opprestt with griefe), ranne vnder the
table bemoning the happy losse of his most kind
vexation, and making as though hee would kisse

her with a most louing embrace. To make all
sure, he brake her necke. The neighbours pittying
the mans extreame passion, in compassion told
him that his wife was not dead, and that all this
was done but to make tryall of his loue towards
her : whereupon they called her by her name,
bidding her to rise, and that shee had fooled
it enough with her husband. But for all their
calling, shee lay still ; which made one of the
women to shake and jogge her ; at which the
woman cried, Alas, she is dead indeed ! Why this
it is, quoth the husband, to dissemble and counter-
fet with God and the world.

### (89.) [1]

A PLANTER of a Colledge in Oxford possessing
some crums of Logicke and chippings of Sophistry,
making distribution of bread at the Schollers
table, one of the Schollers complained vnto him
that the bread were dough baked : Why, quoth
hee, so it should bee ; what else is the definition
of bread, but dough baked ?

### (90.)

A MISERABLE fellow in the country did once a
yeare vse to inuite his neighbours to dinner, and

---

(1) In the old ed. this jest is numbered 90 by an error in the nume-
ration, which runs through the remainder of the piece. It is here
corrected.

as they were one time sate, hee bade them welcome, saying, that there was a surloin of beefe,
that the Oxe it came from cost 20 pound, and
that there was a Capon that he paid 2 shillings
6 pence for, in the market : at which, a country
yeoman sitting against the capon, fell to and cut
off a legge of it (the rest of the guests being not
yet past their roast beefe) ; to whom the man of
the house said : My friend, I pray thee eate some
of this same surloin.  O sir, God forbid, quoth the
fellow, I am but a poore man, an oxe of 20 pound
price is too deare meat, a Capon of halfe a crowne
will serve my turne well enough, I thanke you.


## (91.)

A RICH man told his nephew that hee had read a
booke called *Lucius Apuleius of the Golden Asse*,[1]
and that he found there how Apuleius, after he had
beene an asse many yeeres, by eating of Roses
he did recouer his manly shape againe, and was
no more an asse : the young man replied to his
vncle : Sir, if I were worthy to advise you, I would
giue you counsell to eate a salled of Roses once
a weeke yourselfe.

(1) This rich gentleman had probably perused Lucian's work in the
old version by Adlington, first printed in 1566, and frequently republished
between that date and 1639.

(92.)

A FELLOW, hauing beene married but fiue weekes, perceiued his wife to be great with childe, wherefore she desired him to buy a cradle. Shortly after he went to a Faire and bought ten cradles; and being demanded why he bought so many, he answered, that his wife would haue vse for them all in one yeere.

(93.)

A GENTLEMAN vntrust and vnbuttoned in a cold winter morning, a friend of his told him that it was not for his health to goe so open in the raw weather, and that he mused it did not kill him to goe so oft vntrust : to whom the other replyed : Sir, you are of the mind of my Silkeman, Mercer, or Taylor, for they finde fault as you doe, because I goe so much *on trust*, but it is a fault I haue naturally from my parents and kindred, and my creditors tell me that I doe imitate my betters.

(94.)

A JUSTICE of the Peace committed a fellow to prison, and commanded him away three or foure times, but stil the fellow intreated him. Sirrah (said the Justice), must I bid you bee gone so

many times, and will you not goe ? The fellow
answered : Sir, if your worship had bidden mee to
dinner or supper, I should in my poore manners
not haue[1] taken your offer vnder two or three
biddings, therefore I pray you blame me not if I
looke for foure biddings to prison.

### (95.)

A GREAT man kept a miserable house, so that his
seruants did alwaies rise from the table with empty
panches, though cleane-licked platters : truely, said
one of his men, I thinke my Lord will worke
miracles shortly, for though he practise not to
raise the dead, or dispossesse the diuell, yet he
goes about to feed his great family with nothing.

### (96.)

ONE said that Bias the Philosopher was the first
Bowler ; and that euer since the most part of
Bowles doe, in memory of their originall, weare
his badge of remembrance, and very dutifully hold
Bias.  Now to tell you, this Bias was one of the
7 Sages or Wise men of Greece.  My authors
to proue him the inuenter of Bowling, are Sham-
rooke, a famous  Scithian  Gimnosophist  in his

(1) Old ed. reads *to haue.*

ninth booke of Rubbing and Running; of which
opinion Balductus the Theban Oratour seemes to
bee in his third Treatise of Court performances :
the likeliest coniecture is, that it was deuised as
an embleme to figure out the world's folly and
vnconstancy; for though a childe will ride a
sticke or staffe with an imagination that hee is on
horsebacke ; or make pyes of dirt, or houses of
cards, feed with two spoones, and cry for three
pieces of bread and butter, which childish actions
are ridiculous to a man : yet this wise game of
Bowling doth make the fathers surpasse their
children in apish toyes and most delicate dog-
trickes. As first for the postures : first, handle
your Bowle: secondly, aduance your Bowle :
thirdly, charge your Bowle : fourthly, ayme your
Bowle: fiftly, discharge your Bowle : sixtly, plye
your Bowle : in which last posture of plying your
Bowle you shall perceiue many varieties and
diuisions, as wringing of the necke, lifting vp of
the shoulders, clapping of the hands, lying downe
of one side, running after the Bowle, making long
dutifull scrapes and legs (sometimes bareheaded),
entreating him to flee, flee, flee (with pox on't
when 'tis too short) : and though the Bowler bee a
gentleman, yet there hee may meet with attendant
rookes, that sometimes will bee his betters six to

foure, or two to one. I doe not know any thing fitter to bee compared to bowling then wooing or louers ; for if they doe not see one another in two dayes, they will say, Good Lord, it is seuen yeeres since we saw each other! for louers doe thinke that in absence time sleepeth, and in their presence that hee is in a wild gallop. So a Bowler, although the Allye or marke bee but thirty or forty paces, yet sometimes I haue heard the Bowler cry rub, rub, rub, and sweare and lye that hee was gone an hundred miles, when the bowle hath beene short of the blocke two yards—or that hee was too short a thousand foot, when hee is vpon the head of the Jacke, or ten or twelue foot beyond. In a word, there are many more seuerall postures at bowles then there are ridiculous idle tales or jests in my booke. Yet are the bowlers very weake stomackt, for they are euer casting : sometimes they giue the stab at the alley head, but, God be thanked, no bloud shed; and sometimes they bestow a Pippin one vpon the other, but no good Apple, I'l assure you. The marke which they ayme at hath sundry names and epithites, as a Blocke, a Jacke, and a Mistris : a Blocke, because of his birth and breeding, shewing by his mettle of what house he came ; a Jacke, because he being smooth'd and gotten into some

handsome shape, forgets the house hee came of,
suffering his betters to giue him the often salute,
whilest hee, like Jacke sauce, neither knowes himselfe, nor will knowe his superiors. But I hold a
Mistresse to be the fittest name for it; for there
are some that are commonly termed Mistresses,
which are not much better then mine Aunts : and
a Mistris is oftentimes a marke for euery knaue to
haue a fling at ; euery one striues to come so neere·
her that hee would kisse her, and yet some are
short, some wide, and some ouer, and who so
doth kisse, it may perhaps sweeten his lips, but I
assure him it shall neuer fill his belly, but rather
empty his purse. So much for bowling, that I
feare mee I haue bowled beyond the marke.

### (97.)

A MINISTER, riding into the west parts of England,
happened to stay at a village on a Sunday, where
hee offered kindly to bestow a Sermon vpon them :
which the Constable hearing, did ask the Minister
if he were licēced to preach. Yes, quoth hee, that
I am ; and with that hee drew out of a box his
Licence, which was in Latine. Truly, said the
Constable, I vnderstand no Latine, yet I pray you
let mee see it ; I perhaps shall picke out heere and

there a word. No, good Sir, quoth the Minister, I will haue no words pickt out of it, for spoyling my Licence.

## 𝔄 𝔒𝔩𝔦𝔫𝔠𝔥.

A COUNTRY MAN being demanded how such a Riuer was called, that ranne through their Country, hee answered that they neuer had need to call the Riuer, for it alwayes came without calling.

A FELLOW hauing his booke at the Sessions, was burnt in the hand, and was commanded to say : God saue the King. The King! said hee; God saue my Grandam, that taught me to read, I am sure I had bin hanged else.

## 𝔄 𝔱𝔬𝔶 𝔱𝔬 𝔪𝔬𝔠𝔨𝔢 𝔞𝔫 𝔄𝔭𝔢.

IN Queene Elizabeths dayes, there was a fellow that wore a brooch in his hat, like a tooth drawer, with a Rose and Crow[n]e and two letters : this fellow had a warrant from the Lord Chamberlaine at that time to trauell with an exceeding braue Ape, which hee had ; whereby hee gat his liuing from time to time at markets and fayres. His Ape did alwayes ride vpon a mastiffe dog, and a man with a drum to attend him. It happened that these foure trauellers came to a towne called Looe, in Cornwall, where the Inne being taken, the drum went about to signifie to the people, that at such a Inne was an Ape of singular vertue and quality, if they pleased to bestow their time and money to see him. Now the townsmen being honest labouring Fishers, and [of] other painfull functions, had no leasure to waste either time or coyne in Ape-tricks, so that no audience came to the Inne, to the great griefe of Jack an Apes his master : who, collecting his wits together, resolued to aduenture to put a tricke vpon the towne, whatsoeuer came of it ; whereupon hee tooke pen, inke and paper, and wrote a warrant to the Mayor of the towne, as followeth :—

*These are to will and require you, and euery of you, with your wiues and families, that vpon the sight hereof, you make your personall appearance before the Queenes Ape, for it is an Ape of ranke and quality, who is to bee practised through her Majesties dominions, that by his long experience amongst her louing subjects, hee may bee the better enabled to doe her Majesty seruice hereafter ; and hereof faile you not, as you will answer the contrary. &c.*

This warrant being brought to the Mayor, hee
sent for a shoomaker, at the furthest end of the
towne, to read it : which when he heard, hee sent
for all his brethren, who went with him to the
towne Hall to consult vpon this waighty businesse.
Where after they had sate a quarter of an houre,
no man saying anything, nor any man knowing
what to say : at last a young man, that neuer had
borne any office, said : Gentlemen, if I were fit to
speake, I thinke (without offence, vnder correction
of the worshipful) that I should soone decide this
businesse ; to whom the Mayor said : I pray, good
neighbour, speake, for though you neuer did beare
any office here, yet you may speake as wisely as
some of vs. Then, sir, said the young man, my
opinion is that this Ape carrier is a gybing scoffing
Knaue, and one that doth purpose to make this
towne a jesting mocking stocke throughout the
whole kingdome : for was it euer knowne that a
fellow should be so impudent audacious as to send
a warrant, without either name or date, to a Mayor
of a towne, to the Queenes Lieutenant, and that
he with his brethren, their wiues and families,
should bee all commanded to come before a Jack
an Apes ? My counsell is, that you take him and
his Ape, with his man and his dog, and whip the
whole messe or murrinall of them out of the

towne, which I thinke will be much for your credit, if you doe.

At which words, a graue man of the towne being much moued, said : My friend, you haue spoken little better than treason; for it is the Queenes Ape, and therefore beware what you say. You say true, said master Mayor; I muse who bad that saucy fellow come into our company. I pray thee, my friend, depart; I thinke you long to haue vs all hanged. So in briefe hee was put out of the doores, for they were no company for him. Well now what is to bee done in this matter? Marry (said another Senior), wee see by the Brooch in the mans hat that hee is the Queenes man, and who knows what power a knaue may haue in the Court to doe poore men wrong in the country? Let vs goe and see the Ape, it is but two pence a peece, and no doubt but it will be well taken; and if it come to the Queenes eare, shee will thinke vs kinde people that would shew so much duty to her Ape; what may she thinke wee would doe to her Beares, if they came hither? besides, it is aboue 2co miles to London, and if wee should bee complained on, and fetched vp with Pursiuants, whereas now euery man may escape for his two pence, Ile warrant it would cost vs ten groats a peece at the least. This counsell passed currant,

and all the whole droue of the townsmen, with
wiues and children, went to see the Ape, who was
sitting on a table with a chaine about his necke;
to whom master Mayor (because it was the
Queenes Ape) put off his hat, and made a leg;
but Jacke let him passe vnregarded. But Mistris
Mayoresse, comming next in her cleane linnen,
held her hands before her belly, and, like a woman
of good breeding, made a low curtsie, whilst Jack
(still Court-like), although [hee] respected not the
man, yet to expresse his courtesie to his wife, hee
put forth his paw towards her and made a mouth,
which the woman perceiuing, said: Husband, I doe
thinke in my conscience that the Queenes Ape
doth mocke mee : whereat Jacke made another
mouth at her, which master Mayor espying, was
very angry, saying: Sirrah, thou Ape, I doe see thy
saucinesse, and if the rest of the courtiers haue
no more manners then thou hast, then they haue
all bin better fed then taught : and I will make
thee know before thou goest from hence, that this
woman is my wife, an ancient woman, and a
midwife, and one that may bee thy mother for age.

In this rage Master Mayor went to the Inne
doore, where Jack-an-Apes tutor was gathering
of money, to whom hee said: Sir, doe you allow
your Ape to abuse my wife ? No, sir, quoth the

other, not by any meanes. Truly, said the Mayor, there is witnesse enough within that haue seene him make mops and mowes at her, as if shee were not worthy to wipe his shooes, and I will not so put it vp. Jacks tutor replyed : Sir, I will presently giue him condigne punishment : and straight hee tooke his Flanders blade, his whip, and holding his Ape by the chaine, hee gaue him halfe a dozen jerks, which made his teeth daunce in his head like so many virginall Jackes. Which master Mayor perceiuing, ranne to him, and held his hands, saying: Enough, enough, good sir, you haue done like a Gentleman, let mee intreat you not to giue correction in your wrath : and I pray you and your Ape, after the Play is done, to come to my house, and sup with mee and my wife.

(101.)

*This Tale I writ on purpose to sticke in the teeth of*
*my proud, sqeamish, nice, criticall reader.*

A COUNTRY man brought his wiues water to a Physitian, saying : Good·morrow to your worship, master Confusion. Physitian thou wouldst say, said the other. Truly, said the fellow, I am no scholler, but altogether vnrude; and very ingrum, and I haue here my wiues water in a potle pot, beseeching your mastership to cast it. So the

Physitian tooke the water, which hauing put into
an vrinall and viewed it, hee said : My friend, thy
wife is very weake.  Truly, quoth hee, I thinke shee
bee in a presumption.  A consumption thou wouldst
say, said the Physitian.  I told you before, the
fellow replyed, that I doe not vnderstand your
allegant speeches.  Well, quoth the Doctor, doth
thy wife keepe her bed ?  No, truly, sir, said hee ;
shee sold her bed a fortnight since.  Verily, quoth
the Doctor, shee is very costiue.  Costly, said the
man, your worship sayes true, for I haue spent all
that I haue vpon her almost.  Said the Doctor : I
doe not say costly but costiue ; and I pray thee
tell mee, is shee loose or bound ?  Indeed, Sir,
said the man, shee is bound to mee during her
life, and I am bound to her.  Yea, but I pray
thee, said the Doctor, tell mee in plaine termes
how shee goes to stoole.  Truly, said the fellow, in
plaine termes shee goes to stoole very strangely, for
in the morning it is so hard that your Worship can
scarce bite it with your teeth, and at night it is so
thin that you might eat it with a spoone.

### (102.)

[SOME] good fellowes hauing well washed their wits
in wine at a tauerne, one of them was importunate
to bee gone ; to whom another of them said : I

pray thee be patient, talke no more of going, for if thou wilt sit still but a little, thou shalt find that we shal all be gone, though wee stay here.

(103.)

AN IDEOT, who dwelt with a rich vncle he had, was by a Courtier begged for a foole; which the foole perceiuing, ranne home to his vncles Parlour, which was fairly hung with Tapestry hangings, and in euery one of the hangings was the figure of a foole[1] wrought. So the foole watching his oportunity, that no body was in the Parlour, hee tooke a knife and cut the fooles pictures out of euery hanging, and went and hid them in a hay mow, which when his vncle came in and saw, hee was

(1) See Thom's *Anecdotes and Traditions* (Camden Society, 1839), p. 7. One of the Stories which Sir Nicholas Lestrange includes among his "Merry Passages and Jests" is an account how the Lord North begged old Bladwell for a foole (*though he could never prove him so*). "Old Bladwell" was probably a member of the wealthy Norfolk family of that name, and no doubt the Lord North had a pecuniary object in begging him for a fool, or otherwise in proving him *purus idiota*. In many countries persons of unsound mind are still treated with that revolting inhumanity which was once their lot among us. The "jests" recorded by Taylor and Lestrange (the latter quotes his mother as his authority) reveal a curious state of society and of the law. But statistics might easily be produced to show that at a very much later epoch matters had not greatly improved in this respect. No doubt, the practice which prevailed, even in the time of Charles II., of "begging men for fools," gradually expired; but the laxity with which proofs of a person being *purus idiota* were received, remained a scandal to English legislation long after the reign of the Domestic Fools had come to an end. See Additional Notes and Illustrations to this volume.

very angry, [and] demanded who had spoyled his hangings. Ah nunckle, said the Ideot, I did cut out all the fooles, for there is a great man at Court that hath begged me for a foole, and he would haue all the rich fooles he can heare of, therefore did I cut them all out of your hangings, and I haue hid them, where I thinke he will not find them in hast.

## (104.)

A FELLOW being scoulded at by his Wife, would make her beleeue he would drown himselfe : and as hee went toward the riuer, his wife followed him desiring him to forbeare, or at the least to let her speake with him. Well, quoth hee, speake briefly, for I am in haste. Then, husband, said shee, seeing you will drowne your selfe, let mee intreat you to take my counsell, which is, that you cast not your selfe into this shallow place here, for it will grieue my heart to see how long you will bee a dying; but goe with me a little way, and I will shew you a deepe place, where you shall be dispatched presently.

## (105.)

A WOMAN in Scotland lay dying, to whom her husband said : Wife, now thou art about to leaue mee alone, I pray thee tell me with whom shall I marry. Shee replyed : are you in haste to marry before the breath bee out of my body, then marry the deuil's dam. Not so, wife, said hee ; I haue had his daughter already, and if I should match with his mother too, then I should be guilty of incest.

### (106.)

THERE was a Gentleman that was of a very hasty disposition, so that hee would fret and chafe almost at all things, and be seldome pleased with any thing, and withall was a great Tobacco taker. And as one time hee beat and kick'd his man, the fellow ran from him, and told one of his fellowes that hee thought his master was transformed into Brawne, for hee was all Choller, and that hee thought the reason of his kicking was, because hee dranke Colts-foot among his Tobacco.

### (107.)

A DOCTOR of Physicke in Italy asked a waterman,[1] if hee might goe well by water ouer the River Po. The fellow told him, Yea ; but the Doctor, when hee came to the water side, and saw it was a little rough weather, was very angry, and said : You Watermen are the veriest knaues in the world, for

(1) Old ed. has *watermen.*

to gaine sixpence you care not to cast a man away. To whom the Waterman replyed: Sir, it appeares wee are men of a cheaper function and better conscience then you; for you sometimes will not cast a man away vnder forty, fifty, or one hundred crownes.

### (108.)

ONE borrowed a cloake of a Gentleman, and met one that knew him, who said: I thinke I know that cloake. It may be so, said the other, I borrowed it of such a Gentleman. The other told him that it was too short. Yea, but, quoth he that had the cloake, I will haue it long enough, before I bring it home againe.

### (109.)

A POORE woman's husband was to be hanged at the towne of Lancaster, and on the execution day she intreated the Shrieue to be good to her and stand her friend. The Shrieue said that he could doe her no hurt, for her husband was condemned and judged by the Law, and therefore hee must suffer. Ah, good Master Shrieue, said the woman, it is not his life that I aske, but because I haue farre home, and my mare is old and stiffe; therefore I would intreat you to doe me the fauour to let my husband be hanged first.

(110.)

ONE came into a Colledge in a Vniversity, and asked how many Fellowes belonged to the house. Another replyed, that there were more good fellowes than good Schollers, two to one.

(111.)

A FELLOW being drunke, was brought before a Justice, who committed him to prison; and the next day, when hee was to be discharged, hee was come to the Justice againe, who said to him : Sirrah, you were not drunke the last night. Your Worship sayes true, said the fellow. Yea, but you were drunke, said the Justice ; and you did abuse me, and said I was a wise Justice. The fellow replied : If I said so, I thinke I was drunke indeed, and I cry your Worship mercy, for I will neuer doe you that wrong, when I am sober.

(112.)

A SPANIARD hauing but one eye chanced to meet a man in the field, where, drawing both their Rapiers, the other man with an infortunate thrust strucke out the other eye of the Spaniard, whereat the blind man suddenly cast downe his Rapier saying : *Buonas noches*, which in the Spanish tongue is, Good night.

### (113.)

A REUEREND Preacher once reproued his Auditors for sleeping at his Sermons, but [y]et (said he) I pray you do not refrain coming to Church, though you doe sleepe ; for God Almighty may chance to take some of you napping.

### (114.)

A SAYLOR was absent on a voiage three yeeres; in the meane space, his wife had a boy 20 months old to entertaine him withall at his returne. The Saylor sayd : Wife, whose childe is this ? Marry, husband (quoth she), it is mine, and God sent it me in your absence. To which the man replied : I will keepe this childe, because God sent him, but if God send mee any more on that fashion, he shall keepe them himselfe.

### (115.)

A YOUNG fellow being newly married, hauing bin from home, came suddenly into his house, and found his wife at foule play with another man. The poor young Cuckold ran presently, and told his wiues father all the businesse, who replied

thus : Sonne, I married her mother, and I tell
thee plaine that thy wife seemes to bee her
daughter in conditions as well as feature, for I
haue taken her mother many times in that manner,
and no warning would serue her, till in the end
age made her leaue it, and so will thy wife doe,
when she is old and past it.

### (116.)

THREE Gossips in a Tauerne, chatting ouer a pint
of Sherry, said one of them : I muse whereabouts
a Cuckolds hornes do grow; quoth the second : I
thinke they doe growe in the pole or nape of
the necke ; verily, quoth the third, I doe thinke it
to bee true, for my husbands bands are always
worne out behind.

### (117.)

ONE called a W**** lazy jade. Content yourself,
quoth another, as lazy as shee seemes, she is able
to carry a man quicke to the diuell.

### (118.)

A COMPANY of Neighbours that dwelt all in one
rowe in one side of a street, one of them said :
Let vs be merry, for it is reported that we are

all Cuckolds that dwell on our side of the street (except one). One of the women sate musing, to whom her husband said : wife, what, all *amort ?* Why art thou so sad ? No, quoth she, I am not sad, but I am studying which of our neighbours it is that is not a Cuckold.

### (119.)

A GENTLEMAN, being in a house of iniquity, or Couzen-German to a Bawdy-house, the roome being very darke, he called a lowd for a *light Huswife;* to whom a wench made answer : I come Incontinent.

> *He cals for* light, *she vnderstood him right,*
> *For shee was vanity which made her* light :
> *She sayd, she would* Incontinent[1] *attend,*
> *To make her Continent, she needs to mend.*

### (120.)

Two Mayds (or seruants) dwelling in a house together, the one of them hauing occasion to vse a steele smoothing Iron, or some such kinde of Laundry instrument, and hauing sought it, and not finding it, said to her fellow : thou dost mislay euery thing in the house, and art so busie a

(1) Orig. has *Inconcinent.*

baggage, that thou canst let *nothing stand;* to which the other answered : and you are so wayward and teasty, that a little thing troubles you, and puts you in a great anger.

### (121.)

IN a time of peace, a Captaine being in company, where after dinner there was dancing, with whom a Gentlewoman was desirous to dance, the Captaine said hee was made to fight, and not to dance : to whom she answerd, that it were good that he were oyl'd & hang'd vp in an Armoury till there were occasion to vse him.

### (122.)

ONE asked a huffing Gallant why hee had not a Looking-Glasse in his Chamber. He answered : he durst not, because hee was often angry, and then he look'd so terribly that he was fearefull to looke vpon himselfe.

### (123.)

THERE was a fellow that (not for his goodnesse) was whip'd at a Carts-tayle, and in his execution he drew backward, to whom a Gentleman (in pitty) said : Fellow, doe not draw backe, but presse forward, and thy execution and paynes will be the sooner past and done; to whom the Rogue answerd: It is my turne now; when thou art whip'd, doe thou goe as thou wilt, and now I will goe as I please.

### (124.)

ONE said, that hee had trauaild so farre that he had layd his hand vpon the hole where the winde came forth; a second said, that hee had beene at the farthest edge of the world, and driuen a nayle quite thorow it; the third replide, that he had beene further, for hee was then on the other side of the world, and clencht that nayle.

### (125.)

THERE was a Pope who, being dead, it is said that hee came to heauen gate and knock'd. Saint Peter (being within the gate) asked who was there. The Pope answered: brother, it is I, I am the last Pope deceased. Saint Peter said: if thou be the Pope, why dost thou knocke? thou hauing the keyes mayst vnlocke the gate and enter. The Pope replied, saying, that his predecessors had the keyes, but since their time the wards were altered.

### (126.)

A RICH Miser, being reuiled by a poore man whom he had oppressed, the rich man said: Thou dogge leaue thy barking. The poore man answered, that hee had one quality of a good dogge, which was, to barke when hee saw a thiefe.

## (127.)

A MAN being deeply in play at dice, hauing lost much money, his sonne (a little lad) being by him, wept. Quoth the father: Boy, why dost thou weepe? The boy answered, that hee had read that Alexander the Great wept when he heard that his father (King Philip) had conquered many Cities, Townes, and Territories, fearing that hee would leaue him nothing to winne ; and I weepe the contrary way (quoth the boy), for I feare that my father will leaue me nothing to loose.

## (128.)

AN Oppressor hauing feld all the trees in a Forrest, which for a long time had beene the reliefe of many poore people, sayd, that it was as good as a Commedy to him to see the trees fall ; to whom a poor man said : I hope as thou makest a Commedy of our miseries, that three of those trees may be reserued to finish a Tragedy for thee and thy children.

## (129.)

ONE lamented his friends hard fortune that, being raysed to a place of honour, was growne sencelesse, forgetting all his old familiar acquaintance, and so farre from knowing any man, that he knew not himselfe.

## (130.)

THE Plough surpasseth the Pike, the Harrow excelleth the Halbert, the Culter exceedeth the Cuttleaxe, the Goad is better than the Gunne; for the one sort are the instruments of life and profit, and the other are the engines of death and all kindes of calamities.

## (131.)

A POORE man is in two extremes : first, if he aske, he dyes with shame ; secondly, if he aske not, he dies with hunger.

## (132.)

ONE, being in office, was reproued for negligence ; his excuse was, that it was his best policy to be idle : for if he should doe ill he should displease God, and if he should doe well he should offend men : to whom one answered : you ought to doe your duty, for in well doing you shall please God, and in ill doing you shall please men.

## (133.)

WOMEN take great pleasure to be sued to, though they neuer meane to grant.

## (134.)

ONE said that Suiters in Law were mortall and their suite immortall, and that there is more profit in a quicke deniall then in a long dispatch.

## (135.)

A TRAUAILER was talking what a goodly City Rome was, to whom one of the company said, that all Rome was not in Italy, for wee had too much Rome in England.

## (136.)

A COUNTREY fellow came into Westminster Hall, when one told him that the roofe of it was made of Irish wood, and that the nature of it was such, that no spider would come neere it, and he said (further) that in Ireland no Toad, Snake, or Caterpiller can liue, but that the earth or the trees will destroy them. Ah (quoth the Countrey man), I wish with all my heart that the Benches, Barres, and Flooring were all made of such earth and wood, and that all Coaches, Barges, and Wherries, were made of Irish Oake, that all our English Caterpillers might be destroyed.

### (137.)

MASTER Thomas Coriat (on a time) complained against mee to King James, desiring his Majest that hee would cause some heauy punishment to bee inflicted vpon mee, for abusing him in writing (as he said I had); to whom the King replide, that when the Lords of his honourable Priuy Councell had leisure, and nothing else to doe, then they should heare and determine the differences betwixt Master Coriat the Scholler, and John Taylor the Sculler : which answere of the King was very acceptable to Master Coriat. Whereupon I made this following petitiō to the King—

TO
### THE KINGS MOST
## *EXCELLENT MAJESTIE.*
The humble petition of *John Tailor*, your
Majesties poore Water-Poet.

Sheweth,

Most Mighty Monarch *of this famous Ile,*
(*Vpon the knees of my submissive minde*)

*I begge thou wilt be graciously inclin'd,*
*To reade these lines my rusticke pen compile:*
*Know (Royall Sir)* Tom Coriate *workes the wile*
*Your high displeasure on my head to bring;*
*And well I wot, the sot his words can file,*
*In hope my fortunes head-long downe to fling.*
*The King, whose wisedome through the world did ring,*
*Did heare the cause of two offending Harlots,*
*So, I beseech the (Great) great* Britaines *King,*
*To doe the like for two contending Varlots.*
*A brace of Knaues your Majesty implores,*
*To heare their suites as* Salomon *heard whores.*

## 𝔄 𝕽𝔦𝔟𝔟𝔩𝔢=𝔯𝔞𝔟𝔟𝔩𝔢[1] 𝔬𝔣 𝔊𝔬𝔰𝔰𝔦𝔭𝔰.

THE space of a fortnight from the Bearbaiting, 2 houres and a halfe from the Windmill, about 4 of the Clocke in the forenoon, a little after supper in the morning, betweene old mother Maudlin, of the parish of Ideots, plaintiffe, of the one party, and Gosip Gillian, of Gossips hall, in the parish of Twattlebrough, of the other party, defēdant. A matter in controuersie depēding of issues, where- upon it was constulted by the right reuerend matron,

(1) See *Mery Tales and Quicke Answeres,* No. 39, and *note; Comodie of Patient Grissil,* 1603 (Shakesp. Soc. ed. pp. 88, 89) ; and *Timon,* a play (Shakesp. Soc. ed. p. 26).

madam Isabel, that Katherin should go no more a maying with Susan in the coole of the Euening before sun rising; whereupon Lister tooke the matter in snuffe, and swore by the crosse of Andries bugle bow, that Jone should jogge to Nans house to borrow her poking sticke. Vpon this Philiday starts vp very jeparately, and commands Marget to make haste to Rachels house and borrow a doozen of left-handed spoones. Now old Sibill all this while sate mumping like a gib cat, and on the sodaine she starts vp and thrusts Charity out of doores, to take vp her lodging where she could get it; Doll being much offended to see Marget inuited to Precillaes wedding, by no meanes could suffer Abigaile to breake her fast before she got victuals. Presently Betrice whispers Cisily in the eare softly, that al the company heard it, and bad her tell Alice that vnlesse she tooke heed, the pot would run over and the fat lye in the fire; at this Mary clap'd her hands together, and entreats Blanch to tell her Cozen Edith how she should say that Luce should say, that Elizabeth should doe the thing shee wots of. Amy hearing all this, with a judiciall vnderstumbling capacity, at last tells Parnell that her daughter Rebecka was gone to lie at her Aunt Christians house in Shooing-horne Alley. Now in the heat of all this businesse

Barbara tells Frances how there is good ale at the
labor in vain. The matter being brought to this
passe, Winifrit saies that her god-daughter Grace
is newly brought (God blesse the child), and that
Constance, the Comfit-makers wife, at the signe of
the Spiders leg must be Godship ; out, alas ! saies
Temperance, what haue I forgot ! I should haue
bin an houre agone at Prudences, the Landresse,
to haue taken measure of a payre of Cuffes for
her maid Dorcas. Now to conclude the businesse,
Martha protests that shee will neuer trust Tomasin
againe while she liues, because she promised to
meet her at Pimlico and bring her neighbour
Bethya with her, and came not. Neuerthelesse
Faith went to mother Redcaps, and by the way
met with Joyce, who very kindly batled her penny
with her at a fat pig. Wel, quoth Sara, all this
winde shakes no corne, and I should haue bin a
starching mistresse Mercies lawne apron, and like
a good huswife I am prating heere. Neighbours
and friends, quoth Arbela, seeing the matter drawes
toward so good a conclusion, let's een haue the
tother pinte before we go ; truly, saies Jane, the
motion is not to be misliked, what say you, gossip
Vrsula ? Truly, saies Ellin, I would go with you
with all my heart, but I promist to meet Lydia at
a Lector, that we might take a neighbourly nap

together. Vpon this rose a hurly-burly, that the whole assēbly dispersed themselues diuers wayes, some one way, some another ; and in conclusion, the businesse was all wisely ended as it was begunne.

.

**Finis.**

# CONCEITS, CLINCHES, FLASHES,

## AND WHIMZIES.

*Conceits, Clinches, Flashes, and Whimzies. Newly studied, with some Collections, but those never published before in this kinde. London. Printed by R. Hodgkinsonne for Daniel Frere, and are to be sold at the signe of the red Bull in little brittain.* 1639. 12°.

Of this volume, a recent discovery in this class of literature, only one edition, and of that edition only one copy, is known. Until the book accidentally fell into the hands of Mr. Halliwell, it had never been seen by bibliographers; but in 1860, Mr. Halliwell reprinted six and twenty copies of the new literary curiosity, and thus it became to a certain extent accessible to those, who are interested in the existing remains of early English literature. The collection is remarkable in two respects, first on account of the previously unnoticed mention of Shakespeare, at p. 49, and secondly because the bulk of the anecdotes here brought together are original, which is hardly ever the case in such compilations.

Of the Author of these facetiæ nothing whatever is known; from the commendatory verses prefixed to the book he appears to have been a friend of Thomas Rawlins, the poet and dramatist; but beyond this we have no clue. From the Address to the Reader it is perhaps allowable to infer that the following pages represent a selection from the Table Talk of the Author and his friends.

It is just possible that the anonymous compiler was John Taylor, the Water Poet, who published a collection entitled: "Bull, Beare, and Horse, Cut, Curtaile, and Longtaile. With Tales of Buls, Clenches, and Flashes, as also here and there a touch of our Beare-Garden." Lond. 1638, 8°. Although there are several anecdotes reported in the following pàges which can scarcely be new to the reader, it is to be recollected that they are here found in their original shape and, in many cases, for the first time.

The edition of this work issued by Mr. Halliwell (London, 1860, 4°) is a reproduction of the old text without any improvements, and with very numerous errors. In the present edition, both the text and the pointing have been considerably amended, the original having, apparently, been very carelessly got up, and exhibiting several corruptions in the language, and a punctuation more than usually negligent and faulty. A few notes have also been added. It is necessary to state that the copy used (which is, as the reader is already aware, the only one known) is deficient of two leaves between Jests 231 and 232 ; but in a publication, where each paragraph is complete in itself, this *hiatus* is of far less importance than in the case of a connected or continuous narrative.

# TO THE READER.

GENTLE Reader, I here present thee with the pro-
ducements of some vaporing houres, purposely intended to promote harmlesse mirth ; I wish thee as
merry in the reading as I and some other of my
friends were in speaking of them ; do but laugh at
them, and I am satisfied, for to that (and no other
purpose) they were intended.

## Farewell.

3                                   *M*

# To the Author on his Conceits.

FRIEND, *thy conceits, flown from the downey nes*
  *Of thy rich fancy, lighted on my brest;*
*Where (let me tell thee true, for 'twere a sin*
*To flatter any, much more flatter him*
*I hold my friend) I found such ample store*
*In thy pure mine of gold and silver ore,*
*I became conscious that I sure was bound*
*Now to disclose to th' world what I had found,*
*And render to the readers; no close end*
*Could stop me from being theirs or thy true friend.*

T. RAWLINS.

# Conceits, Clinches, Flashes and Whimzies.

### 1.

AN idle justice of Peace is like the picture of Saint George upon a signe-post with his sword drawne to no purpose.

### 2.

Hee that speakes great gunpowder words may be compared to a deepemouth'd Dogge, or bee sayd to have a tympany in his tongue.

### 3.

A Souldier said hee had been in so many battels and had been so battered with bullets, that hee swore hee thought hee had a mine of lead in his belly.

### 4.

Lovers oathes are like marryners prayers; when once the heate is over, they are not the same men.

5.

Women are like dead bodies for surgeons to worke upon, because they tell a man his imperfections.

6.

Musitians may be compared unto Camelions, because they live by ayre.

7.

One said it was a difficult thing to perswade a multitude (especially in a City where they are for the most part strongheaded) to any reason.

8.

One was called foole for asking what Country man a ploughman was; because it is knowne, said one, they were all borne in Hungarie.

9.

One asked a man whether he had swallowed a Doctor of Phisickes bill, because hee spoke such hard words.

10.

The philosopher's stone had need turne all mettals to gold, because the study of it turnes all a mans gold to other mettall.

## 11.

One asked a poet where his wits were? He answered a wool-gathering. The other replyed, there was no people had more need of it.

## 12.

One asked whence choller was discended? One answered that shee was the daughter of a great mans porter, begot of a kitchin wench in the time of a feast.

## 13.

One asked another why hee loved woodcoke so extreamly? The other answered, why not I as well as you? for I am sure you never go abroad but you carry one under your cloake.

## 14.

One asked why a Knight tooke place of a Gentleman. It was answered, because they were Knights now a days before they were Gentlemen.[1]

## 15.

One said the midwives trade of all trades was most commendable; because they lived, not by the hurts of other men, as Surgeons do, nor by

(1) This jest is a sneer at the profuseness which James the First and his successor exhibited in the creation of knights, as a means of raising money.

the falling out of friends, as Lawyers do ; but by
the agreement betwixt party and party.

### 16.

One said a good Client was like a study gown,
that sits in the colde himselfe to keepe his Lawyer
warme.

### 17.

One said the fees of a pander and a punie
clarke are much alike ; for the pander had but
two pence next morning for making the bed, and
that was a penny a sheet.

### 18.

A woman was commending a boyes face.  Pish,
quoth another, give me a man's face ; a boyes face
is not worth a haire.

### 19.

One compar'd a domineering fellow to a walking
Spurre, that keeps a great jingling noise, but never
pricks.

### 20.

One said it was unfit a glasier should be a Constable, because he was a common quarreller.[1]

(1) A *quarel* was the old term for a pane of glass, and *quareler* was
synonymous with *glazier*.

## 21.

One said he had received a shee-letter, because, saith he, it hath a young one in the belly of it.

## 22.

One asked the reason why Lawyer's Clearks writ such wide lines. Another answered, it was done to keepe the peace, for if the Plaintiffe should be in one line and the Defendant in the next line, the lines being too neare together, they might perhaps fall together by the eares.

## 23.

One sayd hee was so tender hearted, that he could not find in his heart to kill a louse ; another answered that it proceeded only from faintheartednesse, because hee had not the heart to see his own blood.

## 24.

One said a rich,widdow was like the rubbish of the world, that helps only to stop the breaches of decayed houses.

## 25.

A master spoke in a straine his servant understood not, whereupon the servant desired his

Master rather to give him blowes then such hard words.

### 26.

Those that say gallants put all upon their backs abuse them; for they spend a great deale more upon their bellies.

### 27.

One said it was a strange fashion that we had in England to receive money with wives, and give money for wenches. It was answered that in ancient time women were good, and then men gave money for their wives; but now, like light gold, they would not passe without allowance.

### 28.

One perswaded another to marry a w**** because shee was rich, telling him that, perhaps, she might turne. Turne, said the other, she hath been so much worne that she is past turning.

### 29.

One put a jest upon his frend. O, said his friend, that I could but see your braines, I would even hug them for this jest.

### 30.

One asked why Sextons did use to weare black. It was answered that in regard of their office they were to meddle with grave matters, and did therfore weare black.

### 31.

One, seeing another weare a thred-bare cloake, asked him whether his cloak was not sleepy or no? Why do you aske? said the other. Because, said hee, I thinke it hath not had a nap this seven yeeres.

### 32.

One asked what was the usuall food of citizens wives. It was answered, though they loved flesh beter then fish, yet for temperance sake they would so dyet themselves that at noon they fed only upon carp, at night on cods head, and when they went abroad, a little place would content them better then any other thing.

### 33.

One wondred much what great Scholler this same Finis was, because his name was almost to every booke.[1]

(1) This is the earliest witticism of the kind which I remember to hav seen. In a broadside, entitled "The Parliaments Knell," and printed

## 34.

One asked what he was that had a fine wit in Jest. It was answered, a foole in earnest.

## 35.

One hearing a Usurer say he had been on the pike of Teneriff (which is supposed to be one of the highest hils in the world), asked him why he had not stayd there, for he was perswaded hee would never come so neere heaven againe.[1]

## 36.

A Citizen begins a health to all the Cuckolds in the world ; the Gentleman, to whom the health was presented seeing him with his cap in his hand, said, what doe you mean, Sir? pray ye, remember your selfe.

## 37.

One asked a foot-boy why he was so affected with linnen stockings? He answered, because he was troubled with running legges.

about 1647, the author is described as *Mr. Finis.* The disputed question as to whether Shakespeare's plays were written by *Mr. Preface* or *Mr. Finis* is well known.

(1) This story, in a variety of forms, is in many of the jest-books.

## 38.

One sayd to another that his face was like a popish almanack, all holydayes, because it was full of pimples.

## 39.

One sayd it was a good fashion that was worn now a dayes, because the Taylers had so contrived it that there was little or no waste in a whole suit.

## 40.

One said a jellous wife was like an irish trouze, alwayes close to a mans tayle.

## 41.

One said an Apothecaryes house must needs be healthfull, because the windowes, benches, boxes, and almost all the things in the house, tooke phisick.

## 42.

One said a Physitian was naturall brother to the wormes, because he was ingendered out of mans corruption.

## 43.

One gave a fellow a box on the eare, the fellow gave him another. What doe you meane? (sayd he that gave the first box) I did not lend you a box, I freely gave it you. The other answered, he was a gamester, and had been alwayes us'd to pay the box.

### 44.

A Gentleman that bore a spleene to another meets him in the street, gives him a box on the eare ; the other, not willing to stricke againe, puts it off with a jest, asking him whether it was in jest or in earnest ? The other answers it was in earnest. I am glad of that, said he, for if it had been in jest, I should have been very angry, for I do not like such jesting ; and so past away from him.

### 45.

One that was justly jealous of his wife said, prethee, leave these courses, for if thou dost not, they will, ere it be long, make me horne mad.

### 46.

One sayd to a gentleman that was too full of complement : pray you, Sir, do not spend so much wit ; if you be so prodigall of it, you will, ere it be long, have none left for your selfe.

47.

There is nothing, sayes one, more revengfull then hemp : for if a man once beat it, especially in Bridewell, 'tis a hundred to one but it will be the death of him shortly after.

48.

Hee that sweares when he loseth his mony at gaming, may challeng hel by way of purchase.

49.

One askcd which were supposed to be the two fruitfullest acres of ground in the whole Kingdome. It was answered, Westminster Hall and the old Exchange.

50.

It was asked why fat men did love their ease so much. Because, sayd one, the soule in a fat body lyes soft, and is therefore loath to rise.

51.

One asked why yong Barristers used to stick their chamber windowes with letters. Because, said another, it was the first thing that gave the world notice of their worships.

### 52.

One having dranke a cup of dead beere, swore that the beer was more then foxed; another, demanding his reason : quoth he, because it is dead drunke.

### 53.

Usurers live, sayes one, by the fall of heires, like swine by the dropping of acorns.

### 54.

One sayd a prodigall was like a brush that spent it self to make others goe handsome in their cloathes.

### 55.

One wondred what pleasant kind of oratory the Pillory had in him, that men lov'd to have their eares nail'd to it.

### 56.

One said : suppose all the women in the world were like patient Grizell; then, sayd another, we might make Christmas bloks of the cuckingstooles.

### 57.

An Antiquary, says one, loves every thing (as Dutchmen doe cheese) for being mouldy and worm-eaten.

### 58.

One said a Player had an idle imployment of it. O, you are mistaken, sayd another, for his whole life is nothing else but action.

### 59.

One asked his friend how he should use tobacco so that it might do him good ? He answered : you must keepe a tobacco shop and sell it, for certainly there is none else find good in it.

### 60.

A simple fellow in gay cloths, sayes one, is like a Cinnamom tree ; the barke is of more worth then the body.

### 61.

If a man be Cornelius, sayes one, he must be Tacitus too, otherwise he shall never live quietly.

### 62.

One entreated a prisoner to do him a curtesie, telling him that hitherto he had found him a fast friend, and he hoped hee should find him so still.

### 63.

A gentleman riding on the way would needs turne back to kisse his wife that was behinde him ;

he was therefore commended for a kind husband,
• in regard he was before, to kisse his wife behinde.

### 64.

One asked whether such a man were wise or no?
It was answered that he was otherwise.

### 65.

One perswaded a Scholer that was much given
to going abroad that he would put away his cushion,
and it would be a meanes to make him sit harder
to his study.

### 66.

One said poetry and plain dealing were a couple
of hansom wenches.   Another answered : yes, but
he that weds himselfe to either of them shall dye
a begger.

### 67.

One sayd he had heard the story of St. George
how he kild the Draggon that would else have de-
voured the maide, and did wonder that men would
devise such lies ;[1] for, saith he, it is held by most

(1) This is a rather lame and wire-drawn version of a story which may
be found in Aubrey's *Remains of Gentilism and Judaism*, (Thoms'
*Anecdotes and Traditions*, p. 101).   Aubrey has preserved the following
verses :—

> "To save a mayd, St. George the Dragon slew,
> A pretty tale, if all is told, be true :
> Most say there are no dragons, and 'tis sayd,
> There was no George : pray God there was a mayd!!"

men that there was never such a man as St. George, nor ever such a creature as a Dragon. Another answers for St. George: tis no great matter neither for the Draggon, whether there were such or no; pray heaven there be a maide, and then it is no matter.

### 68.

A Scholar and a Courtier meeting in the street seemd to contest for the wall ; sayes the Courtier : I do not use to give every coxcombe the wall. The Schollar answered : but I do, sir ; and so passed by him.

### 69.

One asked the reason why women were so crooked and perverse in their conditions. Another answered : because the first woman was made of a crooked thing.

### 70.

A rich Lawyer, that had got a great estate by the Law, upon his death bed was desirous to give twenty pound per annum to the house of Bedlam. Being demanded why he would give it to that house rather then another, he answered that he had got it of mad men, and to them he would give it againe.

3. *N*

71.

One said women were like quick sands, seemed firme ; but if a man came upon them, he fell in over head and shoulders.

72.

Another said a woman was like a peece of old Grogram, alwayes fretting.

73.

One asked why men should thinke there was a world in the Moone. It was answered, because they were lunatique.[1]

74.

One asked why Ladyes called their husbands Master such a one, and master such a one, and not by their titles of knighthood, as Sir Thomas, Sir Richard, Sir William, etc. It was answered that, though others called them by their right titles, as Sir William, Sir Thomas, etc., yet it was fit their wives should master them.

(1) Bishop Wilkins' work, entitled, "A Discovery of a New World," had just (1638) appeared, and had no doubt given rise to a good deal of discussion on this old and whimsical question.

## 75.

One asked, what was the first commodity a yong shopkeeper put off. It was answered, his honestie.

## 76.

One asked why Icarus would undertake to flye in the ayre. It was answered, because he was a Buzzard.

## 77.

Two Gentlemen talking in latin in the presence of a woman, she grew jealous that they spake of her, and desired them to speake english that she might answer them, for she said she was perswaded when men spake latin, although they spake but two words, that still one of them was nought: whereupon one of the Gentlemen sayd presently, *Bona mulier.* She replyed: I know *bona* is good, but Ile warrant ye the other word meanes something that's nought.

## 78.

A simple fellow, being too bold with one that was his superior, was told he might say what he would for that day, because it was Innocents day, it being so indeed.

### 79.

One said a barber had need be honest and trusty, because whosoever employed him, though it was but for a haire matter, put his life into his hands.

### 80.

A suit in Law being referd to a Gentleman, the plantiffe, who had the equity of the cause on his side, presented him with a new coach ; the Defendant, with a couple of horses : he, liking the horses better then the coach, gave sentence on the Defendants side. The Plaintiffe calls to him, and asketh him how it came to passe the coach went out of the right way. He answers that he could not help it, for the horses had drawne it so.[1]

### 81.

One perswaded his friend to marry a little woman, because of evils the least was to be chosen.

### 82.

One asked how it came to passe that hosts had usually red noses. It was answered, that it was

---

(1) This is a very favourite jest, and is found in several of the early collections.

given to them by nature to show to the world an experiment of the vertue of what [t]he[y] sold.

### 83.

A vaine glorious man was bragging that his Father and his Uncle had founded such a Hospitall. One answered, 'tis true, but yet know that your Father and your Uncle were the meere confounders of that Hospitall you speake of.

### 84.

One said a tooth drawer was a kind of an unconscionable trade, because his trade was nothing else but to take away those things whereby every man gets his living.

### 85.

One asked why he that drew beere was not called a drawer as well as he that drew wine? It was answered, that beere made a man to p****, but it was wine made him draw.

### 86.

One said he wondred that lether was not dearer then any other thing. Being demanded a reason : because, saith he, it is more stood upon then other thing in the world.

### 87.

One said a hangman had a contemplative profession, because he never was at work but he was
put in mind of his owne end.

### 88.

One called another rogue.   He answered : durst
I trust thee with a looking glasse, you would quit
me, and condemne yourselfe.

### 89.

A fellow, that had no money in his pocket, was
in a great rage with another, who told him : pray,
sir, do not put yourselfe into too much heat, unlesse
you had more money in your pocket whereby to
quench it.

### 90.

One being asked what countryman he was, he
answered, a Middlesex man.   The other told him
[it] being he was neither of the male sex nor of the
female sex, but of a middlesex, he must then be a
Hermaphrodit.

### 91.

One sayd corne was a quarrelsome creature, because it rose by the blade, and fel by the eares with
those that cut it.

### 92.

Why do Ladies so affect slender wastes? (said one.) 'Tis (replied another) because their expences may not bee too great.

### 93.

One commending a Tayler for his dexteritie in his profession, another standing by ratified his opinion, saying tailors had their businesse at their fingers ends.

### 94.

One, being demanded the reason why he thought the greatest drinkers quickest of apprehension, made this answer: *Qui super naculum bibit ad unguem sapit.*

### 95.

A Poet, sayes one, is a man of great priviledge, because, if he transgresse, it is by a rule, viz., *Licentia poetica.*

### 96.

The severest stoicks (said one) are the greatest Students, because their contracted browes are alwayes bent to study.

97.

Colliers and mine-workers should be well acquainted with all the philosophicall secrets of the
Earth, because they have deeper knowledge in it
then any others.

98.

Tapsters, said one, should bee men of esteem,
because they are men not only of a high calling,
but also of great reckoning.

99.

Tis impossible that Saylers should be rich men,
because they are never so well pleased as when
they go downe the wind fastest.

100.

A woman said of all men she had a desire to
marry a Huntsman, because he would not disdaine
to weare the horne.

101.

Of all knaves there's the greatest hope of a
Cobler, for though he be never so idle a fellow, yet
he is still mending.

### 102.

A Smith, said one, is the most pragmaticall fellow under the Sun, for he hath alwayes many irons in the fire.

### 103.

The neatest man in a Kingdome (sayd one) is a Barber, for he cannot endure to have a hair amisse.

### 104.

Wit bought is better then wit taught, because he that never bought any is but a naturall wit.

### 105.

Tis probable that those women that paint most shall live longest; for where the house is kept in repaire, there is no feare but it will be inhabited.

### 106.

One said that tall men of all others were most happy, because they were neerer heaven then all other men.

### 107.

A squint-ey'd man (says one) is the most circum-spect of all men, because he can look nine wayes at once.[1]

(1) The sailors still say of a squint-eyed person, that "he looks nine ways for Sundays."

## 108.

One said that tal men should be great polititians, because they have an extraordinary reach.

## 109.

One sayd hang-men were very happy, because those men they do most hurt will never be able to render them *quid pro quo.*

## 110.

It is in some sort necessary that some rich men should be Dunces, because the pretenders to learning may get preferment : for the good wits will be able to help themselves.

## 111.

One was saying it was a fine quality to be able to speak wel ex tempore. Why then, said another, we may commend every woman : for they have the most nimble, fluent tongues, and that without study or consideration.

## 112.

Hang-men practice their cunning for the most part on good natur'd men, because they are ready to forgive, before the hurt be attempted.

113.

Hee that hath but one eye is more like to hit the marke he aymes at then another, because he hath a monstrous sight.

114.

Glasiers, said one, must needes be good arbitrators, for they spend their whole time in nothing but composing of quarels.[1]

115.

Carpenters, said one, are the civelest men in a Common-wealth, for they never do their buisinesse without a Rule.

116.

Of all wofull friends a hangman is the most trusty: for, if he once have to do with a man, he will see him hang'd before hee shall want mony or any thing else.

117.

Bricklayers are noteable wanton fellowes, for they have alwayes to do with one trull[2] or other.

(1) It has been already explained, that a square or pane of glass is sometimes called a *quarrel.*

(2) This jest depends on the similarity of sound between *trull* and *trowel.* The two words were very probably pronounced by our ancestors very much alike.

### 118.

Stationers could not live, if men did not beleeve the old saying, that Wit bought is better then Wit taught.

### 119.

Those that carry about with them counterfeit coyne are more nice and curious of it, then of good Gold or Silver: for they cannot endure to have that toucht of all the rest.

### 120.

Gunners are more serious in what they doe then other men : for what they doe they doe with a powder.

### 121.

Muscattiers of all other Souldiers are the most lazie : for they are alwayes at their rest.[1]

### 122.

One, among a company of his companions, who had been drinking very much, by chance let a ****, who, for conceit sake, said to one of his companions with whom he might make bold : pree-thee

---

(1) The rest for the musket is here referred to.

pledge me; he answered, I cannot; he then reply'd : I pray do but kisse the cup.

### 123.

One passing through Cheap side, a poore Woman
desired his charity; he, disregarding the woman,
kept on walking, and by and by let a ****. The
woman, hearing it, said, much good may it do your
worship ; he, hearing her say so, turnes backe and
gives her a tester ; she thank't him, and told his
worship it was a bad wind, that did blow nobody
good.

### 124.

A man walking the street let a great ****, upon
which he jestingly said : cracke me that nut. It
being heard of a waggish wench that was in a
chamber over his head, who being well provided
at that time with a perfum'd chamber-pot, throws
it out of the window upon his head, saying, there's
the kernill of your nut, Sir.

### 125.

One said a Miller was the fittest husband for a
Scold, because when the mil goes, if her tongue
goes ne're so fast, it cannot be heard.

## 126.

One said that Duke Humfrey's guests were the most temperate men in the world, it being known that at his Table there was never any made drunke, nor with his dyet dyed of a surfet.[1]

## 127.

One said Physitians had the best of it ; for, if they did well, the world did proclaime it ; if ill, the earth did cover it.

## 128.

It is a necessary and fit thing that women learn Roman-hand, because (saith one) they were never good Secretaries, nor ever will be.

## 129.

One saw a man and his wife fighting ; the people asked him, why he did not part them. He answered that he had been better bred then to part man and wife.

## 130.

One said that Tobacconists would endure the wars well, for they would never be stifled with fire and smoake.

(1) This anecdote turns, of course, on the familiar phrase "to dine with Duke Humphrey."

### 131.

A drawer for one thing or other is alwayes appearing at the barre but is not punisht, yet notwithstanding 'tis all scor'd up.

### 132.

Scriveners are most hard harted fellowes, for they never rejoyce more then when they put other men in bonds.

### 133.

Smiths of all handy-crafts men are the most irregular, for they never thinke themselves better employed, then when they are addicted to their vices.

### 134.

Those which weare long haire are in the readyest way to make good Fryars, for they may promise to themselves the happinesse to enjoy bald crownes without the help of a Barber.

### 135.

Tapsters are not only very rash but very expert, for they are apt to draw upon all occasions, and yet suffer very few to go away scot-free.

## 136.

Of al diseases the three-quarters harme[1] is most dangerous and most desired : for all women desire to multiply, though they labor ne'er so hard for 't.

## 137.

Fidlers are very unfortunate in their calling, for they never do anything but it is against the haire.[2]

## 138.

Trumpeters are much subject to sickly distempers; for commonly, when they are most in health, they will fall a sounding.[3]

## 139.

One being asked, where he thought al woodcocks remaind in the Summer-time when they are not seene with us, it was answered, in new England.

## 140.

Horse-keepers and ostlers (let the world go which way it will, though there be never so much alteration in times and persons) are still stable men.

(1) *i.e.* the period of parturition.　　　(2) *i.e.* the fiddlestring.

(3) A play on the words *swooning* or *swoning* and *sounding* must be here understood by the charitable reader. Formerly, perhaps, the *w* in *swound* was sometimes dropped in familiar conversation.

### 141.

One said it was no great matter what a drunkard said in his drinke, for he seldome spake any thing that he could stand to.

### 142.

A hypocrite is odious (saies one) to God, to Man, and to the Devill. God hates him, because he is not what he seemes, Man hates him, because he seemes what he is not, and the Devill hates him, because he seems not what he is truly and indeed.

### 143.

One said of all professions, that Stage-players were the most philosophicall men that were, because they were as merry and as well contented, when they were in rags as when they were in robes.

### 144.

Great Eaters are the most valiant men, for they never fight but with a good stomacke.

### 145.

One asked what the reason was that few women lov'd to eat egges. It was answered, because they cannot endure to beare the yoke.

3.                                        O

146.

One, drinking of a cup of burnt claret, said he was not able to let it down. Another demanded why. He answered, because it was red hot.  ˙

147.

A poor man that lived in the Suburbs of London being owner of a little field, had got together so much mony to buy two little fields more of an acre of ground apeece, yet he was said to be rich, because he had purchased More fields.  ˙

148.

One said roaring Gallants were like Pedlers, because some of them did carry their whole estates upon their backs.

149.

One said that some Taylors were like Woodcocks, because they lived by their long bils.

150.

An Oculist is excellent at sleight of hand : for, if he undertake to cure a blind man, he will so do it that the patient shall see he does it.

151.

One said it was dangerous to wrong a Phisitian, because, if he once have to do with a man, he will be sure to make him stinke.

152.

An Inkeeper brag'd he had a bed so large that two hundred Constables had lyen in it at one time, meaning two Constables of hundreds.

153.

He that byes a horse in Smith field, and does not looke upon him, before he buye him, with a paire of spectacles, makes his horse and himself a paire of sorrofull spectacles, for others to looke on.

154.

A prison is a good instrument of reformation, for it makes many rogues and lewd fellowes staid men.

155.

One complaining that his Sonne was a very prodigall, and that he would give an hundred pounds to have him reclaimed, his neighbor, that heard him complaine, answer'd: let him be a French-Tayler, for they make no waste.

## 156.

A wax-chandlers shop being rob'd, one of his friends came to comfort him, and told him he should not be troubled at it, for he durst undertake his goods would come to light.

## 157.

One demanded of a wild yong Gentleman the reason why he would sel his land. Who answered, because he hoped to go to heven, which he could not possibly do, til he forsook earth.

## 158.

In the Common-wealth of Fishes are many officers; Herring the King, Swordfish his guard; Lobsters are Aldermen, Crabs are Constables, and poor Johns the common sort of people.

## 159.

An idle unthrift, having nothing left to maintaine his humor of good fellowship but his bed, sold it, for which being reproved by some friends, he answered that he could never be well, so long as he kept his bed.

## 160.

Coblers may be said to be good men, because

they set men upright, and are ever imployed in mending of soles.

### 161.

Two men seeing a handsome Wench, but thought to be light, pass by in a very poore habit, the one said : it was a wonder to see such a wench so bare ; the other replied, it was no wonder, for she was common.

### 162.

A drunken fellow, returning home towards evening, found his wife hard at her spinning ; she reprooving him for his ill husbandry, and commending herself for her good huswifery, he told her that she had no great cause to chide : for, as she had been spinning, he came home all the way reeling.

### 163.

An ignorant drunken Surgeon that kil'd all men that came under his hands, boasted himselfe a better man then the Parson ; for, said he, your Cure maintains but yourselfe, but my Cures maintaine all the Sextons in the Towne.

### 164.

A merry fellow said the Ale-house was the only

place to thrive in, for he had knowne many a score
made there.

### 165.

Musitians may be said to be the best Philosophers, for they will be sure to keepe time.

### 166.

A woman, that was very imperious over her
husband, was nick-nam'd by a neighbor and cal'd
Mistres Cap, for which she angerlie demanded his
reason, and was answered, because she was always
above her head.

### 167.

The same woman with her riotous humors having undone her husband, and he being broken and
fled, the same neighbor reproving her, she bade
him not medle with what did no way belong to
him, for she had only broken her owne head.

### 168.

A Lady that was painted, tould a Gentleman she
desired much to have her picture done to the life;
to which he answered: you need not that, Madam,
for you are a picture to the life already.

### 169.

A Gentleman whose name was Stone, falling off his horse into a deep water, out of which he got not without some danger, his companion laugh'd at the mischance, and being reproved, answered that no man but would laugh to see a stone swim.

### 170.

A foolish Gentleman, deformed likewise in his person, was called by one a monster. Nay, surely, said another, the Gentleman is meerly naturall.

### 171.

A country fellow asking which way he might go to Bedlam, a Citizen tould him the nearest way was to be mad. Then, said the Country fellow, you horn-mad Citizens may the better direct us that are Country-men.

### 172.

A common wench stepping into a boate fell into the water, and reaching her hand to be helped out, one refus'd it, saying she need not fear drowning, for she was so light, she could never sinke.

### 173.

One threatned a fellow to breake his head with

a stone. I'le assure you (quoth he) it is a hard
matter to breake my head with a stone.

### 174.

A boy seemed much delighted with a Coblers
· worke, commending and admiring his workman-
ship. The Cobler, pleased with the boyes admiration, asked him if he would be of his trade. To
which he answered no ; for though he loved work-
manship he could not endure cobling.

### 175.

One hearing a rich Gentleman (but ignorant
enough) discourse somewhat weakly how much
land there was holden in capite, asked him if his
wit was held in capite, to which he answered no.
The other asked him again, if he had not some fe-
simple held in capite, to which he answered yes ;
and that it did descend to him and his heires
for ever.

### 176.

A Physitian demanded money of another for one
of his patients that was dead long before. He
was answered that it was a worke of charity to

visit the sick; but if he was so earnest for mony, the only way was for him to visit the dead, and then he would never want money more.

### 177.

A rich Stationer wisht himselfe a Scholler; to whom one answered, you are one already, being *doctus in libris.* Nay, said the Stationer, I am but *dives in libris,* meaning rich in pounds.

### 178.

One boasted himselfe to be esteemd a wit, saying the world spoke him to be all wit. One, standing by, that knew him very well, said, is't possible that you are taken to be a wit or one that is all-wit; if you be all wit, then your anagram is wit-all.

### 179.

A Gentleman hawk'd in anothers ground, to which the surly owner shewed himselfe angry, at which the Gentleman spet in his face. What is your reason for that? said the farmer. I cry you mercy, said the Gentleman, I gave you warning, for I hawk'd before I spet.

### 180.

One running hastely with a stick of fire in his hand to light a fagot, another called him rogue, which being angry and demanding his reason, he answered, for that he had a brand in his hand.

### 181.

A patient man, being domineer'd over by his wife that was flying about his eares, desired her not to teare his band, for he would gladly weare it (if she pleased) without cuffs.

### 182.

One was saying that lead was the basest of all other mettals. It is true, said another, but yet it is the stoutest, for the glasier will tell you that it keepes more quarrels asunder then any other mettal in the world.

### 183.

A Joyner on a time tooke a pill, and it so wrought with him, that he had fourty stooles in a minute of an houre.

### 184.

Carriers, said one, are wise men, for they will

not medle with any thing, but they will know of
what moment and waight it is.

### 185.

One whose name was Gun called a woman
wh***. She, being moved at it, had him before a
justice of peace about it. The justice reprov'd him
for it, and deepely charged him not to call her so
againe. As they were going home, the woman
told him : Master Gun, you heard what the justice
said ; I hope, being so deeply charg'd, you will
hence-forward give a better report.

### 186.

One said Painters were cunning fellowes, for
they had a colour for every thing they did.

### 187.

One asked why kitchin-maids went so sluttishly,
in regard they drest themselves as cleanly as they
did their meat.

### 188.

One was holding a stiffe argument with a Grocer
concerning matters of trade. The Grocers wife bid
him leave contesting with her husband, for her

husband was able to shew him a thousand reasons[1] for one.

### 189.

One said to his friend that had been speaking : I love to heare a man talke nonsense ; the other answered, I know you love to heare youre selfe talke as well as any man.

### 190.

One asked why begars stood in the streets begging with broomes in their hands. It was answered, because they did with them sweep away the durt out of peoples sight, which while they had a mind on they would never part with a penny.

### 191.

A Gentleman tooke up some commodities upon trust in a shop, promising the master of the shop that he would owe him so much money. The master of the shop was therewith very well contented ; but seeing that the Gentleman delayed the paiment, he asked the money. The gentleman told him he had not promised to pay him, he had promised to owe him so much money, and that he would in no wise breake his promise, which if he paid him he did.

(1) We have here, perhaps, a clue to the old pronunciation of *raisin*.

### 192.

One said he had been kept still to the schoole, and had been made a scholler, if he could but have learned to have declined *mulier*, and for that . cause was taken from the schoole.

### 193.

One desired upon his deathbed to have his corps when he was dead stuck with Isop,[1] as is the fashion in divers places. One of his neighbors sitting by told him Time was better. Why? said the sick man. Because, said the other, unlesse you be buried in time you will stinke, that no creature will be able to go with you to the grave.

### 194.

One asked another what Shakespeares works were worth, all being bound together. He answered, not a farthing. Not worth a farthing! said he; why so? He answered that his plays were worth a great deale of mony, but he never heard, that his works were worth any thing at all.

### 195.

One was commending of the point-makers for

(1) Hyssop.

good distinct readers, and that they read better then any other people whatsoever. Another asked his reason. He answered, that since the fashion of Cassocks came up, they kept their points, and that was the only way to make a mans reading gracefull.

### 196.

Two Poets being merry in a taverne, the one was desirous to be gone, the other entreated him to stay, telling him that, if he did goe away, he would make a comedie upon him. You shall get nothing by that, reply'd the other, for then I will make a tragedy on thee, and in the latter end of it thou shalt hang thy selfe.

### 197.

One, meeting his friend riding on the way without boots, asked him about what busines he rid. The other told him that his businesse was of great importance, and he was likewise in great haste. I am very doubtfull then, said he, that your labor is lost. Why? said he. Because, quoth the other, you ride of a bootlesse errand.

### 198.

One, being at supper at a friends house, [where] it chanced there was mutton and capers for supper, fell into a discourse of dancing, saying, that he loved it better then any other kind of recreation ; by and by, taking notice of the capers which he had never seen before, [he] tooke one upon his trencher, cut it in the midle, and put the halfe of it into his mouth. The master of the house, observing it, said : Sir, it seemes you love dancing very well, when you cannot forbeare but you must cut capers at supper.

### 199.

A fellow had the pictures of the five senses stolne out of his house, whereupon he came to a justice, and desired that the theeves might be bound to the peace. For what ? said the justice : for stealing your pictures ? Yes, saith he. I thought, said the justice, you had lost your senses, that you talke so idly.

### 200.

One amongst a crowd of people on the top of Pauls steeple had his pocket pickt. What villaines are these, quoth he, to pick a mans pocket in the Church ! Nay, Sir, said another, you are but rob'd upon the high-way.

### 201.

One asked another what gender Hermaphroditus was of.  He answered, of the neuter.

### 202.

One complain'd he knew not how to maintaine his barns.  Be a good husband, quoth another, and your barns will maintaine you.[1]

### 203.

A rude deboist[2] young man was plac'd by his friends with a  Proctor who, observing the mis-behaviour of the yong man, told his parents, he feared their Sonne would never make a civil Lawyer.

### 204.

In some merry company one bid another mend his jests, for they were all crackt.  They ought to be so, said he, for it is no jest, till it be broken.

### 205.

One, sitting by the fire to take tobacco, said the fire was his friend, and presently spet into it: to which one replyed : you doe not well to quench your friends love by spetting in his face.

(1) This story turns on the double meaning of the two words *husband* and *barn* (*bairn*).        (2) Debauched.

## 206.

A sawcy fellow abusing a Gentleman whose name was Fisher, the Gentleman strooke him ; for which being reproved and threatned with an action : is it not lawfull, said he, for a fisher to strike a jack ?

## 207.

Two schollers walking along a River were stiffely arguing a point, and wish'd for a moderator or a booke of some authority. One of them, presently espying an angler sitting on a tree, cryed out : we have our wish ! for yonder is *piscator* upon *ramus*.

## 208.

Two Gentlemen comming into a taverne, one of them called for a quart of claret. Why doe you love claret ? said the other; for my part, I'le see it burnt, before I'le drinke a drop of it.

## 209.

A Gentleman [was] shewing a yong student a part of *Scotus* in this sentence in an old caracter wherein was printed Dominus Scotus in Sententia, and asked him, if he was not Dunce Scotus. No, replied the scholler, that can not[1] be except V[2] be there.

(1) Old ed. has *on not.*  (2) *i.e. u* (you).

3.                                        *P*

### 210.

One said Gallants had reason to be good Schollers, because they were deep in many books.

### 211.

One, seeing a printed booke that was but one sheet of paper, said it was not necessary for any man to libell it, for it did penance in a sheet already.

### 212.

One asked which of the letters in the Alphabet were the most authentique in a Bill or Bond. It was answered, I o v.

### 213.

One asked why men and their wives did not agree better now adayes. It was answered, men were now more learned, and did know that it was false concord that the masculine and femenine gender should agree at all.

### 214.

A Scholler, that had his study hung round with browne paper, was us'd (when any came in to visit him in his study) to say, he did love sometimes to sit in a browne study.

215.

Two being in a taverne, the one swore the other should pledge him. Why then, quoth the other, I will; who went presently downe the staires, and left him as a pledge for the reckoning.

216.

One asked, wherefore a drum was in the wars. It was answered, to stirre up valour in the souldiers. That is strange, said the other, for, wheresoever the victory falls, the drums are sure to be beaten.

217.

One asked why B stood before C. Because, said another, a man must B before he can C.

218.

One asked how long the longest letter in the english Alphabet was. It was answered, an L long.

219.

One asked why some gentlewomen wore feathers in their hats. It was answered, because they were light-headed.

220.

Two (conspired together) whereof one was a

*P 2*

Goldsmith, to steale a silver bole, intending to share the businesse betwixt them, which when they had stolen, he that was the goldsmith, because it should not be known, did gild it over. It was sentenced, when the matter came to scanning, though the other stole it, yet the gilt of the fact lay upon the gold-smith.

### 221.

One comming by a Sexton (who was making a grave for one Button which was a great tal fellow), asked him for whom that extraordinary long grave was. He answered, he had made many longer then that, and said it was but a button hole in respect of some graves that he had made.

### 222.

One said a barber was an active man, for, if he did once take out his combe, he would box a man about the eares, and the man scarce feele it.

### 223.

One said a cooke of all men had the worst digestion, for, as soone as he had eaten his meat, he would be sure to spit his meat up againe.

### 224.

A great tall fellow, whose name was Way, lay

along the street drunke. One went over him, and being asked why he did so, he answered he did but goe along the high-way.

### 225.

A Gentleman (that was us'd to send his letters by a footpost that was an old flegmatick rotten fellow) complained that he suffred much prejudice because his letters came too late to his friends hands ; another standing by told him it was his owne fault, because he did send them by a rotten post.

### 226.

One whose name was You married a woman whose name was You also ; he for this cause was, and ever will be, cal'd Master W.

### 227.

One who had been somewhat bitter to his wife complayned to his neighbour (who was a northern man borne, and spake accordingly), telling him that she was such a peevish woman that he could not endure to live with her : who advised him not to be so harsh to her, but to goe to her and so-lace her, and then she would be more kind to him.

### 228.

One was saying he wondred why the people in Æthiopia did not write straight along as we northern people ; one answered, they writ under the line, and that was the reason of it.

### 229.

A Dyer, who was an idle drunken fellow, was complayning to a Scholler that he had very ill fortune in his businesse, and that commonly those things that he undertook to dye were spoiled. The Scholler told him that the only way to have this amended was to reform himselfe, for he that lived ill could never dye well.

### 230.

One, whose name was Church, was telling some of his neighbors that his wife was with child, and that he never in his life saw any woman so big before : besides, [he] told them that he feared she would dye on child-bed. Whereupon one of them comforted him, saying that there was no cause to feare her death, and for her bignesse that was no wonder, in regard she had a church in her belly.

### 231.

A certaine man was mightily affected with a

woman whose name was Wall, which did use painting very much : his friends did diswade him from comming neere her, telling him they did wonder he was so besotted to set his affections upon a painted wall.

### 232.

One (whose husbands name was Beane) being delivered of two children at a burden, told the midwife she had been so troubled with wind all the time she was with child that she wondred at it. The midwife said it was no marvaile, in regard her belly so long had been full of beanes.

### 233.

One,.whose name was Mild, being in a tavern tooke out a new coyn'd six pence, who, observing the company to take notice of the brightnesse of the peece, told them it was a mild sixpence.

### 234.

One asked what the reason was that some women were so light heel'd now adayes. It was answered, because they did wear corke-heel'd shooes.

### 235.

One, having a play book called the Wits[1] which

(1) *The Wits*, a Comedy, by Sir William Davenant, 1636, 4°.

he much valued, by chance lost it : but while he was chafing and swearing about the losse of his book, in comes one of his friends, who asking the cause of his distemper, it was answered that he had lost his wits.

### 236.

One stood to prove that a brewers horse was a tapster, because he did draw beere; another answered him it could not be, because, though a brewers horse (if he were overladen) would froth, yet he could not nicke.[1]

### 237.

One, reading of a Curranto, said he wondred that men did so affect to lye in paper and yet without sheets.

### 238.

One asked what herbe that was that cured all diseases. It was answered, Time.

### 239.

One, being about to write the superscription of a letter to his mistres, asked a Scholler what termes

(1) A *nicke* is the raised bottom of a beer-pot or beer-can. The deception practised on the consumer by the height of the *nick* led to the use of the verb *to nick* in the sense of *to cheat.*

were best to give her; who told him the Venus
lasse of his affections was a good word. He, mistaking, writ to the Venice glasse of his affections,
which was a truer title then he was aware of.

### 240.

An Upholster was chiding his Apprentice, be
cause he was not nimble enough at his worke, and
had not his nailes and hammar in readines, when
he should use them, telling him that, when he was
an Apprentice, he was taught to have his nailes at
his fingers ends.

### 241.

One, whose name was Rapier, being a man of
a grave calling, yet using to weare a white suite,
was chid for not getting a black scabbard to his
rapier.

### 242.

One asked what that yong man deserved, that
did love alwayes to be in a playhouse. It was
answered, a box.

### 243.

One being at a friends house in the night was
perswaded to stay all night, but denied, saying he

would be gone, because it was moone light.   His
friend told him he thought he had not been so
lunatique as to love to walke in the moone light.

### 244.

One wondred, why there was so many picke-
pockets about the streets notwithstanding a watch
was at every corner.   It was answered, that was all
one, for a pickpocket would as gladly meet with a
watch as any thing else.

### 245.

Certaine Gossips being a discoursing of the Company their husbands kept: troth, sayes one, my
husband is no sooner out of doores but he has as
many about him, as there is to see the great beast
with two paire of horns.

### 246.

A Company of Country fellows disputing of
learning, and what a crooked, hard, and intricat
thing it was to be a good Scholler: truly, sayes
one, and so it is: for I have heard your best
laten is in crooked lane.

### 247.

One questioned which were the greatest wonders

in the world. 'Twas answered, womens and Lawyers tongues, for that they did alwayes lye, yet never ley still.

### 248.

One demanded what creature was most like an Asse. He was answered, a Puritane, in that they had the longest eares.

### 249.

A Coblers wife speaking of the place she liv'd in, before she was married, her prentise mumbling said there was none but wh**** and Bauds lived there. What's that you say, Sirrah? quoth she. Marry, I say there are honester women then your selfe liv'd there.

### 250.

#### On a Puritan.

*Who is't, d'you thinke, this earth doth here inclose?*
*I know not; why, 'tis a disputing nose.*

### 251.

A young lascivious Gallant, wanting money, could not with his credit sell any thing : yet, his Father being but lately dead, at length was checkt by some of his friends for his loose and extravagant life, and withall told that he had base and beastly Associats, that did draw him to ill houses. He, taking this opportunity, answered : truly, friends, your counsell is very good, I will presently go sell my coach and horses.

### 252.

### On a Cobler.

*If any aske why this same stone was made,*
*(Know) for a Cobler, newly underlayd*
*Here for his overboasting; pray condole*
*Him, that translated many a weary sole.*

### 253.

A Steward being set on by a Theefe, who commanded him to deliver, he being a Receiver, the Steward replyed : I hope you will spare me, I being a Receiver also. You shall be, said the Theefe, if you deliver not the sooner.

### 254.

One sitting at dinner, where great store of rude mirth was discoursed and laught at, a prattling youth clapt him on the shoulder, and asked him if he was making verse he was so mute. Who replyed he was. Speake them, quoth he. No, replyed the other. Why you cannot speak them in better company. I suppose so, quoth the modest man, but two fooles at once will be too troublesome.

### 255.

A Scholler cal'd a tayler base fellow in a taverne, who swore he would have him to the court of Honour. If you doe, replyed the Scholler, looke you make your words good, for I would not willingly be the cause of putting it upon record.

### 256.

A Gentleman going along the street was entreated by a poore criple that had wooden legges to bestow his charity : to whom the Gentleman answered, if he would make a hansom legge, he should have a couple of farthings.

### 257.

A company of Gentlemen, comming into a Tavern, whose signe was the Moone, called for a quart of sacke ; the drawer told them they had none : whereat the gentlemen wondring, were told by the drawer, that the man in the Moone always drunke Claret.

### 258.

One, that was skil'd in writing short hand, promised a Lawier's Clarke to teach him his skill, who thanked him for his paines, but told him they could not live by making short hand of any thing.

### 259.

One said a civit cat was a dainty thing to keepe in a house, because her dung was sweet; another said it was true, but yet it was more profitable to keepe a cooke, especially in a deare yeer, because he spitted rost.

### 260.

One asked, why hard wax was so much in request now adayes. It was answered, because the world did wax so hard.

### 261.

A woman, having married an old man whose name was Edward (whom she thought had been very rich, but not worth a penny), being asked what she had by her marriage, answered, an old Edward.

### 262.

A Gentleman, comming in the night to visit an

old man who had a hansom wench to his wife, and suspected to be a little too light, was entreated by the old man to walke into a roome. His wife having a candle in her hand, entreated the gentleman to follow her, who told her he would have her husband (because he was an old man) to follow the light.

### 263.

Two Gentlemen were in a deep dispute, whether the man in the Moone were a gentleman or a cittizen ; it was determined by a Scholler that, when she was at full there was a gentleman in her, but when she appeared like a horne, there was a cittizen in her.

### 264.

A justice of peace sending a Cheat to deserved punishment, the Cheater, bewailing his hard fortune, wished he could as easily learn to commit as the Justice could discover knavery. Why, that you may, said the Justice. Never, reply'd the Knave, without I be put in authority.

### 265.

A Gentleman in wants was advised by his friend to serve a noble man that so he might raise his fortune. That was, said he, to refuse a lesser poverty for a greater; for although I am poore, yet I have my selfe; there I shall not.

### 266.

A french-man, scoffing at the fancies of the English, in admiring their Nation and neglecting their owne, was thus answered: we in England esteemed you, as you in France do our hownds, for pleasure.

### 267.

One scoffingly demanded of a Drawer with a great Crimson face full of high rubyes, when he was at the Barbers. The drawer answered, troth, Sir, I cannot tell well, but to my best remembrance 'twas much about the time your face was brased.

### 268.

A booke-binder disappointing a Scholler of his Books which he had to bind for him, the Scholler, being angry, cal'd him idle Knave; the Binder not long after brought home his books, and having received his mony for them, desired to know of the Scholler, why he cal'd him Knave the other day. To deal plainly with thee, said the Scholler because I would not flatter thee. Why, sir, doe you think so, said the Binder? Yes, faith, replyed the Scholler. Then I waigh not your words much, quoth the Binder, since children and fooles speake what they thinke. I, but they are Knaves (said the Scholler), that speake against knowledge. Indeed Sir, I tooke you for one of them; and so went his way.

### 269.

A foolish mellancholly Gentleman, riding with his man on the high way, suddenly cryed out, his foot, his foot! His man started, and desired him to light, that he might see what 'twas that hurt him. Then pluck off this boot, said he, which being done the man told him, sir, here is nothing. Then, prethee, sayes the gentleman, pluck off the other, for sure one of them pained me.

### 270.

A pretty wench but lately come out of the Country, in her pouledavis and linsi-woolsy petticoats, living in the strand, was seene not long after in her silkes and sattins, and being by one of her country-women demanded how such might be purchased: faith, answer'd she, only for the taking up.

### 271.

A Citizen going out of towne with some of his

neighbors to hunt : pree-thee, sweetheart (sayes he to his wife), pray that I meet not a Diana, and so come home like to Actæon horn'd, or be torne to peeces with the dogs. His wife, thinking he had' closely jeer'd her, and thinking to be revenged, said : truly, husband, whether you meet Diana or no, I'le take order you shall not want.

### 272.

Certaine Gallants being at a taverne, where they spar'd no liquor, insomuch that all were well entred ; but one whose head was somewhat weaker, and therefore lighter, did nothing but spew, and calling for a rekoning, why, says one of his friends, cannot you tell, that have so often cast up, what you have drunke ?

### 273.

A Gentleman, meeting of a married Souldier newly come from the wars, demanded what charge he underwent. The Souldier replyed, a Captaines. Truly, answered the Gentleman, then you may help your wife to an Ancients place, for she can beare stoutly.

### 274.

A fellow going down Ludgate-Hill, his heeles by chance slipping from him, fell upon his breech.

One standing by told him that London-stones were stout and scornfull. It may be so, quoth he, yet I made them to kisse my breech, as stout as they were.

### 275.

A coward told his friend that one gave him a box on the eare, and he did not strike him again, but turn'd the other also to him ; to which his friend answered : sure there was a great fight betwixt you, when blowes were given on both sides.

### 276.

One asked, why Prentices were so briefe with their clubs, when Gentlemen were falling out or quareling in the streets. One replyed it was their opportunity to be revenged on them for medling with their mistresses.

### 277.

A Country farmer, having a pound neere his house, whereat was a Dunghill, which at its full maturity he sold, on the next market-day, amongst other discourse, told his neighbors that he had made as good a market as ever he did in his life, for he had sold all his dunghill by the pound. One replyed : troth, neighbor, you cannot chuse but be rich ; I have one to sell ; pray, neighbor, tell me how you sold a pound, and how many hundred weight there was in it.

### 278.

One asked a Gentlewoman in which part of the house she did use to lye. It was answer'd, that she lay backwards, and did let out her fore-roomes.

### 279.

A company of Gentlemen [were] in a tavern, amongst the rest one whose name was Bramble ; who being very quarelsome, ere they parted, fell to words and so to blowes, and had beaten and scratch't one of the Gentlemen in the face that he bled ; who going home, one of his friends meeting him by the way asked the cause, how he came to bleed so. No great harme, replyed he, onely a Bramble by chance scratch't me.

### 280.

One told his friend, if he would be pleased to go with him he would bring him to a place, where they should have wenches and lobsters by the belly.

### 281.

A shoe-maker sent his man unto a Gentleman, who had ought him money a long-time for bootes and shoes that had formerly been made for him. The servant, comming to the Gentleman, told him his Master would intreate him to send that little money which was due to him as aforesaid, whereat the Gentleman (rather willing to cavell then pay) in a great rage answered : thou rogue ! what, doth thy Master thinke I am running away, that he sends after me for such a trifle as this is ? No, Sir, replyed the servant, my master doth not thinke you are about to runne away ; but he is, and that makes him so earnest with you and others, that he might take his money along with him.

### 282.

A Gentleman invited to his table many guests, and provided for them divers dishes of meate ; amongst the rest, there being a legge of Mutton, one in the company took it, and fell so homely to worke with it, that he pared off all the flesh, and laying it in scraps in the dish, called to a servant to break the bone for him ; which one perceiving, that sat next the gentleman that invited them, jogged him, and shewed him how uncivilly the party had behaved himselfe ; whereupon the Gentleman, a little mov'd, yet unwilling to be too playne, began a tale to the whole table thus : I was, quoth he, not long since with a friend of mine that much

delighted in hunting, and after our sport comming
home he would needs see his dogges fed, before he
would eate anything himselfe, which I labored to
diswade him from, in regard he was in a very faire
new white Satten sute, which might amongst the
dogs receive some hurt, but rather willed him for
that time to suffer some of his servants to do it;
all would not prevail, but into the yard, where the
dogs were kept, he went, whither he was no sooner
come, but one of the dogs, that was all mire and
dirt, fell to ramping on him, and albeit the dogge
spoyled his faire suite, yet he rebuked not the
dogge, but on the contrary cherished him, which
I, perceiving, said to my friend : Sir, what, doe you
mean to suffer a scurvy dog to spoyle such a suite
as that is? Alas, replied my friend, what would
you have me doe to him? you see, as wel as I, he
is but a puppy. Which was no sooner spoken, but
by all the table applied to him, that had so spoyled
the mutton.

### 283.

One asked whence the word *Interpreter* was
derived. It was answered *quasi Inter-prater*, for
one that prated betwixt two that spake severall
languages.

### 284.

One asked why Chambermaids were more troubled with the greene-sicknesse then other women.  It was answered, because they used to lye at their Masters beds-feet.

### 285.

One asked what beast in the world might be said to have the best understanding.  It was answered, a Cuckold.

### 286.

A maid told her Mistresse she must entreat her to keepe  more maids, because she was  much over laid.

### 287.

Printers (saies one) are the most lawlesse men in a Kingdome, for they commit faults *cum privilegio*.

**Finis.**

# ADDITIONAL NOTES AND ILLUSTRATIONS.

## MERY TALES OF THE MAD MEN OF GOTHAM.

*Introduction.*—In a note to the *Merie Tales of Skelton* (ii. 7), I incidentally shewed, that in a "Comedie called a Knacke To Knowe a Knave," 1594, 4°. the anonymous author has introduced "[Kempe's] Applauded merriments of the Wise Men of Goteham." These particular *merriments*, however, appear to have been the invention of the writer, or to have been taken from an earlier and fuller impression of the Tales than any at present known to survive. There is no trace of them in the edition of 1630. Doubtless, many stories were circulated touching this place and its inhabitants, besides those which were admitted into print.

The celebrity of the Gothamite Tales suggested the selection of the name as a passport to mere political squibs and party-pamphlets. Such were "The *Fooles* Complaint to *Gotham* College, and Resolution taken up by Free Subjects in and about London and Westminster," 1643, 4°; and "The Epistle from the Bottle-Conjurers unto the Gothamites." n. d. 8vo. In *Punch* for Sept. 13th, 1856, was printed a copy of satirical verses on the Reformatory Union, under the title of "The River of Gotham."

In 1701, appeared a folio broadside with the following title:—"Advice to the Kentish long-tails by the wise men of Gotham, in answer to their late sawcy petition to the Parliament."

I have been favoured by my friend George Waring, Esq. of Oxford, with the subjoined fac-simile of the title-page of ed. 1630 of the Tales of the Men of Gotham.

# THE
# MERRY TALES
## OF THE Mad-men
## OF *GOTTAM.*

Gathered together by *A. B.* of Phyſicke Doĉtor.

Printed at London by *B. A.* and *T. F.* for *Micha*[*l*]
*Sparke*, dwelling in *Greene Arbor* at the ſigne of
the *Blue-Bible*, 1630.

Ray, in his Proverbs, 1670, says, speaking of these Gothamite legends :—

"Here two things may be observed—

"1. Men in all ages have made themselves merry with singling out some place, and fixing the staple of stupidity and stolidity therein. So the Phrygians in Asia, the Abderitæ in Thrace, and Bœotians in Greece, were notorious for dull men and blockheads.

"2. These places, thus slighted and scoffed at, afforded some as witty and wise persons as the world produced. So Democritus was an Abderite, Plutarch a Bœotian, &c. . . . As for Gotham, it doth breed as wise people as any which causelessly laugh at their simplicity. Sure I am, Mr. William de Gotham, fifth master of Michael House, in Cambridge, 1336, and twice Chancellor of the University, was as grave a governor as that age did afford—."

Everybody is probably familiar with the old nursery tale :—
> "Three wise men of Gotham
> Went to sea in a bowl :
> And if the bowl had been stronger,
> My song would have been longer."

There cannot be the slightest doubt that the tradition, on which these stories of the men of Gotham were founded in the 16th century, is of great antiquity. In the *Townley Mysteries*, edited for the Surtees Society, 1836, p. 88, the men of Gotham have received their share of notice.—*Vide infrâ.*

In the 6th volume of the *Sussex Archæological Collections*, Mr. M. A. Lower furnishes, as I have already mentioned, an account of Andrew Borde, and contends that not Gotham, in Lincolnshire, but Gotham, in Sussex, is entitled to the honour of having given parentage to these Tales. An anecdote, which Mr. Halliwell gives in his *Popular Rhymes and Nursery Tales*, p. 195, of the Mayor of Pevensey, near Gotham, might strengthen the hypothesis of Mr. Lower, if equally silly stories had not been told of the mayors of all the towns in the kingdom.

P. 4. *The First Tale.*
This story is quoted in the *Townley Mysteries*, ed. 1836, p. 88.
> "*Tercius Pastor.* But syr, ye ar bare of wysdom to knawe.
> Take hede how I fare, and lere at my lawe ;
> Ye nede not to care if ye folow my sawe,
> Hold ye my mare, this sek there throwe
>      on my bak ;

Whylst I, with my hand,
Lawse the sek band,
Com nar and by stand
    Both Gyg and Jak ;
Is not alle shakyn owte and no meylle is therin ?
*Primus Pastor.* Yey, that is no dowte.
*Tercius Pastor.* —— So is youre wyttes thyn
And ye look wille aboute, mor nor myn,
So gase your wyttes owte euyr as com in ;
    Geder up
And seke it agane.
*Secundus Pastor.* May we not be fane ?
He has told us fulle plane
    Wysdom to sup.
*Jak Garcio.* Now God gyf you ease, folys all sam ;
Saghe I never none so fare but the *foles of Gotham.*"

### P. 6. *The Second Tale.*

Un autre Paisan, après avoir labouré jusqu'à midi, se mit avec sa charrue sur un âne, pour ne pas fatiguer ses bœufs à la tromer. S'appercevant que l'animal succomboit sous le poids, il descend, met sa charrue sur la tête, et remonte en disant à son âne : *Tu marcheras bien à present, ce n'est pas toi qui porte la charrue, c'est moi.* La distraction est certainement une absence d'esprit, un difaut, une impolitesse dont tout homme qui veut être sociable doit se corriger soigneusement.—*Poggiana,* ed. 1720, ii. p. 237.

### P. 9. *There dwelt a Smith at Gotham.*

It may be just worth while to notice that, among the proverbial expressions current in Nottinghamshire, there is the following :—
    " The little smith of *Nottingham,*
      Who doth the work that no man can."
Whether this gifted individual had any connexion with the Smith described here, it is hard to say.

### P. 14. *The Twelfth Tale.* "There was a man of Gotham."

An adventure of a somewhat similar character forms the leading feature in *Les Cent Nouvelles Nouvelles,* No. 38 (ed. Wright, i. 238).
Compare the Second Novel of the 3rd day of the *Decameron* and the 8th Novel of the 7th day. The present story bears a close resemblance to the latter, which, it may be mentioned, is imitated in the *Cobler of Canterburie,* first printed in 1590. It is, in that collection, called "The

Old Wiues Tale." It is not at all unlikely that the author of the Gothamite Tales was under obligations to Boccaccio, from whom Borde, their putative writer, has borrowed his " Mery Jest of the Mylner of Abyngton," printed by Wynkyn de Worde, and again by Richard Jones, and to be included in a contemplated work by the present Editor on the Early Popular Poetry of England.

---

## TWELVE MERY JESTS OF THE WIDOW EDYTH.

*Preface. John Hankyn.*
Ames, in his *Typographical Antiquities,* and after him Herbert and Dibdin, suppose that this person was identical with *John Hawkyns* who, in 1530, printed (with Pynson's types) Palsgrave's *L'Esclaircissement de la Langue Françoise.*

P. 36. *The Erle of Wyltshyre.*
Henry Stafford, Earl of Wiltshire, K.G. created Earl in 1509; died issueless in 1523. In 1511, he took part in the Jousts appointed to celebrate the birth of the Prince of Wales, only child of Henry VIII. by Catharine of Aragon (see Ellis' *Original Letters,* Second Series, i. 183). This nobleman was a cousin of Edward Stafford, Duke of Buckingham, Lord High Constable of England, who was attainted and beheaded in 1521.

—— *Gup, queane, gup !*
*Gup* is explained by Halliwell (*Arch. Dict.* in voce) to be a contraction of *go up.* In the present passage, it would almost seem to be equivalent in meaning to *gip* or *gep,* which is used by some of our early writers in the sense of *fye !* or, *get along !* In a note to the *History of Tom Thumb,* 1630, in a forthcoming collection of *Early Popular Poetry,* I have brought together what I could find in illustration of this phrase.

P. 37. *Wainsworth.*
Wandsworth, in Surrey, is here intended.

P. 38. *The Lord Chamberlayn.*
Probably, John de Vere, 14th Earl of Oxford, hereditary Grand Chamberlain of England, succeeded his uncle, John de Vere, 13th Earl, 4 Hen. VIII. and died 18 Hen. VIII. From his diminutive stature, he was known as "Little John of Campes."

**P. 43.** *Brandonfery.*

Brandon, near Thetford, Suffolk, is the place meant. There is, or was, a *ferry* there over the Ouse to the Isle of Ely.

**P. 44.** *Bradefolde.*

Perhaps *Bradfield, Magna* or *Parva*, in Sussex, may be the true reading.

—— *heyt, w\*\*\*\*, heyt.*

See a note to *Peele's Jests*, vol. ii. p. 364, in explanation of the term. *Brock Heyt*, in the present passage, and *hayt*, used by Chaucer in the *Freres Tale*, appear to be synonymous. The passage in Chaucer is as follows :—

> "Thay seigh a cart, that chargid was with hay,
> Which that a carter drof forth in his way.
> Deep was the way, for which the carte stood,
> This carter smoot, and cryde as he wer wood,
> 'Hayt, brok ; hayt, scot ; what, spare ye for the stoones?'
> The fend,' quod he, 'yow fech body and bones.'"

—— Coulme.—*Colne-Earls*, between Halsted and Colchester, is the place which the writer intended. It formerly belonged to the Veres, Earls of Oxford, and being the most considerable of the four places of the same name in the neighbourhood, was sometimes distinguished as *Great Colne.* Here was founded by the Veres a Priory.

—— *In an house of my Lord of Oxenforde.*—

John de Vere, 14th Earl of Oxford, ob. 18 Hen. VIII.

**P. 56.** *In all the town she was not worth a q.*

A Q is here used, doubtless, in the sense of *a half-farthing*, for which it stands equivalent in the old college accounts at Oxford. See Nares' Glossary, ed. 1859, art. Q.

**P. 64.** *Towton.*

I am not aware of any such place in *Sussex ;* but *Tooting*, in Surrey, was formerly known as *Towting* or *Towton*, and was celebrated for many fine seats of noblemen and gentlemen. The truth is, doubtless, that the widow travelled from Southwark to Tooting in the carrier's cart.

**P. 94.** *And kissed her twice, and chirked like a Sparow.*

Chaucer has introduced a passage into the *Sompnoures Tale* (Works, by Bell, ìi. 107) which the writer of the present tract might be supposed, from the singular resemblance, to have seen :—

"The frere ariseth up ful curteysly,
And her embracith in his armes narwe,
And kist hir swete, and chirkith as a sparwe
With his lippes—"

---

## PASQUIL'S JESTS.

P. 27. *How madde Coomes, when his wife was drowned, &c.*
No. 55 of *Mery Tales and Quicke Answeres* has been laid under contribution here ; but the latter is merely copied from the fabliau of " Le Vilain et sa Femme," printed in the third volume of Le Grand, ed. 1829, p. 181.

P. 36. *Of one that lost his purse.*
This is an imitation of No. 15 of *Mery Tales and Quicke Answeres,* and at p. 17 we have a story, which is borrowed from No. 16 of the same work. See also the *Pleasant Conceits of Old Hobson,* 1607, p. 35 of present ed. The original of all these anecdotes is, probably, the fabliau of " Le Marchand qui perdit sa Bourse" (Le Grand, ed. 1829, iii. p. 66).

P. 45. *The subtilty of a Lawyer repayd, &c.*
This is taken from *Mery Tales and Quicke Answeres,* No. 45. The editor of the *Family Jo Miller,* 1848, 12mo, p. 139. has the following remark on the story, which is extracted from the *Mery Tales,* &c. in that work. "This 'Merrie tale' is the longest lived in our collection. It had been dramatized, and appeared in print as early as 1474, when it is spoken of as an old piece, entitled, *Maitre Pierre Patelin.* Brueys modernized it in 1706, changing the title to *L'Avocat Patelin,* from which is taken our well-known farce of the 'Village Lawyer.'"

P. 47. *Cuckoo time.—i. e.* May, when the Cuckoo is supposed to sing throughout the day ; but he makes his first appearance in April. This bird is scarcely surpassed in celebrity by any of the feathered creation, if we may judge from the frequency with which he is mentioned by our writers, and the prominent position accorded to him in rural superstitions. His very important and close connexion with connubial matters is well known, and in the *Schole house of Women,* 1542, the writer, desirous of expressing a state of perpetual cuckoldom, figures the cuckoo "singing

all the year." See *Remains of the Early Popular Poetry of England,*
vol. iii. An account of this subject may be read in the last ed. of Brand's
*Popular Antiquities,* ii. 196, *et seqq.* In *Polimanteia,* 1595, 4°; sign K 4,
*verso,* the Author mentions a supposition on the part of some persons
"that the Nightingall *and the Cuckow* both grow hoarse at the rising of
(*Syrius*) the Dogge-starre." In *the Mery Tales of the Mad Men of
Gotham,* first printed, perhaps, as early as 1540, the third Tale relates
how "on a tyme, the men of Gottam would haue pinned in the Cuckoo,
whereby shee should sing all the yeere."

The following lines, extracted from Halliwell's *Popular Rhymes* and
*Nursery Tales,* 1849, p. 160, embody the ideas of our ancestors respecting
the habits of this bird :—

> " In April,
> The Cuckoo shows his bill ;
> In May,
> He sings all day ;
> In June,
> He alters his tune :
> In July,
> Away he'll fly ;
> Come August,
> Away he must !"

---

## PLEASANT CONCEITS OF OLD HOBSON.

Introduction.—*Flourdew,* the husband of one of the characters in the
*Muses Looking Glass,* by T. Randolph, 1638, was a haberdasher of small
wares.

P. 15. *Lanthorne and Candle light.*
See a woodcut at p. 76 of Mr. Collier's *Bridgewater Catalogue,*
1837, 4°.

P. 20. *How Maister Hobson proved himself a Poet.*
See vol. ii. 215 and 363. In *Notes and Queries,* 2 S. vii. 147, and
3 S. v. 215, may be read some communications on this subject. In
Camden's *Remaines of a Greater Work,* first printed in 1605, 4°, the
epitaph is given with variations as that of "Sir John Calf, Lord Mayor
of London." No person of that unpropitious name is known to have

filled the chief magistracy, and it seems probable that a sneer was intended by this facetious composition on some civic dignitary, whose real
name has not come down.

P. 23. *Matches.*
In a note to the *Merie Tales of Skelton* (ii. 7), I have inadvertently
mis-stated that it was for lucifer-matches that Hobson sought a patent.
The error, however, almost corrects itself ; but I did not detect it, till
the volume was worked off.

P. 27. *To whom Maister Hobson replyed againe : we may better, &c.*
"When there was a feare of Invasion, some schollers in Cambridge
were talking merrily how they would shift, and where they would hide
themselves. ' Well,' sayes one (that was Bachelor of Divinitie, but never
appeared in St. Marie's), 'you have provided for yourselves, but nobody
takes care of me.' ' Yes, faith,' sayes another, ' I'le hide thee where
I'le warrant thou shalt nere be found.' ' Where's that?' sayes he.
' Why in St. Marie's pulpitt,' sayes the other ; ' The safest place for
thee in the world, for [if] ever any man lookes for thee there, I'll be
hanged.'"—*Merry Passages and Jests*, collected by Sir N. L'Estrange
[Thoms' *Anecdotes and Traditions*, p. 36].

P. 31. *How one of Maister Hobson's men quited him, &c.*
It has been already pointed out that this tale is in *Mery Tales and
Quicke Answeres*, No. 54. But it is also in *Poggiana* :—
"Un pauvre Batelier qui n'avoit rien gagné de tout le jour s'en re-
tournoit tout triste chez lui, lorsque quelqu'un l'appella pour le passer
dans sa barque. Le trajet se fit gayement. Mais le Batelier ayant
demandé son payement, le passager protesta qu'il n'avoit pas un sol sur
lui, mais qu'il lui donneroit un conseil qui lui vaudroit de l'argent. *Bon !*
dit le Batelier, *ma femme* et mes enfans ne vivent pas de conseil. N'en
pouvant tirer d'autre raison, il demanda enfin quel étoit donc ce conseil?
*C'est*, dit-il, *de ne jamais passer personne sans vous faire payer par
avance.*—POGGIANA, ed. 1720, ii. p. 210.

P. 33. *Of Maister Hobson riding to Sturbrige Faire.*
This is one of the *Facetiæ* of Poggius :—
"Antonio Lusco dont on parloit tout à l'heure étoit un homme à bons
contes. Il dit un jour qu' étant allé à Sienne avec un Venitien fort
simple, peu accoûtumé à monter à cheval, ils coucherent dans une
auberge, où il y avoit quantité de Cavaliers. Quand il fallut partir,
chacun prend son cheval, sans que le bon Venitien branlat de sa place.
Antoine lui ayant demandé à quoi il s'amusoit, pendant que tous les

3. R

autres étoient déja à cheval, ' Je suis,' *ait-il*, ' prêt à partir, mais comme
je ne saurois reconnoître mon cheval entre tant d'autres, j'attens que tout
le monde soit parti, parce que celui qui restera, sera le mien.'"—*Poggiana*,
ed. 1720, ii. p. 197.

P. 36. *How Master Hobson was a judge betwixt two women.*
This brings to mind a good story related by Roger North in his " Life
of Lord Keeper Guilford," ed. 1826 :—

"Mr. Serjeant Maynard had a mind to punish a man who had voted
against his interest in a borough in the West, and brought an action
against him for scandalous words, spoke at a time when a member, to
serve in the House of Commons for that borough, was to be chosen.
And, after his great skill, he first laid his action in the county of Middlesex : and that was by virtue of his privilege, which supposes a serjeant
is attendant on the Court of Common Pleas, and not to be drawn from
the county where the court sat. And then, in the next place, he charged
the words in Latin, that, if he proved the effect, it would be sufficient ;
whereas, being in English, they must prove the very words to a tittle ;
and those were a long story that used to be told of Mr. Noy, and all the
cock lawyers of the West. And this was tried before his lordship [Chief
Justice North] at the *nisi prius* for the Common Pleas for Middlesex.
The witness, telling the story, as he swore the defendant told it, said that
a client came to the serjeant, and gave him a basket of pippins, and every
pippin had a piece of gold in it. " Those were golden pippins," quoth
the judge. The serjeant began to puff, not bearing the jest: so the
witness went on, " And then," said he, " the other side came and gave
him a roasting pig (as it is called in the West) and in the belly of that
there were fifty broad pieces." " That's good sauce to a pig," quoth the
judge again. This put the serjeant out of all patience ; and speaking to
those about him, " This," said he, " is on purpose to make me ridiculous."
This story being sworn, the judge directed the jury to find for the
serjeant ; but in the court, the judgement was arrested, because the
words were but a land story, and went, as mere merriment, over ale,
without intent to slander."

P. 38. *Of Maister Hobson's rewarding a poet for a bookes dedication.*
Scot, in his *Discovery of Witchcraft*, 1584, ed. 1651, p. 263, relates.
the original of this story, taking it, doubtless, from *Mery Tales and
Quicke Answeres*, No. 23.

P. 40. *How Maister Hobson gave one of his servants the half of a
blind man's benefit.*
This tale, in various forms, is found in many collections. It occurs in

the English *Gesta Romanorum*, ed. Madden, p. 468, where, however, the consequences do not fall quite so severely on the victims, *twelve* stripes being divided between three instead of sixty between two.

P. 44. *How Maister Hobson answered &c.*
Poggius, in his *Facetiæ*, gives an anecdote of a Milanese living about his own time, who, having heard somebody speak of the death of the Paladin Orlando, ran to his wife and communicated the intelligence as a piece of the latest news.

---

## CERTAYNE CONCEITS AND JEASTS.

P. 3. *A certaine fool came unto King Phillip, &c.*
"One begg'd of Queene Elizabeth, and pretended kindred and alliance, but there was no such relation. 'Friend,' says she, 'grant it be so, do'st thinke I am bound to keepe all my kindred? Why, that's the way to make *me* a beggar.'"—*Merry Passages and Jests*, collected by Sir N. L'Estrange [Thoms' *Anecdotes and Traditions*, p. 16.]

P. 9. *One buying a horse, &c.*
In Marlowe's *Faustus* (Works, by Dyce, ii. 63-4-5), the conjuror plays a trick on a horse-courser by selling him an animal which he enjoins him by no means to lead into water; but the fellow tries the experiment by riding his acquisition into a pond, and the horse is immediately transformed into a truss of hay.

---

## TAYLOR'S WIT AND MIRTH.

*Introduction.* Many of the articles in Taylor's *Wit and Mirth* were appropriated, of course without acknowledgment, by the editor of the *Tales and Jests of Mr. Hugh Peters*, 1660, 4°. Such is the case with Nos. 7, 30, 32, 35, 39, 40, 48, 55, 59, 62, and some others. The transfer of this stolen property to his own pages did not cost the plagiarist much trouble: for he has seldom done more than change the names; and Hugh Peters' [sixty] Jests are, in fact, merely a selection from Taylor's book with certain alterations and a few additions for the nonce. In the *Diverting History of Tom of Chester*, printed in the *Palatine Anthology*, 1850, 4°, many of the articles appear to be borrowed from Taylor.

**P. 9.** *An old Painter, &c.*

Gray, in his *Elegy written in a Country Churchyard*, alludes to the "frail memorials [of the humble tenants of the graves, &c.] with uncouth rhymes and shapeless sculpture deck'd : "—

> "Their name, their years, spelt by th' unletter'd muse,
> The place of fame and elegy supply;
> And many a holy text around she strews,
> That teach the rustic moralist to die."

This story appears in the following form in "The New & diverting History of Tom of Chester, containing his witty pranks, jests, &c." (see *The Palatine Anthology*, 1850, p. 119). "An old painter, at the repairing of a church in Chester, was writing sentences of Scripture upon the walls. By chance Tom came into the church, and reading them, perceived much of false English. Old man, said Tom, why don't you write true English? Alas! Sir, quoth he, they are poore simple people in this parish, and they will not goe to the cost of it."

**P. 10.** *Opposite.*

This word is here used merely in the sense of a person facing you at an eating-house table ; but it also occurs in some of the dramatists as an equivalent for *rival.* Thus in *A Cure for a Cuckold*, Act III. sc. 1, Lessingham says :—

> "Yes, I have no opposite i' th' world but
> Yourself: there, read the warrant for your death."

**P. 12.** *— Saying that her husband was in heauen, &c.*

"*Clown.* Good madonna, why mourn'st thou?
  *Olivia.* Good fool, for my brother's death.
    *Clo.* I think his soul is in hell, madonna.
    *Oliv.* I know his soul is in heaven, fool.
    *Clo.* The more fool, madonna, to mourn for your brother's soul being in heaven."—*Twelfth Night*, Act I. sc. 5.

*—— Though my Daw doe not speake, yet I am in good hope that he thinks the more.*

"—for in faith [said Martin] I shall neuer abide that Jacke, while I liue. Upon these words away went her husband, and though he said little, he thought the more."—*Pleasant History of Thomas of Reading*, by T. Deloney, circa 1597, ed. Thoms, p. 34.

**P. 17.** *A souldier vpon his march, &c.*

The anecdote here told by Taylor reminds one of an entry made by Evelyn in his *Diary* under date of the 3rd December, 1651, in which he gives the following account of an accident which befell a friend :—

"Sir Lewis Dives dined with us, who, relating some of his adventures, showed me divers pieces of broad gold which, being in his pocket in a fight, preserved his life by receiving a musket-bullet on them, which deadened its violence, so that it went no further, but made such a stroke on the gold as fixed the impressions upon one another, battering and bending several of them; the bullet itself was flatted, and retained on it the colour of the gold. He assured us that of a hundred of them, which it seems he then had in his pocket, not one escaped without some blemish."

P. 26. *A Nobleman of France, &c.*
A somewhat similar story is told in the *Laird of Logan.* It is as follows :—"As the Paisley steamer came alongside the quay at the city of the Seestus, a denizen of St. Mirren's hailed one of the passengers: 'Jock, Jock I distu hear, man ? is that you or your brither?'"
This jest is not unsimilar in its point to the nursery rhyme :—
" Ho I Master Teague, what is your story ?
I went to the wood, and killed a tory ;
I went to the wood, and killed another.
Was it the same, or was it his brother ? "
Halliwell's *Nursery Rhymes of England*, 6th Edit. p. 7.

P. 35. *A man [was] riding through a village, &c.*
A curious illustration of this jest occurs in a passage in *A Cure for a Cuckold*, Act IV. sc. 1 :—
"*Compass.* I don't think but that the cucking-stool is an enemy to a number of brabbles that would else be determined by law.
"*Pettifog.* 'Tis so indeed, Sir. My client that came in now sues his neighbour for kicking his dog, and using the defamatory speeches *come out, cuckold's cur.*"

P. 38. *Sixe gentlemen riding together, &c.*
" A Gentleman overtakes in the evening a plaine country fellow, and ask't him how far it was to such a towne. ' Tenne miles, Sir,' sayes he. 'It is not possible,' sayes the gentleman. 'It is no lesse,' sayes the fellow. 'I telle you it was never counted above five.' ''Tis tenne indeed, Sir,' sayes the fellow—and thus they were arguing *pro et con* a long time. At last sayes the countryman to him : 'I'le tell you what I'le doe, Sir, because you seeme to be an honest gentleman, and your horse is almost tyr'd, I will not stand with you, you shall have it for five ; but, as I live, whosoever comes next shall ride tenne.'"—*Merry Passages and Jests*, collected by Sir Nicholas L'Estrange [Thoms' *Anecdotes and Traditions*, p. 32].

Andrewes, in his *Anecdotes*, ed. 1790, p. 406, quotes a story from the *Thuana*, which has the aspect of being an imitation of the one in Taylor. It is related of an old judge, who had been told that the distance from one place to another (in Gascony) was two leagues, and who, finding it a very tiring journey, ordered it to be registered in the archives of the province, that it was *six* leagues between the two points. See *Constable's Miscellany*, vol. x. pp. 114–15.

P. 57. *A Fellow hauing beene married, &c.*
The case of this "fellow" was not by any means so desperate as that of the luckless husband, whose story is given in *Les Cent Nouvelles Nouvelles* (ed. Wright), No. 29. "Veezcy," says the latter, addressing his assembled friends, who have come to drink the health of the newly-married couple, and who are at a loss to comprehend the man's desponding looks, "pour un pouvre coup que j'ay accollée ma femme elle m'a fait ung enfant. Or regardez, si a chacune foiz que je recommenceraj elle en fait autant, de quoy je pourraj nourrir le mesuage?" "Comment! ung enfant?" dirent ses compaignons. "Voire, vrayement ung enfant, dit-il; veezcy de quoy, regardez." Et lors se tourne vers son lit et leve la couverture et leur monstre et la mere et l'enfant. "Tenez," dit-il, veezla la vache et le veau, sois-je pas bien party?" The fact was that the lady had prudently laid, with the assistance of a third party, the foundation of a family just three quarters of a year before her union with the hero of this tale; and the latter, to his astonishment and dismay, discovers that the desired pledge of affection is ready-made to his hand.

P. 62. *A Clinch.*
A similar witticism occurs in the *Demaundes Joyous*, printed by Wynkyn de Worde in 1511, 4°. :—
"*Demand*. How many straws go to a goose's nest?
*A.* None, for lack of feet."

P. 69. *An Ideot that dwelt with a rich vnckle, &c.*
The following additional illustrations of this subject may be offered:—
"The Lord North begged old Bladwell for a foole (though he could never prove him so), and having him in his custody as a lunatick, he carried him to a gentleman's house one day that was a neighbour. The Lord North and the gentleman retired a while to private discourse, and left Bladwell in the dining-room, which was hung with a fair hanging. Bladwell walked up and down, and viewing the imagery, spied a foole at last in the hanging, and, without delay, draws his knife, flies at the foole, cuts him clean out, and lays him on the floor. My Lord and the gentleman coming in again, and finding the tapestrie thus defaced, he

asks Bladwell what he meant by such a rude uncivil act : he answered : 'Sir, be content, I have rather done you a courtesy than a wrong, for if ever my Lord North had seen the fool there, he would have begged him, and so you might have lost your whole suit.'"—*Merry Passages and Jests,* collected by Sir N. L'Estrange [Thoms' *Anecdotes and Traditions,* p. 7].

"A Knight held to be a very wise man in his life, left behind him a sonne and heyre that was none of the best witted, to inherit his land : who was beg'd for a foole, and summoned into the Court of Wards for his answer. When question was made unto him what hee would say for himself, why his landes should not be taken from him, hee said : 'It is reported that my Father was a wise man, and begot a foole to inherit his estate after his death : who can tell but that I, a foole, may beget a wise man to inherit after me ?' His answer caried it, and he and his remaine in possession of the same revenues unto this day."—*Pleasant Taunts, Merry Tales, &c.* (circa 1620).

"There came vnto this Citty an Italian Earle, of the house of Anquilora, called Emelio who, desiring to haue a Foole with him, promised a great Almes vnto their house, if they would giue him a mad-man, who, hauing lost his fury, might entertaine him with sport. Those of the Hospital fayled not to promise him one, and withall to bring him to his lodging some of their most peaceable mad-men."—*The Pilgrime of Casteele,* 1621, p. 73.

R. Clay. Son, & Taylor, Printers, London.